A COUNTRY CALLED CHILDHOOD

A Country Called Childhood

A Memoir

DEEPTI NAVAL

ALEPH

ALEPH

ALEPH BOOK COMPANY
An independent publishing firm
promoted by *Rupa Publications India*

First published in India in 2022
by Aleph Book Company
7/16 Ansari Road, Daryaganj
New Delhi 110 002

ISBN: 978-93-90652-62-4

5 7 9 10 8 6 4

Printed in India

To Mama and Piti . . .

Memory rushes back at times

pulls me by my finger

eggs me on, and says

come, let's go . . .

inside those dark chambers

where you stood in the light

rejoicing in a life

yet to unfold . . .

Contents

A Note about the Book

When I started to write about my childhood, I thought of it as not just a regular book where I tell people about all that I lived through. Rather, I wanted to recreate my childhood for the reader. I wanted to take you through those corridors of memory, setting up things the way I remember them. In that sense it is not a typical memoir—it is more like a screenplay. This book could simply be titled, 'Stories from my Childhood'. And it would be apt. Because I feel life is all about stories; that I am the sum total of all the stories that impacted me since I was a little girl, stories from my early days. It is stories that fill me up with life—make me what I am— stories that make me look at life the way I do, stories that make my world come alive. If it were not for the stories that came down to me from my mother, my father, and from all the people around at the time I was growing up, then who would I be? What would I be without the stories that crept into my heart, found a nesting place, and stayed in there forever?

Stories . . . I don't nurture them, they nurture me.

Prologue

The Dance of Songs

It's getting dark in the city of Amritsar. Shops are shutting down. Street lamps come on, casting dim yellow pools of light. Rickshaws and bicycles hustle to make their way home. A handcart loaded with gunny bags wobbles down the street. Even Dwarka's kite shop is winding up. The old Sardar tailor pulls his rickety shutter down, gets on his bicycle, and pedals away. Shahni's voice can be heard; she's urging her buffaloes home. Grubby little boys, the mochis, play outside in the gully, and behind the threshold of the phaatak, the big iron gate, two little sisters, Bobby and Dolly, go about their lives.

This scene seems like it's from hundreds of years ago but it actually dates back to 1956. It's one of my earliest memories in which I am almost four years old. It's the street I remember the most, the street on which I lived.

A little girl darts out of her house crying, 'I want to go to my Mama!'

'Come back!' shouts Mai Sardi, my nanny, from inside the big gate.

'No, I want to go to my Mama!'

'Your Mama has gone to the cinema; you get in here at once!'

'I will also go to the cinema!' she retorts, and runs down the street.

Suddenly, something stirs in the air. There's a muffled grunt in the sky, and the breeze changes. The sky turns red. Tin sheds begin to flap and rattle; the smell of wind on earth. It's a dust storm!

Stray pieces of paper littering the ground outside the bookbinder's shop fly up and float in the air. Bicycles fall in a slow, studied motion along the wall of the cinema hall. The wooden shutter of Gyaan Halwai's shop tilts and slips out of its clamp. He stands with his arms outstretched, holding it with all his malai-lassi strength against the wind, his lungi threatening to fly off. A rickshaw puller pedals backwards and sideways. The world seems to slant at the edges. Dust storms the streets. Mai Sardi's voice cuts through the mayhem. 'STOP! I say . . . Get back, girl . . . It's dark!'

The girl is not coming back. She runs all the way to the end of the street and suddenly finds herself in the middle of Katra Sher Singh Chowk in front of Regent Talkies surrounded by huge cinema posters. The posters begin to tear from the whiplash of the wind. *Szarrr . . . szar szar szar szarrrrrrrr . . .* Faces of actors and actresses fold up and slap against the dry whitewash of the decrepit cinema hall. Unable to keep her eyes open from the dust, wind, and tears, the little girl hides her face in her sleeve. At her feet swirl particles of dust, torn scraps of paper, bright orange and pink trimmings from the tailor's shop . . . and gather momentum. She stands still for a while, watching the little merry-go-round around her dotted rubber booties until her eyes fall upon something.

Across the street, the plotwallah is doing a tandav! He is the skinny man who sells little leaflets with the plot and songs of Hindi films printed on them. A strong gust whisks away the sepia coloured leaflets from his hands and flings them into the wind. They soar in the air, going up and up in circles, dodging the poor man's attempts to retrieve them. Tossed into the wind, the yellowed sheets somersault, now diving to his feet, now rising as if to sudden applause! He leaps and plunges by the side of the road, slapping his arms around, hurling himself at the musical notes. One leaf slips into two and two into four, till the songs dance above his gaunt, lanky frame. He dances with the songs, the poor plotwallah, trying in vain to hang on to his only means of livelihood, as it slips away into the grainy air.

No one notices the little girl as she stands in the middle of the chowk, enthralled by the dance of songs; her large eyes fill with tears, but she forgets to cry.

'There you are, *marjaani!*'

Mai Sardi steps forward, scoops me up in one sweeping movement, lodges me onto her hip, strides down the street, and puts me back inside the house where I belong. As we enter, my grandmother rises from her chair pointing a finger at me.

'NO little girls from good homes *ever* go out to cinemas on the street!'

SECTION I

BEGINNINGS

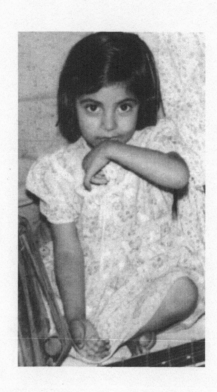

1

Sinister Sadhus and Baleful Bats

It was during the winter rains that I arrived. I was born on 3 February 1952 at the V. J.—Queen Victoria Jubilee Hospital located at one end of Company Bagh in Amritsar.

'It was a very disturbed, stormy night,' recalls my mother. 'The night you were born it rained incessantly. I was lying in a little corner room of the hospital with you, a tiny bundle, next to me on the cot. The room was filled with water. It leaked everywhere. A cold wind blew in from the slit in the window. There was a furnace

My first photo.

in the room, but no one was around to light the firewood. The long sprawling corridors of the old Victorian red brick structure lay empty in the thrashing downpour.'

Dr Sant Ram Dhal, the doctor who delivered me, had wound up and left for the day. Mai Sardi, who managed the house, and would later be my nanny, had dropped off the tiffin and returned home. So had my father after his evening visit. The ward was dim and deserted.

'In the wee hours of the morning, while it was still dark, a sadhu baba came knocking on my door,' said Mama. 'But I was too weak to get up from my bed. If I did, I'd have to wade through the ice-cold, waterlogged room to get to the door. The sadhu kept knocking for a long time, begging, but I could not help him. Finally, he left, cursing.'

'What was the curse, Mama?' I would ask whenever she'd tell me this story.

'I don't remember, beta,' she would say. 'He cursed me, *not you*, my doll.'

The night I was born continues to fascinate me with all its dramatic elements—the freezing cold, the dimly lit corridors, the deserted ward, the deluge, the ominous sadhu, and his curse ...

∽

As a toddler, I likely did quite a few odd things, but there was one habit that takes the cake and embarrasses me to date. It's a story my mother most loved to tell everyone about me. When I was tiny, and we'd go to visit my maternal grandparents, I would often end up in my nani's kitchen in search of sugar to satisfy my budding sweet tooth. A pattern soon emerged.

'Badi Mummy, thhodi cheeni de do!' (Badi Mummy, please give me some sugar) I'd say, my hand extended before her.

'Cheeni nahin hai, chal ja!' (There's no sugar for you! Go!) Badi Mummy would rebuke me with a smile.

Then, like clockwork, I would reply, 'Achcha, faer thhoda loon hi de do!' (Okay, then give me some salt!)

Can you imagine? I mean, how did that work? How could I be asking for sugar, and the next instant be ready to settle for salt? This still appals me. I don't know what went on in my little head at the time, but in later years, I felt so sheepish listening to this story that I swore to myself I would *never* compromise to this extent. On *anything*! *Ever*!

∽

Such stories aside, my first proper childhood memory has to do with the boy with a bowl. One evening, Mama along with some other women had gone to a house in the neighbourhood to distribute milk to needy children. I decided to tag along to do my first bit of social work. I was little then, and clung to the pallu of my mother's sari as she went about her mission of mercy. The little boy with the dark complexion was even littler. Just as the ladies finished distributing the milk and were about to climb down, he appeared at the bottom of the narrow staircase, a small bowl in his hand, looking up expectantly.

'Oh, no! There's no more milk left, bachche ... it's all finished.'

The boy just stood there looking up at us, his eyes large and luminous in his dark face, dressed only in a dirty banian, the rest of his skinny body as naked as the day he was born.

'Why have you come so late, my child?' Mama asked, feeling sorry for the little one.

'My ... my mother ...' he began breathlessly, panting from the effort of climbing the three steps to get inside the building.

'My mother did not have a katori ... she had to borrow it ...'

His eyes shone with pale anticipation.

'But the milk has finished,' Mama repeated, holding on to my hand.

The small dark face grew darker.

In that moment, at age four, I experienced a hollow feeling in my stomach as I stood looking at this tiny human being who seemed not more than two years old.

This image would remain with me for a long time to come. It was the first time I felt empathy for someone. I remember recognizing this as a new emotion. While feeling sorry for him, I was watching myself watching the boy and feeling his pain. This perhaps was my first lesson in acting—taking a mental note of an experience and storing it away. In my later years, I would draw upon this emotion and use it in many ways.

Sitting at a roadside cafe on Thirty-third street and Lexington Avenue, he'd suddenly appear before me—the boy with the bowl. Sometimes I was looking at life from the top of the staircase, and at other times, I was the little boy with the small dark face with large luminous eyes, standing at the bottom of the stairs with an empty bowl in my hand.

∞

My early childhood was a very enjoyable time of my life, full of laughter, fantasy, adventure, and incident. My closest companion was my sister, two years older than me. Her pet name was Bobby. We were 'Bobby & Dolly' for the kids of our neighbourhood and for our cousins who arrived from Delhi during summer vacations. In fact, our names would often be clubbed together, especially when we were being summoned by our parents or other adults: Bobby–Dolly. I feel I was called Dolly just to make it rhyme with Bobby. If I was given to believe that I was cute and doll-like, it was pure humbug. The name Dolly remained glued to me until I was almost ten years of age.

It was Bibiji, my dadi, who chose the name Deepti for me. In

Sanskrit, 'Deepti' means light or glow. It comes from the word 'deep', which means lamp—'diye ki lau', the light of a lamp. However, no

Didi and I.

matter how beautiful and deep, it didn't stand a chance of remaining whole and pristine because of the curious Punjabi trait of mangling perfectly good names into shorter variations, ensuring they don't mean anything any more. We love naming our loved ones Pappu, Teetu, Sweetie, or Bunty. As a result, I was Dolly to all—Raj Aunty's family upstairs who were our tenants, my cousins, Munni next door. The mochis who lived in the gully between our house and the mosque called me 'Dole-li'.

For my parents, however, I was Deepi, a bit shorter than Deepti. I quite liked that—for people close to me, I don't mind being Deepi. But I love the name Deepti. It's not such a difficult name to pronounce, but why would it be pronounced correctly? Everyone ends up calling me either Dipp-tee, or Dipti, never Deepti. If I insist, then friends rub it in saying, 'Okay, Deeep-teee, happy?' No, not a triple e, just a double e ... Deepti. And that's not too much to ask for, is it?

∞

From the beginning I was taught to call my sister 'Didi', making her sound like she was much older, though the age difference between us is precisely a year and ten months. Her real name is Smiti, which in Sanskrit means 'smile'. She had the most beautiful smile on earth, and each time she smiled her eyes lit up like lamps. I liked to think I had a great smile too. The difference was that she was oblivious to it, while I knew exactly the effect I had on people, having practised a variety of poses in front of the mirror in the hat stand.

As a girl Didi was God's good child. In our early childhood pictures

I see the difference between the two of us clearly—she is the all-smiling, trusting, innocent face of humanity, and me, I have this *guess what I'm up to now* look in my eyes.

Actually, I was at a great advantage. Didi, being older, was the one answerable for everything, whereas I was accountable for nothing. She was the one who got reprimanded for every wrong we committed. 'With that innocent face of yours, you can get away with murder!' she'd grumble when she got annoyed with me.

Didi and I in identical clothes.

Mama would dress us in identical frocks, making sure we looked like sisters. During our early schooldays, Didi rode a bicycle with me happily perched on the back seat as she trundled all the way to school, from Hall Bazaar to Majitha Road and back. But she never really resented that, I knew Didi had a soft heart for me. In my favourite photograph of the two of us, we are on a tiny little tricycle, going round and round in the vehra.

When I was small, I was a total chamchi of my sister, trying to do exactly as she said and did. Perhaps this was why for much of our childhood, she treated me as if I was completely stupid. 'You don't know anything!' was her standard remark for me. And it was I, and no one but I, who was responsible for creating this image of myself. Every time she wanted a break from learning her lessons, and felt like a little entertainment, she would summon me.

'Deepi! Chal! Choochi ban ja!' (Deepi! Come on! Now become stupid!)

And I would instantly transform—become a choochi—start babbling in totli zubaan, turning all my Rs and Ds into Ls, twisting the corner

of my frock around my little finger, narrating some fictitious story! 'Ek vaali na, main na, othhe gai si . . . othhe bale loki khale si . . . saale loki dekh lae si . . . saaleyaan ne mela dalama dekheya . . . te bale khush hoae!' (Once I went to this place; there were many people there. They all saw my drama and they loved it!) Didi would enjoy this act of mine for a few minutes and have a hearty laugh, but once she'd had enough of me, she'd suddenly command, 'Achcha bas! Hun thheek ho ja!' (Okay, enough! Now become all right!) And instantly I'd straighten up, become completely normal, at once disconnecting myself from this desperate creature of a minute ago. Both of us would quickly return to our books, me to my impossible maths, and Didi to her geography lessons.

Didi and I in the vehra.

As a performer, I believe these were my beginnings.

When I recall these incidents from my early childhood, I cannot believe that I could be such a moron, forever ready to make a fool of myself at the drop of a hat. At one ishaara, one gesture from Didi, I'd become a choochi and the next moment I'd be thheek.

Besides the primary objective of winning over my sister's heart, I loved the fact that everyone around would find this act of mine rather cute. When people came over, Didi would show me off! With constant practice I became skilled at the art of tutlaana, speaking like a toddler. Whenever I was required to perform in front of a live audience, I would happily do it, no matter how stupid I was expected to look. Whenever Didi would narrate a story or an incident, I would repeat the exact same thing, and then, at the end of it, looking innocently at my sister for final approval, I'd say, 'Hai na bai, Didi?' (Isn't it, Didi?) and she would reward me with that winning smile of hers, 'Haan haan, thheek hai!'

When people ask me where I acquired my craft as a performer, I have no qualms crediting those 'Choochi ban ja! Thheek ho ja!' days as my earliest workshops in acting.

Childhood was all about Didi and I—two sisters in the world—so similar, and yet so distinct.

∞

Hamming it up for my sister aside, the very first time I saw real actors on the big screen left an unsettling impression on my little mind.

It is pitch dark in the theatre. There are people, shadows, sitting around me. On the giant cinema screen, I see swords flashing. Why are those men fighting? Trying to hurt each other! My feet turn inward. The soundtrack is blaring in my ears—the metallic whip of the swords is menacing. My toes curl inside my shoes and stiffen. I feel sick. And scared. I don't like this. I don't want to be here. I want to go home. Where is my Mama? I grope for my mother's hand.

This is my memory of my first film—*Durgesh Nandini*. The year is 1956. I am four years old. I do not remember much about the movie; certainly not the nicer parts. All I remember is the fear that enveloped me during the fighting scenes. I hated the whole thing and felt great relief when the film finally ended. As we got out of the dark theatre that night, I promised myself—I will *never* see another film in my *life!*

Come next summer and all my cousins from Delhi—Indu Bhaiya, Ashu, Babbu, Manju Didi, Alok Bhaiya, and Cheenu—had come to our house, Chandraavali, for their vacations. One evening they were all excited about going to see a movie. I was at once alarmed. I had dreaded the experience the first time. But I couldn't find a way to escape. Mama got me all dressed and sent me off with the rest of the gang. The cinema hall was not far from the house. As we walked down Bhandari Bridge and the theatre came closer, my disquiet intensified. I *had* to do something. I was not going to sit through the horror of watching another movie. Mama saw me lagging behind and waited for me to catch up. One look at my face and she said, 'Oh my God! What's the matter? You look ill!'

There was my chance. If only I could convince my mother how unwell I was. That night on Bhandari Bridge I did my first bit of real acting. I looked deep into my mother's eyes. With a 'save me if you can' look on my face, I whimpered, 'I feel terrible, Mama! I have a very bad pain in my stomach. I cannot walk another step!'

Mama looked at me with great empathy.

'Oh, you poor thing!' she said, feeling disappointed for me. 'I'll have to send you back home, then.'

Wow! It had worked! Mama promptly called Mai Sardi walking excitedly up ahead with everyone else, and asked her to take me back. I felt bad for Mai Sardi, but my little act had been so convincing my mother actually believed me!

Later that evening, when the gang returned from the theatre, I was horrified to see them jumping with excitement. The boys sprang all over the place, gyrating in this strange, jerky manner (hero style, they called it), singing songs from the film, and talking animatedly about the romance between the hero and the heroine. The film they had seen was *Tumsa Nahin Dekha* and it didn't have any fighting at all! In fact, it had a lot of song and dance and was great fun to watch. What the hell! I had missed out on the opportunity of seeing the great star of the time—Shammi Kapoor. I ended up feeling quite stupid about the whole episode and for days I suffered pangs of regret, so much so that I promised myself—I will *never* miss the chance of seeing a film again, and *never* again in my life will I ever do *acting*!

∞

Some of the clearest memories of my life that remain with me are from those early days and I remember them with great nostalgia and affection.

One of my favourite rituals was the periodic cleaning of my ears by my mother. A sweet tingling, a liquidy headiness, would course through my body as I put my head on my mother's lap, tilted to one side, the hydrogen peroxide going down one drop at a time into the ear. Mama would sit on a jute mat in the sunlit veranda purposefully holding a glass eyedropper with a black rubber tip in her hand—one, two, three, four, five—five drops, and then we'd both wait...a cool tremble would run through my bones as Mama would hold my head to her knee, waiting for the tincture to work its magic. I could lie there forever. Then slowly, as if coming out of a trance, I'd sit up, tilting my head to the other side, letting the black muck flow out on to the cotton swab in Mama's hand.

'There...see? How dirty your ears were?'

In most of my memories I tend to conveniently omit Didi from the scenario, imagining that whatever was happening was between me and my Mama, but my sister was always around.

Didi and I took turns lowering our heads on to Mama's lap, after scrambling for who'd be the first to go, the slippery chiffon folds of her sari soft beneath our necks, then the slow count to five...and then, finally, when the euphoria ended, carefully raising our heads, sitting up slowly, trying to prolong those few magical moments. 'Please clean some more, na, Mama, please...' I'd end up pleading with my mother, for which I'd get my nose pinched to a peach-pink. *Ouch!* Each time my mother was taken over by a sudden outburst of unreasonable love, an emotion called laadh, she'd pinch my nose so hard, I'd go *ouchouchouchouch*, trying to get out of her clutches, my best tactic being simply burying my face in her bosom. Mama would laugh heartily and grab my nose again, pursing her lips, grinding her teeth, shaking it real hard, a gesture I couldn't get her to stop doing for years to come. I couldn't for the life of me understand what warped pleasure she got from disfiguring her daughter's perfectly shaped nose. If she kept pinching it the way she did, I was afraid it would soon start looking like a pakoda! But Mama would laugh and that was the good life, a moment that existed just between the two of us, mother and daughter.

∽

A similar ritual involved Jeet who used to work in our house at the time. Every Sunday, both Didi and I would squat on the floor in the white afternoon sun, towels around our shoulders, all set for Jeet to give us an oily head massage with thick sarson tael. Though hired as a cook, she soon developed a special bond with Mama and became not only indispensable to the running of the household but also an integral part of our family. In my recollection of Jeet, I see her scurrying about the house, her short, podgy figure in salwar kameez with the dupatta trailing behind her. Jeet was everywhere—wobbling across the vehra, scuffing her feet on the ground—the queen of the kitchen, singing as she went about her daily chores.

'Good heavens!' exclaimed Mama one day when she noticed that both Didi and I had got lice in our hair. She instantly set Jeet to the task of delousing our hair. I had brought the lice home first, contracted from God knows where. Didi then got it from sleeping on the same bed as me. The ordeal went on for days.

The lice-picking afternoons came in the form of white powder mixed with mustard oil rubbed vigorously into our scalps. We girls weren't allowed to walk about the house once our long strands were tied up, wrapped in white muslin, and kept in place with safety pins. This was so the wraps wouldn't unravel in the night as we twisted and turned in bed, kicking each other. In sleeveless white cotton chemises, we lay curled up, facing each other—two pairs of skinny legs, knees touching knees, heads touching heads—and giggle a whole lot before we finally tired and fell asleep.

Next morning when it was time to get the lice out, Jeet patiently sat with us under the hot sun on the first terrace, splatting the miserable vermin between her two thumbnails. She'd squish the tiny black things and brush them off, red-streaking the white muslin spread on her lap.

'Ayyiieee!' she'd squeak, and a tiny shiver would run down my spine.

'Show! Show!' I'd turn my head in disgusted excitement each time we heard a faint, succulent tick between the collision of two nails.

'No need!' Jeet would retort, nudging my head back to the front.

Serves them right, I'd rejoice triumphantly, the bloodsucking beasts.

One afternoon, Mama came up to check on our progress.

'The girls won't sit still, Phabiji', Jeet complained. 'They keep shuffling.'

Mama sat down. 'When I came back from school one summer with a head full of lice, do you know what my father did to me?'

'What?'

'He got hold of a razor and shaved off all my hair.'

'NO!!!' Didi and I choroused.

'And I sat and howled that whole evening holding my chopped hair in my lap.'

All at once I wanted something similar to happen to me. Just as dramatic. I visualized myself with a bald head, sitting in the dark on the staircase with my long strands stretched before me on my lap, and fat, sticky tears falling in slow motion . . . just like Mama.

'Sit quietly and keep your head straight!' Mama said. 'Don't make me do to you what my daddy did to me. From a pretty little girl do you want to start looking like a funny little boy?' I was never in two minds about that. The thought didn't amuse me one bit. I'd hate to be a boy! I loved being a girl. The only boy I liked was my adorable little doll, my golliwog.

∽

Among the many oddities that fascinated me, I especially loved polishing the kitchen vessels to a high shine, a chore that I'd look forward to on my frequent strolls to the kitchen. Whenever Jeet turned her attention from doing the dishes at the sink to whatever was cooking on the brass pump stove, I'd sink my hands into the bowl of ash placed there and give the smoke-blackened pateelas a vigorous scrub until they shone a silvery white. Both Didi and Mama made fun of me, '*Eh lae!* There she goes again—her hands in the ash. How can any sane person enjoy cleaning utensils with raakh?' But I didn't care, I loved it.

∽

It was the same fascination that made me look forward to the days on which the kaliwallah, an itinerant polisher of blackened vessels would pay a seasonal visit to the house.

'*Phaande kaleeee kara laaaawwww . . .*' was a most welcome call at Chandraavali, one that made me run across the vehra to the big phaatak where Jeet hauled out rusted, blackened pateelis to clean. I'd plonk myself on the threshold, next to the heap of utensils, waiting for the wizardry to unravel. The kaliwallah would place a pateeli upside down on the burning coal flame of his sparkle machine, while rotating it with his left hand. Then he'd take powder on a cloth and scrub the inside of the pateeli creating smoke clouds, and within a few seconds, the black pateeli would turn to a sparkling white—Like *chhoo-mantar*! Every time the kaliwallah came to the gully, I'd go hunker down beside him, waiting for the magic show to begin.

∞

We weren't allowed in the sun forever though. Mama made sure we didn't stay out too long in the scorching heat of the summer afternoon. It was mandatory for us to get back indoors and lie under the shade of the bamboo chicks in the veranda for our siesta.

It was difficult for us to stay away from the burning courtyard though, its white hopscotched grid on the floor, the *satapoo* a favourite with all little girls. I'd always get the feeling that by not being out there, I was missing out on something major happening on a hot summer day. But we'd inevitably get ordered inside, buntae clutched in our hands.

Lying on the cool darkened floor I'd carefully place the little glass marbles real close to my face, turning them round and round and watch, for a long time, the colours intermingle, the jingle on the terrazzo floor tickling my ear. The floor made a sound, if you put your ear real close to it, an earth sound, and I'd lie wide awake on the bamboo-shaded mosaic, listening deep within, for a world I imagined existed below.

The marbles still come alive, clear, sparkling, in all their splendid colours, floating timeless, in their blues and their greens.

∞

Life in Chandraavali was mostly blissful, except for a certain time in the evenings when bats came whirling into my life. The creatures hiding by day, came flitting around at night, darting sharply from corner to corner, menacing in their frenzied flight. The wooden beams in the high ceiling of our veranda were a haven for the winged creatures. A bat would come careening in, and spin overhead—round and round and round at terrific speed. I'd shriek and duck under my father's writing table with the swiftness of a cat. Blinded by the light, the bat would be trapped, unable to escape, until Mama got up and switched off the lights.

As for Didi, she would simply close her book and keep sitting calmly at the far end of the veranda, waiting for the lights to come back on. Once that happened, she'd go back to her book, as if nothing of consequence had happened. I would eventually crawl out from under Pitaji's table, casting apprehensive looks at the ceiling. I could swear the bats never came from the outside but had a secret hiding place in the veranda of our house, and that wasn't a comforting thought.

Mama had once told me a story about a bat that got stuck to Badi Mummy's forearm. Everyone tried to get it off, but the bloodsucking creature wouldn't let go, and when it did, the skin on her arm also came off with it. It was the most horrifying bat account I'd heard as a child. Ever since, I've been petrified at the thought of a bat clinging to my skin and sucking my blood! Thinking back, I suspect Mama never told Didi that story, otherwise she wouldn't have been sitting through it all so unruffled, as if living with bats was a way of life.

It wasn't just the bats that one had to live with. There were other living creatures that inhabited the veranda. I distinctly remember what I would later refer to as a 'conference of lizards'. The reference was to a bunch of agitated geckos that were to be found on the top right corner of one of the walls. After a brief, frenzied nodding of heads and wagging of tails, they'd disperse, move to various corners, and take up strategic positions. From there they'd fix a beady eye on the poor insects bumbling around the light bulbs. As they started to stalk their prey, they'd grow so still, that it would get the adrenaline racing in my veins. I'd be on edge, waiting ... Sure enough, before the light-stunned insect was even aware of what was happening it would disappear down the maw of one of these creatures.

One evening, Didi was immersed in a dictionary, reading aloud: 'Salamander: a mythical being, especially a lizard or other reptile, thought to be able to live in fire.' She then repeated loudly, 'A lizard or other reptile ... Salamander—a mythical being.'

Mama, walking into the study, said, 'Words in dictionaries are to be looked up, not mugged up.' Bunny, my young cousin, living with us at the time, gazed dreamily at the wall above the garden. I sat with my drawing book, colouring in the pages with my crayons.

The next afternoon, a small net cage was suspended from a wooden beam near the terrace door. Inside, a gecko scrambled about, making the contraption sway like a pendulum. Bunny struck a match, twisted a sheet of paper, and set it on fire. He then held the burning paper under the makeshift cage. Just then, Didi arrived on the scene and screamed.

'What on earth are you doing?'

'Checking!'

'Checking what?'

'If this lizard is a salamander!'

'Mythical, you idiot!' Didi stormed, 'Stop. This instant!'

She snatched away the burning paper and stamped it under her foot.

'How dare you torture the poor thing! Go look up the word "myth" in the dictionary. A myth is a widely held but false belief or idea.' She said, and jerked open the cage. The frightened lizard scuttled out and, through the latticed rectangle in the wall, disappeared into the gully.

∽

Munni and I spent a lot of time together. She was the neighbour's daughter, literally the girl next door. She and I were the same age, with just a day between us. Munni, me, and Didi, often made up a threesome and Mama would often say, 'Munni is my third daughter.' She loved it when Pitaji fondly called her 'Munni-Atta-Gunni'.

One of Mama's favourite stories about Munni is when she caught the four-year-old marching down the street along with her brother Binder, wearing just a kachhi. Mama was scandalized.

The threesome: Didi, Munni, and I.

'Where do you think you're going, wearing just underwear in the middle of the bazaar? Get back inside *this* minute!' Mama said, grabbing the little tyke, and marching her off to her mother. 'How can you let your daughter amble down the street wearing just a kachhi? Send her to *my* house, instead. Let her play with my girls, but *never* again, on the street, without clothes!'

From that day onwards, Munni was forever in our house.

Once, Mama reprimanded her for something and banned her from coming to our home. I don't remember what she had done to deserve such a drastic punishment. The next thing we knew, Munni was standing at the top of her terrace overlooking our courtyard, throwing cow-dung cakes into our house. That was Munni's way of venting her frustration.

∽

When Didi wasn't around, Munni and I would frequently amuse ourselves by sliding down the thhada, the raised, step-up porch of the house facing the street. A homeless man called Phaa, lived by the drain that flowed under the arch of the thhada. He must have had a proper name at some point in his life but now he was simply known as Phaa, meaning brother. We kids called him Shudai, the madman. Whenever, we stepped out, he would make a strange noise.

'J-j-j-j-j-j' was a familiar hissing sound we'd hear in a real low octave each time we stepped in and out of the house from the main entrance. Phaa wasn't intimidating in any way, so we mostly chose to ignore him.

The thhada had a flight of steps leading down to the street bound on either side by stone ledges. Munni and I liked to slide down the ledges, something we'd often do just for kicks. We'd scurry back up, and again come zipping down. We must have slid down those ledges hundreds of times, with Phaa hissing away, providing the background music. Occasionally, we'd see him pull out his head from under the arch and peep at us with one eye, the other forever hidden behind his tousled locks.

One day, as Munni and I were playing on the thhada, happily oblivious to the homeless man's existence, things changed. I came sliding down the ledge, legs dangling on either side, when suddenly he sprang out from under the arch and grabbed my foot. I clutched on to the ledge and shrieked in taar saptak, hitting an all-time high pitch, while he went 'J-j-j-j-j' in

the mandra saptak, the lowest octave. I kicked in the air and jerked my
legs trying to yank my foot away, but it was caught in an iron grip. His
grimy hair flopping all over his face, one eye peering through, he kept
hissing *'J-j-j-j-j-'* and grinning vacantly, hissing and grinning. Petrified, I
kept screeching, desperately holding on to the ledge with both my hands.
Munni shrieked from the other end. He was no playful creature, this one,
like Mai Kodhkirli, the other lunatic in the neighbourhood, living across
Hall Bazaar. *He* meant *harm.* My screams brought Mama tearing out of
the house. 'Shoo! Get away! *Get away!* You!' When she was unable to free
me, the shopkeepers across the street dropped whatever they were doing
and came hurtling to my rescue. As they grabbed him, and hustled him
away, the hissing intensified, *'J-j-j-j-j-jj-jj-jjj-jjjj - jjj . . jj . . . j . . . j . . .'*
then slowly faded.

Dishevelled and frightened beyond belief, I must have been a sight.
Mama slapped my clothes back in place. I gathered my ruffled self together
and hid behind my mother, who was deeply distraught. Munni, too, looked
terrified. That's the day Shudai was taken away from under the porch.
The bazaarwallahs went into close conference right in the middle of the
street, and it was decided that he be handed over to the lunatic asylum.

'What is a *paagal khaana?*' I asked, next morning, sitting at the breakfast
table. My father looked up from his newspaper. Mama didn't want to
answer that one. 'Eat your toast,' she said. Didi, however, had a smirk on
her face. Looking up from the Blondie & Dagwood strip, her lips parted
in a gorgeous smile as she said, 'A place *you* may quite like!'

2

The House by the Mosque

Our house in Amritsar, which was named Chandraavali, was a corner
house, opening on to the street on one side via the thhada while the
other side opened to the maseet-waali-gully, a small lane that ran between
our house and the back of the mosque.

Bauji, my paternal grandfather, bought the house in 1933 from a
barrister called Shaikh Mohamed Umar, Bar at Law. His brother had
built the mosque, and Shaikh Mohammed constructed his house next
to it. When he died, the property was divided between his two wives.
Pandit Gyan Chand Sharma, my grandfather, bought the larger portion of
the house, and Pandit Devraj Shastri, Munni's father, bought the smaller
section. Separating the two halves was a towering wall with a door in
between, which was bricked in once the Pandits moved in with their
families, turning their sections into Brahmin homes.

The Chandraavali house was a looming, four-storey structure built on a large five hundred square yard plot on the outer edge of the walled city. It had fourteen rooms and countless windows, half of them opening to the street, and the rest to the courtyard where I spent many sunlit afternoons playing hopscotch on the bricked floor. The house was whitewashed a sultry yellow and the woodwork painted a grey-blue. The main house comprised a large hall, our hall kamra. In the centre of the hall kamra sat a deep blue sofa, a three-seater placed across from the mantelpiece. On the mantel stood a brass vase and a wooden plate, which looked like it was sliced out of a tree trunk, with a landscape painted on it. The wall above the mantel held a painting of my paternal grandparents, Bauji and Bibiji, 'a fine work of art', as Mama always pointed out. Other rooms of consequence were Bauji's study opening to the street, next to which was my parents' room that faced the pillared veranda, its high roof a haven for bats. In the middle of the veranda was the hat stand that stood like a character, a witness to my coming of age, but about that, a little later.

Beyond the veranda was the courtyard or the vehra. To the right of the vehra was the towering wall where the door between the two sections had been bricked in. To its left was our bathroom, the gusalkhaana, and the empty cowshed we used for parking bicycles. Further left was the phaatak, the huge wrought iron gate that opened to the maseet-waali-gully. Cut into this big gate was a smaller gate that had an iron latch with a rope attached to it hanging outside the kitchen. Every time there was a knock on the phaatak, I'd run and pull the rope, so the metal lever would go up allowing the visitor to enter our courtyard by bending just a wee bit.

It was in this courtyard that my Mama's bougainvillea blazed all through the year, its magenta flowers flooding the vehra, a visual memory of the house that is deeply embedded in my heart. There was also the raat ki rani, the night-blooming jasmine that my mother so loved. She would take me across the vehra counting the little white buds glowing in the yellow kitchen light. 'Deepi, look, how the tiny flowers are blooming! Now the whole house will be filled with their fragrance!'

Under the bougainvillea, was kept a little milk katori for the stray cat that prowled between our house and Munni's. Behind that was the kitchen where Jeet was often heard humming and, at times, trilling while chopping onions and potatoes. To the right of the kitchen was our room—

Didi's and mine—a room we were to share all through our growing
years. Next to the kitchen, was a small granary, where, along with the
dals, chawal, and atta, Mai Sardi kept her tin boxes filled with rag dolls
dressed in tiny, ivory-coloured salwar kameez, their hair made of black
wool. These tin boxes were a mystery to my mind; they intrigued me no
end. I often wondered why all these dolls were kept in boxes. On the *one*

Maseet-waali-gully

day that they escaped their tin
prison and lay spread out on
the terrace to get some sun,
a sudden hailstorm beat them
down, reducing them to rags.
No one had remembered to
pick them up. Later I saw Mai
Sardi collecting the soaking
wet dolls and throwing them
into a gunny bag. After that
day I don't remember seeing
the little cotton dolls nor the tin box, their home where they once lived.

To my child's eye, the house in Amritsar had a strange character;
there was something mysterious about it. From time to time, when you
least expected it, it changed in shape, colour, texture, even in the way it
felt. When I think of the house, I feel I am looking at the artwork of a
wacky set designer. Some of this was no doubt due to my hyperactive
imagination but a lot of it was also because of the eccentric and novel
way in which it was built. There were staircases hidden everywhere, eight
in all, going down and across like a crossword puzzle. There was one
right outside my parents' room that led nowhere, the passage in which it
ended having long been locked and abandoned since the tenants moved
in upstairs. Sometimes when I'd be upset, I would go and crouch in its
dark end.

The stairs next to the kitchen led to the two terraces on different
levels. The first flight opened to a large terrace adjacent to the study
room, where Didi and I spent much of our time closeted with books—
she studying, and me, daydreaming!

I called it the Green Room, first, because it was painted a leafy,
lime-green, and secondly, because the name sounded like the backstage

of a theatre and had the element of drama to it. It was in this Green Room that I'd spend a lot of my time with actors and actresses—cutting pictures out of film magazines and sticking them on the inside of my books' cupboard. Mama would come up from time to time to check up on us and seeing the clutter in the room, she'd usually get mad.

'What are these socks doing here with your books?' she would demand. 'Get up right now, *you dirty pigs*, and clean your room!'

'You dirty pigs' was my mother's favourite cuss words for us, a phrase we didn't really mind. We'd heard it so many times, we had got used to it. I figured there was a certain amount of affection hidden in there.

It was the Green Room where we slept through the winter months, the furnace keeping us warm at night. All rooms in the house had furnaces. Even the terrace outside the Green Room had an open hearth furnace built into the yellow wall, something I found quite dreamy and surreal.

Just before you entered the Green Room there was a steep dark staircase on the right, plunging down to another dead end. It had perhaps once opened into the mochi gully. To my mind there was a great mystery about this staircase. Every time I ran to the Green Room, I'd pause for just a moment, and peer into the darkness below. A tiny ripple would run down my spine when I looked into those murky depths and I'd quickly move away. I would imagine all kinds of sinister characters living down there, characters that came alive only at night.

∽

In my mind, the person with whom the Green Room and the terrace are most intrinsically entwined is Mai Sardi, my nanny, whom I loved dearly. She was a Brahmin widow from Sultanwind, who turned up at our house one winter, and stayed on many a season looking after me. Mai Sardi always wore a long mal-mal shawl over her head and white salwar kameez. On winter afternoons, she'd sit in the warm sun on the terrace, cotton wool spread all around her, pulling out quilts, mending the old razais—a seam here, a stitch there.

Often, as she worked, she would chat with Raj Aunty, our tenant, sitting at her window across the courtyard. I loved the sound of the language, the Punjabi dialect in which they spoke, its cadence and rhythm. They could talk for hours together under the white winter sun filling quilts with cotton wool or sifting lentils for small grey stones. The conversation ranged from what happened last summer during someone's marriage ceremony in the village, to the satsang nights in the neighbourhood, when women would hurriedly wind up their daily chores—feed their husbands, put the children to sleep, clean up their kitchens—then go and stay up all night listening to some enlightened being speak eloquently about 'moh-maya', and how to free oneself from desires, expectations, and disappointments in the human cycle of birth and death.

I remember Mai Sardi being around me until I was about six. Then, suddenly, she was gone. Later, Mama told me that one day, as my father was returning home on his bicycle through the gully, he saw Mai Sardi slap me for some infraction. That very instant, he asked her to leave. I don't remember what I'd done to provoke Mai Sardi's wrath, nor do I remember being hit. I do remember I missed her a lot, as she was the closest to me all those baby years. But now Mai Sardi was no longer there and I was left with just my golliwog.

∽

Going up another angular flight of stairs from the first level would find you standing before the most amazing sight. The dome of the mosque suddenly rose up before you, with the white-from-the-sun walled city for backdrop. It was from this uppermost terrace, the dhoore kotha or barsati, that one discovered the city—a fleet of rooftops ending in the blaze of the sunburnt skyline. All houses had their drama, and for me, the most dramatic aspect of the Chandraavali house was this barsati. From here the city looked like a Pahadi miniature, all perspectives clear and visible—the houses, their interiors, the banisters, courtyards, inner and outer views into windows clear and transparent—all terraces ending in the whiteness of the summer sun, scorching through clear glassy skies. It is on this barsati that I'd spend my girly years, dreaming about life.

∽

It was here that I'd immerse myself in happier pursuits. As a girl I loved watching the pigeons fly. I'd throw a stone at the dome of the mosque, and off they'd go flying, making a wide circle in the sky ... then return to the dome flapping back into their original positions. As soon as they nestled

back in, under the cement petals that fringed the dome, I'd throw another
stone, and there they would go again, soaring into the blue sky, the sound
of their beating wings music to my ears.

Khairuddin Masjid

I would linger on the barsati, the roofed part of the terrace, for hours with
a book in my hand, reading . . . though 'daydreaming' is a more accurate
word. During the winter months, the cold could not dissuade me. I'd
run up at the slightest pretext, sneaking away from the real world to be
with the friend I'd made up there—the stray cloud. For hours I could
sit just gazing at the sky. If anyone had ever seen me those days sitting
on the barsati, talking to the clouds, they would've surely concluded the
poor child's mental state was unsound.

When the rains set in, and the world was dripping wet, I'd still hang
out there, snuggled up under the tin shed, mesmerized by the cloud
formations. I'd see faces and forms taking shape as the clouds glided
across the sky.

Endlessly I could sit up there, lost in my own little world. My sojourns to the barsati were a constant source of irritation for my mother, who'd often look for me all over the house, usually to no avail. There were times when I could hear her calling out to me, but I wouldn't answer. I imagined the terrace had a ladder that reached all the way to a high place in the skies, a place I could climb to and hide among the clouds.

∽

One day there was great excitement in the neighbourhood.

'Baddal aaya! Baddal aaya! A cloud has come!'

A single stray cloud did not float away with the rest, it stayed back, lingered ... Slowly, it moved down, turned the corner of Hall Bazaar—a gigantic white, fluffy blob, drifting into our street. A splendid apparition! Everyone stood spellbound! Little boys playing gulli-danda stopped in their tracks, the wooden gullis slipping from their hands and falling to the ground. Men and women, old and young, gaped and gasped in astonishment. From the tikkiwallah's stall, it glided past Shahni's tabela. Sardarilal managed to keep his turban from falling as he stopped milking his buffalo and rose, his feet squelching in the sodden, cow-dunged earth. The old Sardar tailor left his Usha sewing machine and stood at the edge of his wooden plank above the naali, captivated by the vision. Scruffy urchins ran down the maseet-waali-gully, their feet bare, wide grins on their faces and brightness in their eyes. They disappeared into the cloud, giggling, splashing its whiteness around.

'Baddal aaya! Baddal aaya!

Mai Kodhkirli, the madwoman of Hall Bazaar, came running down the street, arms flapping in the air, dispersing the brilliant flocculence into fluid streaks of white.

By now the cloud was quite close to where I stood spellbound on the thhada. The enormous white presence glided towards me and curled itself around my bare feet. I was ecstatic! A woolly, moist nothingness tickled my skin, my eyelashes. The sky had reached out to me! The cloud had travelled all the way down and entered my life, become part of my world. I was enraptured!

∽

For months, Amritsar was hot and arid. The summer was usually long, stretching from early May till the end of July, when the monsoons finally arrived. All through the summer months we slept on the barsati. On days of sweltering heat when the nights were still, we'd sprinkle water on our beds and lie down under the open sky waiting for the breeze to start blowing. In the house next door there were other ways of dealing with the breezeless nights. Munni's mother would say, 'Pur gino, pur! (Name the towns ending with 'pur'). So, the kids would start counting— Gurdaspur, Kanpur, Jabalpur, Saharanpur, Ferozepur, Rampur, Sultanpur, Hoshiarpur, Lyallpur—and sure enough, twenty-one purs would bring in the breeze.

৵

One recurring ordeal for me that took place in the house I grew up in, was getting up in the middle of the night to relieve myself. Doing su-su at night was a nightmare! In order to pee, it was necessary to climb down two flights of stairs in the dark. I would wake my father up and Piti would hold a table lamp across the banister, face down, directing the light towards the huge wall of the vehra to light up the floors below. The stairs would only be dimly lit but it was better than nothing, and I would walk down all the way to the ground floor, talking to my father as I went.

On the night that I am recalling here, something had changed. Perhaps there was a sudden chill in the air. Summer had slipped away without warning, and when I woke up in the middle of the night, I wasn't sure if it was from the uncontrollable urge to pee or from the sudden drop in temperature.

I walked to the door that led to the staircase, and began climbing down. As always, the table lamp lit up the courtyard below, but there was no light in the stairs. I groped my way down in the dark, dragging one foot at a time, feeling my way to the edge of each cement step before lowering the other foot, holding on to the walls on either side.

'Don't switch off the light . . . until I tell you, okay?' I called out to my father, 'and please stay right there!'

'I'm right here, holding the lamp for you, my dear . . . Now go on, there's nothing to be scared of!'

Whatever light the lamp managed to throw on the wall was insufficient to light up anything properly. Instead, it made the place appear eerier, creating shadows that swayed in slow motion. And I knew ... I knew there were things here lurking in the dark, things that appeared only at night when everyone was fast asleep. One flight down and I came level with the tiny storeroom that contained the giant trunk that held our winter quilts. That trunk looked more like a creature out of a horror movie, than a harmless piece of luggage. Steeling myself, I hurried past the door of the terrace. That's when I heard something move. I stood still. On the faintly lit terrace I saw a bearded old man, full of menace, bloodshot eyes, long teeth, and gnarled hands, his long fingernails painted red. He sat there amidst the cotton and spools of yarn, his mouth open in a terrifying carmine grin.

A chill ran down my spine. A cat leapt from the furnace and disappeared into the dark.

'Piti ...' I quavered, 'I can't go down ... It's too dark ... Please come down with me ... You'll fall asleep, I know ...'

'I won't ... I'm still holding the lamp, aren't I?'

'But you are not *talking* to me ...'

'I'll keep talking, all right? But hurry now and come back fast—good girl!'

I shut my eyes tight; I was determined not to let the old man reappear. With both my hands on the walls, I continued to climb down slowly, my heart pounding in my chest. I groped my way through the curve of the narrow stairs, dragging my palms along the chipped walls where the paint had flaked off, creating an uneasy sensation beneath the fingertips.

'Pittiiieeee ...!'

'Yes, yes ...'

I finally arrived at the bottom of the staircase. The huge wall on the left loomed overhead, a giant yellow triangle of light playing saviour.

I stood still in the vehra, peering into the dark to see if any figure would emerge from the veranda or the corners of the house invisible to me in the darkness.

'Piti! ... You've gone to sleep!'

'I haven't, beta. Are you done yet?'

'No, I'm going to ... just keep talking to me!'

In the cool autumn night, little beads of sweat started to appear on my neck. I held my breath and moved towards the phaatak. The gully outside the house was asleep. I looked at the latrines, it was pitch dark. No way was I going to step in there!

'Pitteee ...' I called, and the huge yellow triangle on the wall nodded. At the gate, still holding my breath, I squatted at the drain, momentarily forgetting the terrors that lurked in the dark. *Aah*! What relief! The joy of peeing in the open made the whole ordeal worth it.

Then, something moved. I held my breath again as I heard footsteps coming closer. In the slice of light flooding in from under the gate, a shadow moved towards me. The low grunt of a drunken man returning home. I froze.

'Pit ... teeee!'

No reply. Only the light of Piti's lamp wavered against the courtyard wall, reassuring me of my father's presence. The footsteps shuffled past and disappeared into the gully; a whiff of fresh breeze wafted in again. I shivered ...

Suddenly, I felt the shadows waiting for me in the dark had slithered up right behind me, their breath on my neck. I panicked. Piti hadn't answered. He had gone to sleep! How could he? I was all alone now.

'Piteeeee ...'

Springing up, I shot across the length of the vehra, where the bougainvillea stood drooping, and began galloping up the stairs.

'Pite e e e e ...' My voice was now weak with fright. As I ran, my hands slapped both sides of the chipped walls—Dhap! Dhap! Dhap! Dhap! The shadows leapt behind me, looming overhead, clamouring for me. As I bolted around the corner of the Green Room, all the demons living inside that monster of a trunk crawled out, dancing to alien drums, a music that deafened my ears!

I bounded all the way up, two steps at a time, never once looking back. The grotesque, grinning goblins were close at my heels; creatures of the dark, shrieking and screaming, breathing down my neck where my two pigtails flung and hit against each other! Dhum! Dhum! Dhum! Dhum! I could feel the dread creep up my back, my ears, my ankles, between the sweaty joints of my knees! Outside the storeroom the bearded old man with his bloodshot eyes and red smile, was waiting for me. As I sped around the curve, he pounced at me. I swerved and kept pelting up the stairs. He followed, just one touch away, but I kept charging onwards, till I emerged on to the barsati, breathless and panting.

'Good girl!' Piti lowered the lamp from the banister and finally switched off the light.

'See! ... I told you ... it was *nothing!*'

∽

Occasional terrors aside, one of the things I found most fascinating about our home in Amritsar was the mosque next to it, just fingertips away, a narrow gully separating the two. Khairuddin Masjid, the biggest mosque in eastern Punjab, was built in the year 1876, seventy-six years before I was born in the house next door. My memory of the house is entwined with the maseet's dome, its minarets, and the mellifluous sound of the azaan, unexpectedly stirring something within you.

In 1952, the year I was born, the maseet was a dark, deserted place since most Muslims in Amritsar had left for Pakistan during Partition. No one lived there, except for the pigeons that fluttered around the blackened dome. And then, in 1956, when I was around four years old, the first maulvi returned to the maseet. My memory of that October day is vivid. The cold was beginning to set in but we hadn't yet moved downstairs. In the wee hours of the morning, while it was still dark, I suddenly heard a wail ...

'*Allaaaaah hu Akbaaaaarrrrr ...*'

It filled the sky with startled pigeons.

'Azaan ... ?' my father murmured as he got up from his bed and looked over the edge, peering at the maseet. In the dark, he could faintly discern a lone maulvi standing in the centre of the compound, his voice raised in prayer, breaking the silence of the deserted sanctuary. A sudden wind surfed the terraces. Pigeons winged their way up, making primordial circles in the sky. Didi and I woke up, and went and stood next to our father. Mama came up the stairs and gazed at the scene below. The autumn wind wafted, stirring dry leaves around the mossy pond of the maseet. A window slowly opened in Raj Aunty's house. Mochi Bhagwan Das ambled into the gully looking startled; a few more windows opened down the street, framing sleepy faces. People slowly woke up to the muezzin's call that rang out faintly in the dark. Shahni's buffaloes were the only ones that remained unmoved.

'*Azaan ...*' whispered Mama, '*Hai ...* How beautiful ...'

That night, before going to sleep, my father, for the first time ever, spoke about the maseet as he remembered it from his boyhood days. There was a time he said, after 1947, when there was not a single Mussalman in Amritsar. Not one. But, before Partition, the maseet was a vibrant, flourishing place. There would be 'dhuandhar taqreeraan', impassioned sermons over the loudspeaker. The tiny entrance to the maseet in front of our phaatak was reserved for women. Come Friday hundreds of them would enter through this back door for jumme di namaz, all wearing black burqas. Although the maseet was active all the time, my father said, their prayers never clashed with our havans.

Once the maseet reopened, the notes of the azaan went up in the air five times a day. The muezzin summoned the people for namaz, but there were no Muslims left in the area to come and pray. I would listen intently to the notes of the azaan. They were different from the saat sur Masterji had been teaching us in the music class, and almost sounded out of sur to my newly attuned ears. But there was something compelling about the notes—it was as if someone from far out in the wilderness was calling you back home ...

The off-key notes slowly became a part of our lives; I'd even begun to find them musical. Over time, I began to see a few worshippers in the maseet—men in long shirts and salwars wearing tiny white caps.

I'd perch up on the chhajja, the edge of the terrace for a top angle view of the maseet, my nose pressed to the concrete. We kids were forever curious about the maulvis who'd hoist up their salwars and wash their goray-goray feet in the pond, before they started to pray.

'Didi! Come! Look! They're coming out now ... they're washing their feet in the pond, see!'

'Such white feet! ... How fair they are ... and how fat!'

'What are you girls peering at?' Mama would ask, each time she caught sight of us hanging over the chhajja.

'Look, Mama? Their skins are so pink, they look like Kashmiris!'

'Okay, now get down. It's improper. They are maulvis, pious people. Stop spying on them.'

My sister and I would constantly look for excuses to go into the maseet and look around. We would sometimes throw a ball at the dome and then go running all the way around to the Hall Bazaar entrance to ask for the ball back. It seemed like a perfectly valid excuse to enter the mosque. But we never succeeded. All we wanted was to go inside once, just once, inside *our* maseet, as we considered it. We couldn't understand why we weren't ever allowed to step inside. But no! Girls weren't allowed, we'd be told firmly. How unfair was that! When I think back, as a child, the magic of the maseet continued to have a grip on me, and I felt a great longing to go inside the holy shrine and explore its forbidden spaces.

Once, on our return from a holiday, I entered the house, sprinted across the vehra, ran straight up to the terrace and for once ... stood stunned! A spotless white dome stood dazzling before me against the blue September sky. Wide-eyed, I gaped. The maseet was no longer dark and weather-streaked. It had been painted white! Whiter than anything white I'd ever seen. I was enchanted!

Seasons changed. A white moon shone behind the third minaret. There was something mysterious about the stillness of the pond at night. At times, the mochi kids sneaked into the maseet late at night and snooped around the dark dome. It felt eerie, watching them from the terrace.

One time, when the maseet was completely deserted, I saw a young girl in a black burqa strolling around the dark dome. An old man could be seen calling out to her for meals; he was probably her grandfather. When I'd go up to sleep at night, I would look out for her. She seemed to be the same age as me. One evening I saw her step inside the tiny entrance to the dome. To my mind, she was a girl of mystery. No one knew where she'd come from. On the few days that she was there, I did see a fire burning in the corner of the mosque—there was nothing other than that to mark her presence. Had she come from Pakistan? I wondered. My gaze would follow her strolling around the dome. I could have easily called out to her from across the ledge, but I never tried that. She, too, looked towards me from time to time but nothing beyond that. And then, one day, the fire went out and the girl was gone. I never saw the mystery girl again. This has remained for me one of the strongest images of the maseet—the image of a young girl walking around in a black burqa.

∞

My fascination with the maseet, as is quite clear, had little to do with religion. Similarly, I was entirely fascinated with the faqir who came down from the hills every winter. In the wee hours of the mornings, I would hear him singing in the gully. It would still be pitch dark outside and we'd be nicely tucked in our razais when, as if in a dream, his voice would filter in, wafting through the cold and the fog, faint and distant at first, and then closer and clearer, the words resonating through the still-dark-from-the-night gullies.

Othhe beej lae taranaan vaali kiyaari
In that place plant a bed of melody

Jithhe papaan vaale khet beej laye
Where you have sown fields of sin

Jivein mavaan noon puttar piyaare
As mothers love their sons

Phagat piyaare rab noon
God loves his disciples

Kai tar gaye kiyaan ne tar jaana
Some have swum across, some will reach there

Jinnane tera naam jappeya . . .
Those who have chanted your name . . .

The voice seemed to come from another world—the perfect melody, the complete harmony, the eternal philosophy . . . the ultimate note to be woken up by. Yet, there was something sad in those notes. Those words that he sang haunt me even today, his clear, full voice beckoning from the distance with a strange magnetic force.

The stars would still be out when I'd sometimes get out of my warm bed, step onto the cold floor, walk down to the kitchen, open the tin jar, fill up a big bowl of flour and shiver my way up to the big gate.

'Dede bachche, Babba pher agle siaale aayega tere darvaaze!'

(Give, my child, this old saint will return to your door only next winter!)

I'd open the iron latch, groping in the dark, and there, standing outside, would be the faqir with a long grey beard and a dark shroud around his head, holding open a sack into which I'd pour the flour, my eyes burning with cold and curiosity. 'Seesaan Biba!' he'd say gratefully, then turn away, singing. I'd crawl back into bed, and lie awake in my razai listening to the faqir's song, to the sound of other doors unlatching and latching, till the voice weakened at the turn of the gully. The faqir's song would slowly fade into the distance but the words would linger . . .

Kai tar gaye kiyaan ne tar jaana
Jinnane tera naam jappeya . . .

These words would resonate in my heart years later, in another city, another country, another time when in the middle of the night I'd suddenly find myself lying awake in bed, hearing the same note, the same voice, the same words:

Othhe beej lae taranaan vaali kiyaari
Jitthe papaan vaale khet beej laye . . .

Now, when I think of the faqir in the gully, I recall that it was his faqiri, asceticism, that fascinated me. I wanted to know more about his life. He came down to the plains in the winter, but where did he live the rest of the year? Where did he come from? Did he have a family? Had there perhaps been a woman in his life? Had he left a child behind somewhere in a home and crept out in the dark, to wander forever, like Gautama Buddha from chapter 11 of my history book? It was the minimalism that I felt most drawn to—the bowl, the shroud, the song, and nothing more . . .

3

Republic of Mochistan

We had an assortment of neighbours, some of whom I grew very close to like Munni, and others I was intrigued by like the mochis who lived in what I called the Republic of Mochistan. Our nearest neighbours were the Sharmas, who had a top angle view of our entire life. Strictly speaking, they couldn't be described as neighbours because they lived in the upper three storeys of our house overlooking our courtyard and the two terraces. Every time we looked up, a couple of faces quickly fled from the windows. Suraj Narain Sharma owned an electric appliance shop in Hall Bazaar called Philips Radio, and he lived upstairs with his wife Raj, and their five children: Baby and Shobha, the two girls, and Gogi, Kaalu, and Pappu, the boys. The family had been living in that part of the house ever since the great earthquake of Quetta in 1935 had driven them out of their home and forced them to migrate to Amritsar. Sharma Uncle, a thorough gentleman, was a tall, handsome man, while Raj Aunty, a most affectionate woman, was petite, uneducated, and rather plain to look at. They seemed such a mismatched couple that when I was older, I'd often wonder how matchmaking was done those days. Though the Sharma kids went to a different school, we all sort of grew up around each other; I was constantly running up to Raj Aunty's house for any little thing, as she pampered me no end.

∞

Sharing a common wall with us, the wall that was bricked in once the Muslim family left for Pakistan, was the house of Pandit Devraj Shastri, Munni's father, who along with his brother, Pandit Jagan Nath Mishra, owned the Krishna Pharmacy known for making Ayurvedic herbal medicines. Devrajji, was refined and scholarly with a calm and endearing personality. Phaiyaji, as Munni would call him, was the gentlest soul I ever knew. When extremely anguished he would curse, 'Arre O andhe ke putra! Buddhi ke shatru! (Oh, son of the sightless! Enemy of knowledge!) Once, when he came over to our house he found Mama reprimanding us for something, and said to her, 'Little girls are like flower buds, you should never be harsh with them.' I always regarded his children, Munni, Binder, Vibhu, Sudhakar, and Diwaker as part of my own family.

Munni's parents were another odd couple. Devrajji was rather good looking for a pagdi- and achkan-clad pandit, but his wife, whom we only knew as Chaanji, was an unlettered woman, whom I will forever remember as sitting on the floor in front of the firewood stove serving endless cups of tea to each family member through the day. Though we had entirely different home environments, and there was a huge cultural chasm between Munni's mother and my Mama, we were never allowed to make anything of it, and Munni, Didi, and I were forever in and out of each other's homes.

Munni had a soft and sweet voice, though she was barely audible. Her expression, while she sang, was so tender it was good enough to just watch her singing. She also played the harmonium beautifully. I could always hear her playing the instrument, sitting in her barsati room visible from our house. She could play any song; you named it and she'd play it. If Munni and I had one thing in common it was our love for music. We shared songs and exchanged plots, the handmade leaflets bought

Munni

from the plotwallah at Regent Talkies. Songs that we could not find in the plots, we jotted down from the radio, hurriedly scribbling away, as though writing shorthand!

On the upper floor of Munni's house was a large, very dark, mysterious place full of huge black drums where Ayurvedic medicines were made. Those giant cylindrical barrels would be filled with a sticky, grainy substance. Very often while playing we'd go hide behind those dark drums amidst the steam and heat of the dank cellar. The place smelt of a strange herbal formulation called Chyawanprash, supposedly good for one's health. In the evening, after the workers were gone, we kids would sneak in and out of the factory playing hide-and-seek. Amreeka, the helper in charge of the place, would sometimes dab the black paste on little scraps of paper for us to lick. The thick substance felt strange on the tongue and I could never really decide if I liked the taste of it or not.

∞

Other than our neighbours, the people who most frequented our house were Pitaji's friends, Gyaniji and Sunderlalji. Dalip Singh Uncle, the DSP of Amritsar, would come over for long stays and occupy our study room upstairs.

Gyaniji

Moolchand Uncle, who had been Bauji's munshi all his life and was now my father's secretary, was more family than staff. Then there was Iqbal Chand, Pitaji's peon in the office. Professor Kumar, a colleague of Pitaji's, would sometimes come home with his wife. I was particularly fond of Kapoor Singh Uncle, a thorough gentleman and a kind, noble soul. He was Piti's close friend from the Lions Club and they shared an interesting intellectual bond. But of all these people it was Gyaniji who held a special place in our lives. A remarkable man, and hugely intellectual, he was selflessly devoted to our family. In my father's words, 'I learnt a lot from him. He groomed me and was my greatest well-wisher, greatest philosopher, guide, and friend. An ordinary looking man, he had a very distinguished mind. He taught me rigour in life. "Speak to the point, and speak with strength, whatever you speak!" he would say.'

∞

Shahni's buffaloes form a major part of my visual memory of life in our little gully. During the rains their shiny black skins formed a lovely backdrop to my view of the street from the Green Room balcony. Shahni and Sardarilal, her husband, ran a tabela, the buffalo shed right outside our gate in the large open plot of land adjoining the maseet. Every morning we would wake up to the sound of buffaloes being prodded to eat their chaara before the milking began. I knew their entire routine by heart: Sardarilal, Shahni, their children—Rupa, Bhalli, Bimbo, and Rita—would get busy feeding, bathing, and then milking the buffaloes. The rest of the day the buffaloes seemed to do nothing but lounge around. While going to school and coming back, I'd see them doing jhugaali, sitting around lazily, masticating in the sun. They chewed their food *really* slowly, not that they ever did anything at speed. A huge tub was placed in the gully outside our bathroom where the buffaloes would drink water. The tap in our gusalkhaana ran for hours every afternoon to keep the tub filled.

Shahni's buffaloes had distinct personalities, or so I imagined. Each one of them had its characteristic traits and I could distinguish one from another quite effortlessly. I even had names for them—Fatso, Brownie, Ganga, Charlie, and Jaddo. My favourite was Brownie, who was more brown than black. One season, Brownie fell ill and started to look bony and emaciated, more like a cow. Whenever I'd return from school, I'd go straight across to the tabela to look her up. For days, Brownie lay in one corner of the shed, barely having the energy to chew her cud. The family did their best to nurse her back to health but sadly she didn't make it. I was distraught at her demise. But I recovered from Brownie's death soon enough, as I had found another buffalo to dote on—Charlie.

∞

Of all the neighbours we had, the ones that fascinated me the most belonged to the forever-cussing cobbler clan that we were strictly forbidden to mix with—and understandably so—the mochis. As far back as I can remember, the mochis had always lived between our house and the mosque, in their narrow, labyrinthine world. Uprooted from Pakistan, across the border of Rajasthan, they had fled during the chaos of Partition and ended up in Amritsar. Around twelve families had taken shelter inside the deserted mosque. However, once things settled down somewhat, the local Waqf Board in charge of the mosque, objected to their presence and decided that the mochis would no longer be allowed to live inside the religious sanctuary and would have to shift their dwellings elsewhere. That's when my grandfather opened up the area at the back of our house and asked them to move in. Later that year, the gully behind the Chandraavali house was officially allotted to the mochi community. They set up their little mud shacks and tin sheds, and 'mochi mohalla' was established. We called it 'Mochistan: the splendid Indian ghetto'.

The men mended shoes while the women made chappals and colourful little potlis. Their little ones ran up and down in front of our gate, forever spinning wheels and lattoos, the multicoloured whirligigs. At times the little ones would knock at our gate wanting flowers from Mama's bougainvillea in the vehra and she'd pluck for them fresh blossoms from the burst of magenta, then watch the dark skinny bunch run down the gully, naked, pink flowers tucked behind their ears.

Young mochi boys polished shoes to make a living. They'd line up outside Hall Gate with square wooden boxes, their boot-polishing kits neatly stacked with dark glass bottles, darker brushes, and rag cloths for shoe-shining. To their left was the old tonga stand where the tongawallahs harnessed their horses early in the morning. At this intersection was the multicoloured fruit and vegetable market, along with the newspaperwallah and the cycle stand where the Punjab Roadways buses halted for tea breaks. Babulal was the only boy who worked at home with his father, making chappals for women.

The pradhan of Mochistan was a meek-looking man named Basant Lal Chaudhary. Bhagwan Das, a man with a pockmarked face, owned the first shack in the gully. Other prominent mochis included Badrinath, Tekchand, Nanakchand, Saligram, and Chhaju Ram—part of the group that had migrated to Amritsar in 1947. In 1955, when the Indo-Pak border opened for the first time, they all went to visit friends and relatives across the barbed wire.

Among the women was Naini, Tekchand's wife, who was very adept at her craft, and Tejwati, who stood out with her one blue eye. The other women I recall were Holi, Bhoori, Gango, and Kishan Devi. There was one mochan who was very beautiful; she was Jaangi's mother. Mama would sometimes let her inside the house. She had light eyes and a delicate face. I forget her name now.

The most prominent among all these women was Deoli. Deoli's was the last voice we'd hear before going off to sleep, screeching away into the night, venting her spleen at Nainu Ram, her husband. 'Deoli's mouth is like a volcano, spewing lava!' he'd say. He would come home sloshed from sleazy, dank speakeasies tucked into the narrow gullies of the walled city. Late in the night, he'd stagger back home, rehearsing his defence dialogue.

Back in the gully a blustering whiplash would await him. Without fail, Deoli would cut loose with invective, loud enough for everyone in the mohalla to hear. A barrage of pure Rajasthani cuss words (which I didn't then comprehend) would emerge from their dismal dwelling and rise up to the barsati where we'd lie wide awake under the star-studded sky. Slowly, sleep would take over, and Deoli's voice would recede into the background as the moon emerged from behind the minarets, glimmering in the starry night.

In the morning, Nainu Ram could be seen sneaking out of the gully, walking close to the wall in order to hide his blackened left eye. On nights when she'd sock him in the right eye, he'd be seen walking backwards. He took his punishment from his wife every day of his wretched life, but finally, one memorable night, Nainu Ram retaliated. He hit his wife back. He became such a whirling dervish of fury that it took the entire cobbler clan to restrain him from tearing out his wife's hair. Deoli woke up the next morning, a changed woman.

Deoli and Nainu Ram had six boys and a girl. Tota, Deoli's eldest son, was dark as coal. He would pack his shoebox every morning, go sit at Hall Gate along with the other mochi boys and work till late every evening. But there were days when he'd sit at the corner of our gully buffing shoes, while Didi and I would stand waiting for our school tonga.

It was from Tota Ram that I learnt the art of shoeshine. Watching him, I learnt how to, step by step, polish my black Bata shoes to perfection. First, you smear the polish roughly over the shoe and set it aside. Then you take the brush. The round circular movement of the bristles will begin to spark a shine on the dull leather surface. Thrice the polish goes on the shoe and thrice you brush it. But the job isn't done yet. Not until you have worked on the leather with muslin. You fold the cloth into several layers. Then, holding it from both ends, you give the shoe a rigorous buffing. It is then that the magical moment arrives when the shoe in your hand begins to glisten, like the new calf I once saw emerge from Shahni's calving buffalo.

∞

Possibly the worst thing about the mochi mohalla was the sight of the little mochi boys perched precariously over the drain, defecating, an act that irked my father no end. Despite repeated requests and warnings, the urchins refused to change their ways. Every afternoon as my father peddled home from work on his bicycle, it was a sight to see the tiny tots scatter at approach. I never witnessed the epic tantrum the kids' squatting over the drain brought on, but Gogi told me the story in such detail that I could picture it as though it had taken place before my eyes.

One day, when Professor Naval was setting off for college on his bicycle, he was enraged to see kids, one too many, hunched over the drain along the wall of the house. When he made his displeasure known loud and clear, the mochis retaliated by opening the little back door to the mosque right in front of the Chandraavali gate, the one meant strictly for women. This further disgruntled my father and, for once, the well-mannered Professor Saab threw a fit. In his frustration he started laying about with his umbrella. As he lunged at the kids perched over the drain, they squat-scuttled in different directions colliding with each other, their kachhis between their knees. In this tumult, Professor Saab's books fell unceremoniously from his bicycle, their pages in disarray. The *Collected Shakespeare* lay scattered all over the muddy ground, uncollected.

The mochis were very upset. They argued that if Professor Saab was so worried about the hygiene around his house, shouldn't he object to the buffaloes that fouled the area as well? 'We are just poor people, Saab,' they said, 'Why don't you ask Sardarilal to take his buffaloes back into his territory?' Father grew angrier. He hurled his umbrella at Sardarilal's buffaloes, driving them back into their enclosure. Sardarilal was hugely offended, as Goel of Goel Bakery along with other shopkeepers turned up in support of my father. The fracas grew. It turned into one big imbroglio wherein the entire mohalla got involved. On one side was Professor Saab and the neighbours, on the other, Sardarilal and the mochis.

∽

It took a large cobra to set things back in order. One morning there was a sudden commotion outside the gate. The entire mochi mohalla had gathered there. 'A huge cobra has come from the gully into your house, Bauji; we will catch it and kill it!' they yelled. Mama hurriedly packed Didi and me off to Raj Aunty's house. I watched the whole drama unfold from a top angle, the window of the Sharma residence. Suddenly I saw a black cobra slithering along the wall of our terrace. In its wake came all of Mochistan right inside the Chandraavali house, brandishing rods, sticks, and jhaadus, dry grass brooms, hell-bent on killing the venomous creature.

This was the only occasion I remember when no one in the family seemed to have any qualms about the mochis running all over our rooms, courtyard, veranda, kitchen, terraces. Each time the snake appeared even briefly, the neighbourhood charged after it. Eventually the frightened reptile, in a burst of speed, made good its escape. I was terribly scared of the cobra but nevertheless fascinated by it. I was surprised how a smooth-skinned creature could glide so swiftly over the rough brick wall. How the cobra was eventually caught, I have no idea. My memory ends at the wall.

∽

Some days later, when I returned from school, I saw the big phaatak flung wide open. Within the house a seminar was in progress. My father stood inside the gate with his blackboard placed on Mama's easel. Sitting cross-legged in the vehra before him was a gaggle of little urchins deeply engrossed in what he was saying. The topic was one of utmost importance. Unsurprisingly, this lecture revolved around their habit of defecating in the drain along the house. Father told them at length why it was insanitary, affected the health of everyone in the neighbourhood, and was a foul habit. He suggested they use the public toilets under Bhandari Bridge, or the ones near the bus stop and said persuasively and firmly that they should stop using the drain to relieve themselves. 'Not here in the open . . . Not in *full view* of the public!' Naturally, my father's campaign did not succeed immediately but he kept at it, and eventually managed to convince the mochi mohalla to build toilets and put an end to the unhygienic and self-demeaning practice.

∽

My fascination with Mochistan notwithstanding, it was understood we had to maintain a respectable distance. During festivals like Diwali and Holi when the kids in the neighbourhood got together to have some fun, we weren't allowed to play with the mochis; it was just the way things were. So, on the day of Holi, little toddlers would stand outside the phaatak holding pichkaaris, gaudy plastic water guns, in their hands, squirting red- and yellow-coloured water in the direction of our gate. And we'd end up playing make-believe Holi with them from inside the phaatak, never once stepping out for a direct confrontation.

∽

The one time we had an opportunity to somewhat mingle with those in the gully and witness a Rajasthani wedding was the day Babulal got married with full band-baaja-baraat! All of Mochistan glimmered with fairy lights, flickering between a jade green and an azure blue. Sparklers went off as the baraat entered the gully. At its head was Babulal, returning with his bride in tow, wearing a shiny, printed achkan and holding a silver cardboard sword in his hand, his expression one of a man returning from the battlefield. It was one hell of a neon-lit chaos: the gota-patti ghagras, the dholak, the mithai. Women crowded at our gate insisting that we participate in the festivities. That's the day Didi and I went into the gully along with Mama and watched her gladly receive a thali of laddoos from Babulal's mother, after blessing the newlyweds.

∽

Although our worlds collided but glancingly, looking back I always remember the mochis with great fondness. I cannot end my account about Mochistan without mentioning Lala, Deoli's younger son who sang beautifully. Lala, who walked with a slight limp, would sit at his thhela, a wooden handcart, his baisakhi slanted against the wheel, and sing all evening, sometimes till late into the night. At times he'd recline, one arm beneath his head, looking at the mosque, the moon, the silent pigeons. On rainy nights he could be seen sitting under the handcart, a gunny bag over his head, his knees pulled up to his chest, singing, until everyone in the mohalla fell asleep. Lala didn't talk much; in fact he was the quietest of the mochi boys. Perhaps the only way he knew how to communicate with the world was through song.

Lala wasn't the only one in the gully who made music. At night, as we prepared to sleep under the open sky, the gully would come alive to the sound of music. The mochis would sit up till late, singing, tapping rhythmically on the dholki and khurtaal, and playing the manjira. It was this strangely haunting beat I'd doze off to every single night, gazing at the moon emerging from behind the clouds—listening to the cadence of the mochis' music, their beedi-cracked voices.

4

Nheri Aayi! Nheri Aayi!

A storm is brewing. A tin sheet rumbles in the wind. Dark clouds roll over. Everyone runs to their terraces, rolls up mattresses, and pulls them under cover. There's the scent of rain on earth. These are the images, sounds, smells I so remember, like it was yesterday.

'Nheri Aayi! Nheri Aayi!' was such a thrilling soundtrack during those days when we lived in a country called childhood.

What fascinated me most about the landscape of Punjab were the dust storms. I found them exciting, filled with mystery, creating a sensory experience that was hard to match. I loved the nheri and I'd actually wait for it, almost certain that it would be followed by a torrid downpour of rain. They provided the element of drama to our everyday lives.

Except for the grit that got into my eyes, experiencing a dust storm was thrilling, not least for the way in which it transformed the landscape.

The maseet during a dust storm.

Suddenly, in the middle of the day, the sky would turn pink, then a deep magenta, and finally become pitch black as if the sun had been blown out. My eyes would brighten each time there was another ripple in the air and the wind started to howl. Black clouds rolled over the city, turning day into night, and yellow bulbs blinked to life, lighting up the streets.

One particular dust storm, when I was around ten, is etched in my memory. I am on the terrace enthralled by the spectacle that is beginning to unfold. I see Jeet pulling off the clothes flapping on the clothesline, her expression dark and inward. I hear a sharp crack of a whip, then a low hostile rumble, constant and unnerving. A stray kite caught in the electric wires starts to flutter; the sky reddens. The wind picks up, turns into a squall. Rickshaw pullers scramble about in the dust-stormed street. Scraps of paper whirl and tumble madly in the thickened air. I hear Mama's voice loud and clear.

'Dipeeeee, come down at once!'

'Whhyyyyyy?'

Why did I have to go down when life was happening up here. I stay up on the barsati, watching everything, and I wait . . .

Brief gusts of wind move things around in the world. The tin sheets on the barsati begin to rattle; a rat-tat-tat hammering provides a steady beat to everything else that is going on. The bedsheet on Didi's cot swells up in slow motion, then abruptly folds up and turns over itself. The table lamp beside Piti's bed sways and rolls over onto the floor.

Spreading outward from the horizon, the sky for as far as I can see is an expanse of pink. I look across to the mosque. Beneath the dome I see serried ranks of pigeons squeeze into themselves and wait, their feathers rising and falling in the wind. They huddle together. From the tumult all around they know something is about to happen.

∽

Another image slowly comes into focus—

The sky clouds over as Didi and I wobble up and down the gully. She is teaching me how to ride a bicycle. She holds the bike firmly while I try to mount it. A little boy comes wheelbarrowing, and I fall. I try again, and I run into a wall. The sky rumbles. The weather begins to change . . . we girls rush back home.

Mama grabs her oil sheets from the vehra and runs for cover. 'Baachhad aan vaali hai! It's going to rain!' says Pitaji. That word sends a ripple down my spine—'Baachhad'—the first shower the monsoon wind whips in!

∽

The rains come to Amritsar in July for fifteen days, beating down like Mastana's wedding band. A crack of thunder and the downpour begins. The storm-water pipe from our terrace rapidly floods the courtyard. Mama's raat ki rani slowly wilts and droops to the ground. The buffalo shed, the mochi gully, the tonga stand at Hall Gate, the mosque, the pigeons . . . nothing is spared. It pours everywhere. Little boys make tiny paper boats and float them in the streets. The monsoon is here in full splendour!

Excited, I run up to the terrace and bundle up under the tin shed, watching the shower slanting in from all sides, witnessing the downpour, its serenade on the roof. The houses are just a blur on the horizon, the terraces lacking all definition. Each bricked edge merges into the next. The city is watercolour-washed into the dark-grey skyline.

A song is playing in my head. Eventually it all ends in a song. Sitting on the rolled-up bed, tucked in a corner, I sing my rain songs.

For the cobbler clan, the monsoons were a challenge. Little kids waddled across the gully now turned into a slushy dirt track. We would hear the ghetto dwellers squelching their way through the night, trying to throw plastic sheets over their mud shacks to keep them from dripping. It continues to pour.

Later, when the rain abated, little crawlies came out of the ground, creating squiggly burrows in the mud, etching the sodden earth with their languorous trail. We kids would sprinkle salt on an earthworm and watch it wriggle and coil into itself. As children, we could be innocently cruel.

∽

Monsoons, for all their hold on me, also brought destruction in their wake. There was a flood the city still remembers, the flood of 1955. The Bhakra Dam near Ropar had broken, and there was devastation everywhere. It was the time when Bhandari Bridge was under construction and the walled city was completely immersed in thick, muddy water. People hung on to electric poles to save their lives. According to the Ambarsaris, 'Water was coming in from outside of Hall Gate and rushing towards Lahore at great speed, the speed of a train!'

∽

One monsoon our street got flooded. Three days it had rained incessantly, and finally when it subsided, a sound kept me up till late. It was Lala, wading through the water-clogged street, his baisakhi a muted tick, his limp foot trailing behind like a tired oar . . . and Lala was singing . . .

The next afternoon, as I'm sitting in the Green Room trying to do my homework, something in the street distracts me. I come and stand in the balcony, and watch the flooded street below. I know there's a big khadda, a pothole, in the middle of the road, now invisible in the knee-deep water. Just then, a rickshaw comes wading through the street, fully wrapped in gaudy film posters, ferrying a man with Mastana loudspeakers announcing the next release in town. Oh no! No, NO . . . and it hits the khadda! The loudspeakerwallah is thrown from his seat and plonks into the water. A huge splash, and his Mastana tweeters wash away with the flow. Little urchins slosh their limbs about in the muddy waterway, slapping each other, laughing crazily, chasing the yellow-green tweeters floating towards Hall Bazaar.

∽

One of my most splendid monsoon nights came to me in the shape of a newborn calf that Charlie gave birth to. Late that night there was a banging on the phaatak and a voice called out, 'Come, Shahni's buffalo is giving birth!' Excited, we wriggled out of bed. Mama grabbed umbrellas and covered us in plastic hoods. The lights had gone out and it was raining heavily. We sploshed across the gully and lined up at Shahni's slushy tin shed. There was Raj Aunty, Kishna, and some mochi kids wrapped in gunny bags. Sardarilal stood holding a gaslight in his hand. In the dimly lit night, we all stood waiting for the moment to happen. With the rain pouring down and the lights flickering, it was a long stretched out moment when we witnessed a little calf come into this world, his glassy black skin shimmering in the yellow kerosene lamp.

Even as Shahni was trying to wipe him clean, the calf, almost at once, opened his huge dark eyes and looked at the world around him. Against the backdrop of a streetlight, dripping wet, under a cluster of black umbrellas, we all stood, gawking at him ... till all of a sudden, he slipped out of Shahni's hands and fell to the squishy ground. Everyone gasped. But then, after a few moments of flailing his limbs about, the baby buffalo swiftly swayed upright. Everyone cheered! Fascinated, I looked up at Mama; her eyes were moist. She held us close. Didi softly uttered 'So black,' and I whispered, 'like velvet!' Instantly the little one became my favourite of all the buffaloes.

I knew what I was going to call him—*Black Velvet*.

5

The Walled City

Amritsar was established nearly 450 years ago as Ramdaspur, named after the fourth Guru of the Sikhs, Guru Ram Dasji, the founder of the city. The Guru invited fifty-two traders from nearby cities to settle here, and they dutifully arrived, with their families in tow. These families started the first thirty-two shops in the city, which can still be found in a street popularly known as Batisi Hatta. Its modern name, Amritsar, comes from Amrit Sarovar, the holy pool around Gurdwara Harmandir Sahib, the Golden Temple. Known as Darbar Sahib during those days, it was built in 1604 by Guru Arjan Das, the fifth Guru, who placed a copy of the Adi Granth Sahib within the gurdwara after its completion.

Years later, during his reign in 1822, Maharaja Ranjit Singh began fortifying the city, starting from a wall in the Katra Maha Singh area. Later, his brother, Maharaja Sher Singh, continued with the construction of the wall with the twelve gates, among them the Sultanwind Gate and Chatiwind Gate. When the British annexed Punjab in 1849, Amritsar was a walled city. The British built the thirteenth and final gate—Hall Gate (renamed Gandhi Gate after Independence). It was in one of the lanes off Hall Bazaar that I spent the first eighteen years of my life growing up in the city of the Golden Temple.

∞

Only a stone's throw away from the Golden Temple is Jallianwala Bagh, the infamous public ground where the horrific massacre of hundreds of unarmed Indians by the British took place in April 1919. I have a vivid memory of my first visit to the site with my parents, when I was around eleven. As a child I'd heard of Jallianwala Bagh many a time, mostly from Raj Aunty, but didn't know what had actually happened there. Now, since we were a little grown up, my father decided to tell us about the massacre.

The word bagh means garden and that's what I'd imagined it to be all this while. But this place was in a shambles; it looked like a graveyard.

I remember walking around this empty, rundown space with a red brick wall all around it. Pitaji took us up close to the markings on the wall where the bullets had been fired. I ran my fingers over the narrow bricks, touching each and every hole in the wall, which said 'Goli ka nishaan'. Mama walked us around the well, where women and children had jumped in to save themselves from the bullets. As evening approached, I sat on the steps in the Bagh and thought about the massacre, the way it would have happened. Faded red brick houses lined the back of the wall, their windows opening into the Bagh. I imagined how people living in those homes must have actually seen the horror take place right before their eyes. The brutality of the incident left me numb for days.

That evening, as the family retired to the terrace, and both Didi and I sat around Pitaji's reading lamp reflecting upon the visit to Jallianwala Bagh, my father talked about the role of Khairuddin's mosque in the struggle for freedom.

In Pitaji's words:

'It is said that on 9 April 1919, there was a jaloos in Hall Bazaar in which twenty people were killed by the British. The dead were brought into our mosque and bathed here at the pond. They were Hindus, Sikhs, and Muslims, all. Then their funeral processions were carried out of the mosque, together. It is believed that in retaliation to this event, a jalsa was held at Jallianwala Bagh. The date was 13 April, the day of Baisakhi, when, on the orders of Brigadier-General Reginald Dyer, the brutal massacre took place killing thousands of people.

'It was a national disaster and a turning point in India's history—it fired up the entire nation. Thousands of people, unarmed, men, women and children had gathered there for a peaceful meeting and they get shot at, without a warning! Bhagat Singh, then a young boy of twelve, was so deeply impacted when he visited the site of the massacre, that it cemented his determination to fight against the British.'

'Jaloos nikalde si,' Pitaji said, 'lokaan-ne kapre sut ke jalaaye!' People pulled out all their good English clothes and burnt them on the streets!

Little did I know at the time that my very first role in Bombay would be in a film called *Jallianwala Bagh*, where I would tell the story of this tragic chapter in the history of my hometown.

∽

After Gandhiji started the Quit India Movement, it snowballed into a major campaign during the early 1940s. Crowds took to the streets in agitation against the British: 'Down, down, the Union Jack! Up, up, the National Flag!'

An active participant in the revolution was my bhua, Sneh, who along with other college girls, was ready to fight for freedom in full josh. The girls would rally to get colleges and shops shut down, and parade in the bazaars raising slogans: 'Band Karo! Band Karo!'

Sneh Bhua

Once, as they went around shouting slogans, a huge mob started to follow the girls down the city streets. They felt cornered. How would they go home now, dodging the crowd? The police officers stationed at Jallianwala Bagh, tried to disband them, but the girls didn't budge. Their brothers soon landed up there as well, looking for their sisters. But the girls kept shouting naaras:

'Hindustan Zindabaad! .... Inqalaab Zindabad!'

The police were adamant. 'We'll arrest you if you don't disperse!' Around twenty-five girls were arrested and hauled into a big van. And here comes the interesting part. The girls are being taken to the thana at Qila Gobindgarh, and behind the police van, following in large numbers, are the brothers of these girls, including my father. At the thana, the police serve them tea and biscuits, because they know these girls belong to respectable families. Then, they stand before them with folded hands.

'Bahenji, ais taraan na karo! ... Sisters, please don't do this! We cannot use our hands. We have no way to stop you! We cannot slap you, or touch you. Please don't make things difficult for us!'

The girls are detained at the thana for nearly two hours, but seeing

the brothers bottlenecked outside, the police get frustrated and finally let the girls go. Once released, the girls go right back to the streets, shouting:
'Down, down, the Union Jack! Up, up, the National Flag!'

∽

Our street, on which the Chandraavali house was built, fell between Hall Bazaar and Katra Sher Singh. It was a fairly quiet street compared to the chaos of the inner city. Though the street was first laid out in 1702, most of the houses on it dated from the mid 1720s or later. When I talk here of the street and the neighbourhood in which I grew up, I refer both to the main street and the myriad nameless little lanes and gullies that led away from it, lined with houses, shops, the mosque, and other fascinating odds and ends. Scholars lived alongside tailors, carpenters, buffalo-herders, lassi-makers, and kite-sellers. Ajit Bookbinder a lean young Sardar, who had converted the tiny porch of his house into a bookshop, was the binding factor between the educated and the uneducated.

Having spent my formative years on this street, my story would not be complete if I didn't tell you about the characters that surrounded me. I call them 'characters' because not all were people whom I knew well or interacted with. But when I sit down to write an account of my Amritsar days, they pop up on the screenplay of my life, each playing their part to make the story complete. I am indebted to these people for having given me that 'close to life' quality that is often attributed to my work as an actor.

∽

Dwarka Das guddiyanwallah was the favourite of the children of Katra Sher Singh. He sold kites of all colours and sizes, some with long papery tails that wafted in the breeze against the February skyline. I loved the varied hues of freshly glassed strings wound perfectly around cardboard balls—the yellows, the magentas, the blues! The kite shop was a sudden, unexpected splash of colour in the middle of the colourless street.

I'd forever be running down the road to Dwarka's shop for something or the other: a rubber, a pencil, a sharpener, Morton toffees, jaggery cakes, peanuts, and the occasional gaachni for white-painting the davaat, the wooden slate. After buying what was needed, I'd put my hand out and say, 'Choonga de!' and good old Dwarka would open one of the glass jars on the counter, take out something clenched in his fist and deposit it on my palm—a pinch of chooran, or a tiny sweet wrapped in cheap plastic. 'Eh lae choonga!' he'd say, feigning annoyance.

It amuses me today when I think of it, but we kids believed that choonga was our birthright. If you bought toffees worth two annas, you'd stand around till you got a bit more out of the poor kite seller. That little extra was called choonga—it was a cultural thing—and I'd seen all the other kids do it, so I thought it was my right, too, to demand that extra bit. When I'd buy a kite from him, I'd insist that he strung it too. When we ran out of string, we'd run back to him for more. He'd measure out the taut, glassy string on his palm, criss-crossing it between his thumb and his little finger, counting the length under his breath. Once he finished and was about to cut the string off with his teeth, we'd promptly say, 'Choonga?'

Sometimes, he'd get mad if we were one too many—Munni–me, me–Didi, Didi–Munni, Munni–Binder, Gogi–Pappu, Gigu–Gogi—we came in all sorts of permutations and combinations, huddled around the wooden plank above the drain where Dwarka sat, taking up most of his tiny little showroom, our palms forever extended for more.

'Get away you all! No choonga for you today!'

One day, I got caught by my mother while I was asking Dwarka for choonga. When I got home, she let me have it. 'Don't you dare ask for choonga-voonga like the other kids! You are *not* one of them!' she shouted.

'Yes, Mama . . .'

'Don't you ever be seen putting out your hand out to anyone! For *anything*! Ever!'

'Yes, Mama.'

'Take only what is rightfully yours, and no more!'

'I won't, Mama . . .'

It was a lesson well learnt, and one that would stay with me for life.

∞

The next shop that comes to my mind is Modern Tailor, an establishment right across the street from our house. Sardar Inder Singh, the old darzi, was the one who stitched clothes for Didi and I during our growing up years. The tailor was a tenant of Goel who lived on the upper floor and ran a bakery. Goel of Goel Bakery was a freedom fighter and a staunch Congressman. My father always addressed him as Goel Saab. His daughters, Kechhi and Shoki, were girls we sometimes played with, and later we'd all be in the same music class together.

∾

Among the vanished relics of my time as a child are the kind of pens that were then in use. These were kalams, reed pens, that had to be sharpened periodically with a knife. We bought these pens and ink at Babaji's pen shop, the little store at the corner where we all ended up every now and then to get our kalams sharpened. This is when I was still small, practising handwriting with kalams on the davaat. For one anna, we would fill up eight or nine kalams. I'd often run up to Babaji's for gaachni, then sit down in the vehra with a bowl of water, dilute the round soap-like disc and apply it to freshen my davaat.

∾

Dr Atam Prakash's clinic was another place that I visited quite frequently. I was prone to nasal infections and Mama would send me off to his clinic at any little aberration in my nasal passage. But sometimes Doctor Uncle would come home in case I was running a high fever. He charged five rupees for a house call. Dr Atam Prakash's clinic was as modest as the other businesses on the street. It stood a step or two above the naali, and we'd climb a narrow flight of stairs to a small two-bench room with a curtain, behind which Doctor Uncle treated his patients. I remember him as a gentle, soft-spoken, extremely kind-hearted man, who managed to fix most of our childhood ailments.

I once went to see him because I had a huge, ugly boil in the centre of my left palm. Mama took one look at my hand and ordered me to run to Doctor Uncle and get Kans, his skinny compounder, to apply a poultice on the boil. Every time we girls visited the clinic, Kans would pull us aside, dip a cotton swab in sweet glycerine, and, whether required or not, ask us to open our mouths wide, stick our tongues out, and dab the sticky liquid inside our throats. That little clinic operated on the principle that illness, and more importantly the cure for all illness, was in the mind. Glycerine would sort out pretty much every infection that sprang from the throat, and for practically everything else there was purple tincture. A quick *dab-dab-dab* of the solution, and off we'd go running to the house, and jumping right back into the hopscotch squares. Even today, I can recall the smell of that purple tincture and glycerine, the cure for every single thing!

But this time Doctor Uncle took one look at my hand and casually reached for his scissors. Scissors? I was alarmed. Before I could say anything, he took the scissors from a bowl of boiling water and cut the blister right off. *Khach* went the scissors once, and a gooey fluid squirted out. I stood there looking at a handful of yucky pus. I was so shocked by the suddenness of the surgical procedure that I forgot to cry. Surprisingly, it hadn't hurt me one bit. I was then bundled off to Kans, who very skilfully and neatly dabbed the freshly opened wound with good old purple tincture and wrapped my hand in white gauze.

Back home, I stood in front of Mama waving my bandaged hand in her face, 'It's gone! See! Doctor Uncle cut it off.' Mama was staring at me in disbelief. 'Cut it off? Just like that?'

'Yes! With scissors! Just like that!' I replied, sounding far braver than I had actually been.

∽

Further to our right, opposite the tabela, was Dogra's haircutting salon, where Mama would often take me for a quick crop. Didi always wore her hair long, so she was never required to sit in front of Dogra's veined mirror. Mohni, a studious Sardar boy, the pride of our neighbourhood, lived on the floor above Dogra, with Bae, his Nani. She was an old woman in her eighties, and loved her grandson to death.

Bae was a character who would take on much larger dimensions on the canvas of my imaginary world. I ended up calling her Bebbe and conveniently decided that instead of the far end of the street, she lived right here, on the uppermost terrace of the Chandraavali house, in the open-to-the-winds summer room above the Sharmas' residence.

∽

At the right end of our street was the famous Hall Bazaar, the main marketplace of the city, lined with small and large shops on both sides of the road, throbbing with activity. Opposite Sharma Uncle's Philips Radio shop was Dhruv Uncle's Prabhat Photo Studio, a destination I remember for sentimental reasons. Our family occasionally went there to get ourselves photographed—the regular black-and-white family portraits developed from small square negatives that Dhruv Uncle would later touch up, adding a dash of pink to our cheeks and giving our garments a tinge of aqua. One end of Hall Bazaar gave you a full view of the red brick structure of Hall Gate with the huge clock in the centre of it. The other end, past the main entrance of Khairuddin's mosque and rows of bookshops and woollens, led you to the historical Town Hall square, from where three lanes branched towards the Golden Temple. I'd often come here with Didi and Munni and while they browsed the kiosks for Punjabi juttis, I'd stray towards Malika Da Butt, curious to get a closer look at Queen Victoria's demeanour as she stood in the middle of the square, a pigeon perched atop her crown. It is here, in this city square, that the Partition Museum stands today.

∽

I was happiest when I went shopping with Mama to Hall Bazaar. We had the latest issues of *Woman & Home* in our house and Mama would use patterns from the magazine as a guide to pick up haberdashery at Girdharilal's shop. The old man sold wool in the most beautiful colours. He also sold fabric, lace of all kinds, piping, designs, and knitting patterns. While she perused the stock, I'd hold her brown shopping bag watching intently. There was something sensuous about the way Mama touched the fabric, the soft spools of wool, the laces.

Our shopping expeditions would follow the same route each time. For shoes, we'd stop at Bata, and for our school uniforms, the fabric would be bought at a shop in Chitta Katra, and stitched at Krishna Tailors in Guru Bazaar. The brothers who owned the establishment learnt everything from my mother. 'You tell us, Bibi, whatever you say, we'll do it exactly like that!' and it was Mama who sat with their tailors and explained things in great detail. I remember she had them make her a dressing gown in light grey print in the softest of flannels, a fine Polish fabric she surprisingly bought off a rehri, a random vendor on the street.

Our next stop would be the P. V. Kailash store opposite the Chinese shoemaker in the little market on Cooper Road. At first Mama was hesitant to go there, thinking it was too sophisticated a shop for her means, but then she found they had really good merchandise. It was here that she bought the 'Mum' deodorant she'd read about in *Woman & Home*. In this my mother was way ahead of her times—she was using deodorant when hardly anyone in Amritsar knew what deodorant was.

The dyer, Rang Lal, or Colour Singh, as I secretly called him, was my favourite halt, his wayside adda being the last stop on our list. He chose to work off the pavement in one of the back streets making inroads into the heart of the city. Mama, being very particular about the specific shades she liked, would not trust anyone but Colour Singh to understand and deliver back into her hands the shade she had in mind. I would sit on the bench off the sidewalk, admiring yards and yards of pagdis in vibrant colours spread out in the open, swaying softly in the breeze.

There were three cinemas right around the corner from our house: Chitra Talkies, Amrit Talkies, and Regent Talkies. A little further away was Ashoka Talkies, in the lane below Bhandari Bridge, again within walking distance. New Rialto, one of the oldest cinemas in town, was situated on Railway Road, outside the city wall. It always looked to me like a Punjabi woman with a huge backside.

At Chatiwind Gate, on the outskirts of the city, there was Liberty Cinema and Krishna Cinema. Adjacent to them were City Light and Nishaat Talkies. After the first run, the movies would go to that side of town. There was also Prakash Talkies, which was out of bounds for us girls, unless we went with the family.

There was a small cinema hall in the Cantonment that exclusively showed English movies, frequented by the city's elite. English movies also showed at Ashoka, Chitra, and Nandan Talkies, which was built later.

Chitra Talkies, the grand old theatre in the lane across Hall Bazaar, was built during British times. Just outside the walled city, near Hall Gate, Chitra Talkies was the first cinema hall of Punjab. It was built in 1909 by a wealthy building contractor, Sardar Mahna Singh, known as 'the man who tried to bring the magic of the movies to the people of Amritsar'. The cinema hall also doubled as a theatre as it had a large stage area around the screen on which dramas could be performed, live. Incorporating both Western and Indian elements, the majestic building, painted in deep yellow, had wide staircases, glazed wooden banisters and an enormous central hall with high ceilings, the likes of which could be seen only in English movies.

I saw my first English film at Chitra Talkies. Mama dressed up Didi and me in identical white frocks with pink polka dots, and we went along with Piti to see the classic, *Ben-Hur*. I remember how anxious I felt when the famous chariot race began. The wicked spike protruding from the wheels of the villain's chariot was dreadful to watch. *The Guns of Navarone,* starring the handsome Gregory Peck, was the second English movie we watched at Chitra Talkies a couple of years later.

∞

Life-size poster of Madhubala at Regent Talkies Chowk.

Regent Talkies, the cinema at the end of our street, was just a fleapit claiming to be the best in town for sleaze, a no-no place for 'girls from good families'. Most of the films we saw were at Chitra Talkies or Adarsh Cinema, or even further out at New Rialto, but never next door at Regent *Taakie*. Across the street from Regent Talkies was an important landmark—Mastana Loudspeakers, a shop where yellow and green tweeters with long necks and flat faces gaped from the walls—funny looking gadgets that spoke loud and metallic.

And right there, at Regent Talkies Chowk, stood a life-size poster of Madhubala pasted on the door of the printing press, smiling her slant, seductive smile, enticing all passers-by. The actress stood regal against the shop's flyscreen door, her long plait falling across her bosom. Although her posture was alluring, she had an innocence about her that made men go weak in the knees.

Past Madhubala's inimitable smile was the plotwallah, the character I began this memoir with. The plotwallah was to become an integral part of our lives once we entered our teens. That's when Munni and I, obsessed with Hindi film songs, would no longer have any qualms running back and forth to Regent Talkies Chowk, rummaging through his stack of five by sevens, hunting for song lyrics.

∞

A furlong away from Regent Talkies was the equally grungy Amrit Talkies. There wasn't much difference between Regent Talkies and Amrit Talkies of Katra Kanhaiya, further away. We would never enter that theatre no matter what film was showing there. It was another dingy, run-down hall, one that again wasn't meant for girls from good homes.

Amrit Talkies stood on the cusp of Farid Chowk and Katra Jaimal Singh where a lot of violence had taken place during the days of Partition.

The woman who ran Amrit Talkies died old and alone. The cinema hall had been neglected for a long time, but she loved the dark, grim place. Legend has it that she'd often say, 'I'm going to be back right here, when I die ... under the seats of the theatre ... as a snake. I will live here in my theatre. He lives here, too, my dead husband. He hasn't gone anywhere. He has become a snake and crawls about the theatre in the nights after the last show. I too will be here.'

∞

Katra Kanhaiya used to be a red-light district before Partition. The 'women of jharokhaas', as the prostitutes were called, lived all along these lanes. It was called 'gaane bajaane da bazaar'. The infamous baariyaan vaale makaan all belonged to the nautch girls. Farid Chowk was famous, equal to none other than the Hira Mandi of Lahore. The better category of prostitutes lived in houses on the upper levels. These were women who knew the art of the mujra, spoke chaste Urdu, and were women of great tehzeeb. These girls could forever be seen sitting at their windows, keeping a roving eye on the street below.

∽

According to a family story, Hazarilal, a blind boy from my grandfather's village, who was fond of music, somehow got introduced to these nautch girls. They acquired him for their entourage and converted him to Islam. He played the tabla while they danced. When his uncle and father came to get him, he refused to go back with them. 'Main nahin jaana, mera koi taluk nahin tuhade naal.' (I'm not coming back. I have nothing to do with you.) I always found this account very intriguing—a blind boy, a distant relative, gives up the security of home and family for his love of the arts and becomes a tabalchi, playing to the tune of the nautch girls.

When Partition finally happened and it was decided that Lahore would go to Pakistan and Amritsar would remain a part of India, all these baariyaan vaale makaan quickly emptied out. From Regent Talkies all the way up to Amrit Talkies, entire rows of balconies on the upper levels were left deserted. The women of jharokhaas were forever gone, and so was Hazarilal.

Many years later, when I was writing about all this in New York, I asked my father whether he remembered the women of jharokhaas, and he said, 'They were there, yes, everywhere ...'

'Around the Chandraavali house?'

'Yes ... more around Regent Talkies Chowk.'

'When was it that you became aware of them?'

'I was a boy of fourteen then, or fifteen, and was told to never look up at the balconies. Even if I saw them or if they tried to get my attention, I was to never look above the shops and to keep walking straight. These were not good women, I was told.'

Mischievously, I asked: 'You must have sometimes *wanted* to look up?'

There was a moment's silence, as I wondered if I had gone too far. I was about to clam up, when there was a slight smirk of recall on my father's face, and Piti said, 'Maybe ...'

∽

As very young children, though, the main attraction of Regent Talkies

Chowk was not the cinemas or tales of ladies of ill-repute, or even the plotwallah, but someone far more important to us little girls—Gyaan Halwai, the sweetmaker, who was famous throughout the city for his lassi that came in a tall brass tumbler with a thick layer of malai on top. We kids swore that he used blotting paper for the yummy top layer. Since there were no eateries around our house, every time we had a visitor at home, Mama would send us running to the chowk to buy the famous Gyaan Halwai di lassi.

Another culinary legend in our neighbourhood was the tikkiwallah who stationed himself at the corner where our street met the main Hall Bazaar. He was a short, dark, chubby man who sat on the floor with his chhaabri, making the most amazing aloo tikkis in the world. The end of 1956 saw the adoption of the metric system. Ser became kilo, paa was now 250 grams, and ½ kilo was equivalent to 500 grams. In the year 1957, the currency changed too; the anna became ten paisa, and duanni was abolished forever. For years I could not understand the difference between pauli (four annas) and thhelli (eight annas). Once at the tikkiwallah's corner, after feasting on the crispy, mashed potato patties, I asked him, 'How much?' Flipping the steaming tikkis on the oversized tava, he said, 'Pauli de deyo.' (Give me four annas).

'Naeen, main taan thheli deni! (I will pay only eight annas!) I said, determinedly.

As everybody around me burst out laughing, Didi, embarrassed, pulled me aside. 'Silly! Why are you insisting on paying him eight annas when he is asking for just four?'

Next to him was the kulfiwallah, in his pakki dukaan, where, after relishing the spicy tikkis, we inevitably needed to cool down our burning tongues with the faloode-waali kulfi. That's the part I loved. Having a terrible sweet tooth, I'd really look forward to the cone-shaped malai kulfi, topped with syrupy, fragrant falooda. Interestingly, both these maestros, the tikkiwallah and the kulfiwallah, were called Kishen Chand.

∽

A lot of my childhood memories of Amritsar are associated with the calls of street food vendors. Their vocal range hit every note on the scale, from low bass and baritone to a high mezzo-soprano.

Of all the voices that rose and fell on the streets of my early years, the most distinctive was the kaul-chapni-wallah's lone call in the morning, selling fresh lotus seeds.

'*Kaul chapni lai lao . . . Kaaawwwl chapneeeeeeee!*'

He would call just before the monsoons set in.

Those lotus seed mornings came in the form of tender succulent green kaul chapnis. I'd perch up on our ledge to check if the kaul-chapni-wallah's rickety handcart had turned the corner and trolleyed into our street. Mama would take out a few coins from beneath her pillow and ask me to run and get a whole bunch of lotus pods fresh from the fields. I'd rush back with the bouquet in my hand, breaking open the tiny green fruits, biting into the soft white kernels of the kaul chapni, the mystery fruit of my childhood days.

A short while later, another vendor would call out:

'*Aabu chhalleeeeee . . . Aabu chhalleeeee!*'

I loved the aabu chhallis. I would watch in utter fascination as the rehriwallah pulled out corncobs from his sandbox—a large, mud-coated wooden container with a tiny burner below it. He'd grope about in the burning sand which didn't seem to singe him in the slightest and pull out by the shank a fat, juicy corncob. He'd then peel away the green husk surrounding the soft flesh, squeeze lemon on it, turning it round and round as he did so, before finally sprinkling it with salt and handing it to me. How I loved digging my teeth into the mushy ripe kernels.

Finally, there was Fateh Chand's nightly long drawn-out bawl announcing the excellence of his aam papad— dry mango strips sprinkled with black salt.

'*Maalde - ae - ae - ae . . . Aaam-paapadae - ae - ae - ae . . .*'

He did the rounds of the gullies around half past nine. The minute I heard his call I'd zip across to the thhada to buy the not-so-dry orange and black squares, my taste for aam papad being the sure thing that gave away my Punjabiyat!

✺

Nights in Amritsar were like discovering another city altogether. Once the shops closed down at eight and the bazaars quickly emptied out, it would be time for the pye-dogs to go on the scrounge. The streetlights in

Hall Bazaar would still be ablaze but the inner lanes would be shrouded in shades of cadmium yellow. It was at night that train sounds from down the railway tracks reverberated through the fallen-to-silence gullies.

Aah, those after-dinner walks ... How I loved our nightly strolls, when the bazaar was quiet—no traffic of rickshaws and motorcycles—no noises either. We would walk all the way from the house up to the paan shop on the other side of Bhandari Bridge, where Mama, Piti, and Gyaniji, my father's closest friend and confidante, enjoyed their nightly paan with meethi supari. Didi and I would follow. I walked to geometric rhythms in my head, double stepping over lines or markings on the road.

My father would always be engrossed in a spirited intellectual discussion with Gyaniji over something important, and Mama would walk with the two of us, holding our hands, listening to their daily indulgence. The men would often discuss etymology: the study of the origin of words and the way in which their meanings have changed throughout history. While the rest of the world huddled around paan and beedi shops discussing Partap Singh Kairon and local politics, the decline of etymology as a linguistic discipline was a major concern with my father. I also often heard Piti and Gyaniji discuss the afterlife, a concept that hugely intrigued my father.

During those late evening walks across Bhandari Bridge and back, I noticed my mother's way of looking at life. It was the way she observed and perceived things around her, the way she reacted to situations. One evening, I recall, we saw a drunken man lying in the middle of the road just outside Hall Gate. He lay face down, completely insensible to the world around him. Mama instantly reacted with empathy and wanted Piti to reach out and help him. But my father was sceptical. He looked on out of concern for a while, and then for some reason, decided to let him be, not get involved and prodded us to walk on. I remember the expression on my mother's face at that moment. She looked at my father, perplexed, and couldn't understand why her husband would not do something to help the poor fellow! The moment has stayed with me.

And then, there were the encounters with the old kulfiwallah, stationed at the intersection just outside Hall Gate. On severe winter nights we'd often see him sitting on his haunches, trying to sell kulfis. Each time we passed him by, Mama would notice him and say, 'See how he is sitting out in the cold, poor chap.' Didi and I would both look and empathize with the old man. On our way back, when we'd still find him sitting there, Mama's heart would go out to him.

'*Hai*, look ... He is still sitting there, hoping to find one customer for the last bit of kulfi left in his matka, before he can return home. Poor thing, he must have children to feed—but who will buy a kulfi in this bitter cold so late in the night?'

I'd glance back at the old man, his hands wrapped around the red mal-mal cloth covering the matka, his cold damp fingers white and wrinkled on the inside. I'd stop to look at life through my mother's eyes—something I assimilated from those after-dinner walks. Later, as an actor, I'd be able to draw so much from them.

SECTION II

AN UNLIKELY PUNJABI FAMILY

6

Bauji and Bibiji

Pandit Gyan Chand Sharma, my paternal grandfather, was a leading criminal lawyer in Amritsar. Bauji was born on 12 April 1896. His father, Pandit Shiv Ram, a scholar, hailed from Jalalabad, a small village perched on a sleepy little plateau on the bank of the river Beas, and was an intellectual and a poet who wrote in Persian. Khaaki was his takhallus, his pen name. The word 'khaaki' comes from the Urdu word khaak, which means 'dust'—a metaphor for humility—I am born of dust and I am nothing but dust . . .

Bauji and Bibiji, my paternal grandparents.

Jalalabad, which is now a major centre of the Radha Soami Satsang Beas, was then a predominantly Muslim area. It was an unremarkable village, a mere teela, situated on an elevation about 200 feet high; all the houses were built on top of the mound. In those days there were no buses, so people would go to Jalalabad on foot. Some would ride horses. There were no roads, just a few lanes meandering about, like muddy towpaths. There was barely a bazaar. In the entire village there must have been just five or six shops selling groceries and basic essentials. Bauji later built a concrete house in the village with three rooms and a courtyard. He named it Chandra Nivas (after my father) and would sometimes visit his first cousin, Ganpat Ram, and his son, Dharam Chand, who had made it their home.

A story about my great-grandfather, close to my heart, is one that my father often narrated fondly.

In Pitaji's words . . .

'Once, the Hindu Sabha High School in Amritsar invited the Deputy Commissioner, an English lord, for an inaugural function in the school. In those days, the early twentieth century, when something like this happened—when an eminent Englishman agreed to grace an occasion—people would feel as if God himself was coming to their locality. So, the school called upon Pandit Shiv Ram "Khaaki" from Jalalabad to compose a poem in honour of the angrez dignitary and read it out to him.

'What is of note here is that my grandfather's reputation as a poet had spread all the way to Amritsar. The lalas of the city knew there was a renowned poet called Pandit Shiv Ram "Khaaki" in Beas, and bestowed upon him the honour of welcoming the English lord.'

This always made me proud—my ancestors were scholarly and artistic; my great-grandfather had such renown as a poet and his literary talent was recognized and revered in the field.

∽

I have with me a family portrait, the only portrait in which my great-grandfather is present. In the sepia-coloured image, there are three men in achkans. The photograph dates back to about 1903. On the left is Pandit Shiv Ram, my great-grandfather, light-eyed, fortyish, and on the right is his older son, Kishen Chand, at that time around twenty-one years old. The little boy in the centre is Bauji, my grandfather, who was about seven at the time. What interests me in this picture is the dress code of the three men. Though they belonged to an obscure little village in Punjab, they seem to have a sense of self that transcends their immediate surroundings. They are dressed in long coats and pagdis, in those days a standard dress code for Hindus, regarded as a sign of self-respect. I love the white buttoned-up shirts and the fob chains hanging from the coat pockets. I never fail to be amazed by the little detailing in the studio portrait—the handkerchiefs, hand-embroidered, the little rings in their earlobes, or the bunch of flowers that my grandfather is holding in his lap, and the two black umbrellas slanted on either side of the men.

Bauji was eight years old when his father passed away. His older brother, Pandit Kishen Chand, who was fourteen years older than Bauji, was childless, and brought him up like his own son. He was the patwari of Jalalabad, the village land record keeper, and it was his dream to educate his younger brother and make him a big man.

Bauji first studied in the only school in Jalalabad, which had classes up to the fourth standard. Thereafter, he was educated in a nearby village called Vairowal, about three miles away with classes up to the eighth. According to my father, 'The only way to get to Vairowal was by walking along the bank of the river, a sandy wasteland with a huge expanse of raeta all around. As a boy, Bauji would daily walk those seven miles to school and back, barefoot on the dry riverbank, through thorny, shrubby pathways. At night he would study under the lamp with his choti tied to the fan, in case he fell asleep.'

Kishen Chand, though he could not afford to spend much on family affairs, never backed away from providing for his younger brother's education and did as much as was possible for him. After completing his middle school at Vairowal, Bauji came to Amritsar where he met a man called Lala Sanghar. The Lala was impressed by the boy's dedication to his studies and decided to bear the entire cost of Bauji's education. He lived in the Lala's house and did his matriculation at the Hindu Sabha School. The irony is that the Lala had four sons, but none of them got through school—all of them, hardly fifth-class-pass, ended up working at the Lala's shop.

Bauji then did his BA, and completed his studies by taking tuitions, following which he obtained a BT (Beginner Teacher's) degree and became a schoolteacher. For two years, he was the Second Master at the DAV School in Amritsar. But then he had a change of heart. He did not

Bauji as a young man.

want to remain a teacher all his life. He began studying law, and in 1921, decided to join the Law School in Lahore. The whole day he would teach, and in the evening, he'd take the train to Lahore to attend classes.

Bauji was already married to my grandmother by the time he obtained his law degree, an LLB. When he was to appear for his final exams Bauji developed conjunctivitis in both his eyes and could not read. This is when Bibiji stepped in and helped him pass his exams. She had matriculated, so she could read English. She would sit up with her husband through the night and read to him chapter after chapter of the prescribed syllabus. Not only did Bauji pass his exam, he stood First Class First in the final year of his LLB.

In 1924, my grandfather started his law practice in the city of Amritsar. Soon enough, his career was flourishing, and he became very wealthy. My father told us many stories about those days. Apparently, my Bauji's house was full of people at all times: a bright, buzzing place with young people running around twenty-four hours of the day. There were langars being served all day long. Those who partook of Bauji's hospitality included relatives from Africa; then, there were various clients—Jats from nearby villages would sleep in the vehra of the house as their cases were being heard in the courts. Destitute girls were sheltered in the house. Hazarilal, the blind boy who ran away with the nautch girls, also lived in the house for a few years. It is to those days that this little story belongs, perhaps the only story that my father narrated to us with a lot of heart.

In Pitaji's words . . .

'Amidst all the bustle in the grand house, there was Mataji, a frail old lady who always sat in a corner of the house, and with the rest of her faculties, kept tabs on whatever was going on around her. She was Nihaal Devi, Bauji's mother, and was completely blind. Bauji would bring home a whole lot of coins wrapped in a thaeli, quietly walk up to her and place the thaeli in her lap. The jingle of the coins would startle her. "Putt, eh ki hai?" (Son, what is this?) and Bauji would whisper in her ear, "Bebbe, paise hai ... main kama ke lyayaan ... sambhaal ke rakh lai aapne kole!" (It's money ... I've earned it. Keep it safe with you!) And Mataji would take the slippery velvet sack in her hands and cover it with her shawl in a way that no one got a whiff of the treasure she was hiding. "Kinney hai?'" (How much?) she'd ask in hushed tones. "Lots," my father would whisper back, "Poore chaar sau rupaye!" (Four hundred rupees) and the old woman would shiver with excitement, "Chaaar ... saaaau ...?" Her grip on the bag would tighten, "Achcha, achcha ... don't you worry! I'll look after it, but don't let anyone know I have the money."

'This sweet little game would be played by your grandfather every now and then when he wanted to show how grateful he was to the woman who had brought him into this world. Mataji died in 1947. She had been blind for twenty years. She had borne nine sons, of whom only two had survived: Bauji, the youngest, and Tayaji (Kishen Chand), the oldest.'

∞

In the year 1915, Pandit Gyan Chand Sharma married a woman his equal in all respects, a woman of high education and great strength of character. Manorama Devi Sharma, my paternal grandmother, was born in the year 1900. She hailed from a town called Nava Shehar and lost her mother when she was just a year old. She studied at the Arya Kanya Maha Vidyalaya in Jalandhar where she passed her tenth standard exams and became a matriculate, which was unusual for girls those days. In 1915, she acquired a bachelor's level degree called 'Snatika'. She was a scholar of Sanskrit. Bibiji's

Bibiji as a young woman.

mother, also a Sanskrit scholar, had calligraphed the Bhagavad Gita in her own hand. Bibiji's father was in the Revenue Department of the Punjab government and had retired as a Kanoongo, a level or two higher than a patwari. (Kanoongo is an Urdu word for 'Kanoon ko jaanane waala'—a person knowledgeable about the law). One of Bibiji's forefathers was the Diwan of Kapurthala State. Bibiji's two brothers, a lawyer and a doctor, were both brought up in South Africa. It has been recorded in family history that Bibiji's father was so strict he did not allow her to attend her own brother's wedding in case she was noticed and drew unnecessary attention.

According to my father, Gyan Chand was first betrothed to an uneducated village girl. At the age of nineteen or twenty perhaps, he met Manorama Devi and was very impressed by her. She was a highly eligible girl: good-looking, fair, with sharp, aquiline features. In addition to being highly educated, she belonged to a better family than the girl Bauji was betrothed to. When Gyan Chand broke off the engagement, the girl's family were shattered. Along with some well-wishers they came to meet Bauji. Upon seeing him, the girl's father took off his saafa, the turban men wore in Punjab at the time, and placed it at the young man's feet. He then pleaded, 'Saada qasoor tusi saadi jholi pao!' (Tell us what crime we have committed!) Every time my father got to this part of the story my heart would break. Bauji, however, would not be swayed.

When my grandparents got married, Bauji was a schoolmaster in Amritsar and lived in the heart of the walled city. They had six children. My father, the second child, was their only son. Their first born was a girl named Santosh, then came my father, and after him a string of girls: Saroj, Sneh, Shashi, and Savita.

Bibiji and Bauji were both strong personalities. Though they had opposing views, they never clashed and were able to make a success of their marriage. They were two sides of the same coin. It is interesting to note that Manorama Devi was a staunch Congressi, while Pandit Gyan Chand Sharma, a kattar, hardcore Jan Sanghi, was devoted to the Hindu cause. For twenty years he'd been Zila Sanchalak for the RSS and associated with the likes of Atal Bihari Vajpayee, a fiery youth leader at the time who later became prime minister of India, Guru Golwalkar, and Syama Prasad Mookerjee, founder of the Bhartiya Jan Sangh Party.

Interestingly, according to family history, Syama Prasad Mookerjee stayed at the Chandraavali house the night before he left for Jammu where he was finally arrested and jailed, leading to his death in 1951. Bauji was arrested shortly after the incident and jailed at the Yole camp as he rallied against the mysterious death of Syama Prasad Mookerjee.

Despite being on opposite sides of the political spectrum, Bibiji and Bauji respected each other's beliefs and allowed each other to freely express and exercise their convictions in word and deed.

Mama, Bibiji, Bauji, and Piti.

Being staunch Arya Samajis my grandparents did not believe in idol worship and other rituals. Instead, the only religious activity that took place at home were havans—purification ceremonies performed by the lighting of fire and chanting of shlokas.

Once, in the late 1940s, both Bauji and Bibiji were given tickets to fight local elections by rival parties. In other words, they were up against each other. Bauji was in the Jan Sangh camp and Bibiji fought the elections under the banner of the All India Women's Conference, a Congress affiliate. When my mother went to Gandhi Ground, where the jalsa was being held, she, as a loyal daughter-in-law, would maintain a strict neutrality as she shuttled between the two booths—Bibiji's Congress tent and Bauji's Jan Sangh tent. When people asked who she intended to vote for, my mother would proudly reply, 'Both. I believe in both!'

Political opponents in Gandhi Ground, Bauji and Bibiji would return home every evening to calmly discuss the events of the day, neither in any way treating the other with anything but civility, respect, love, and, most importantly, equality. This is a lesson I absorbed at a very young age—men and women were equal in every respect, even when married to each other—and have always found it hard to settle for anything less.

∝

My grandparents' home, as I mentioned earlier, was always open to the

needy. Women abandoned by their families, orphaned girls, whoever needed support and shelter, was welcomed into the Chandraavali house. Every so often Bibiji would 'adopt' a young orphan girl, provide her with food and shelter, educate her, and then get her married. Bibiji helped find grooms for, and did kanyadaan of, more than seventeen such girls. However, before they were given away in marriage, she trained them to be self-sufficient. My grandmother's

Bibiji in her later years.

ideas of 'settling down' were far ahead of her times.

For most of her life, Bibiji remained actively involved in social work. She was the founder of the Women's Conference in Punjab and did pathbreaking work. She headed the Stree Sahayak Sabha, which promoted widow remarriage. Every time she heard about a woman being ill-treated or thrown out of the house, Bibiji, along with other women, would go over to the woman's house, and persuade her husband and his family to stop mistreating her and convince them to take her back. Long before the term 'feminist' made an appearance in that part of Punjab, my grandmother was a feminist. Remember all this was taking place during the 1930s and 40s when divorce or separation caused untold misery to the women involved. In this way she saved the marriages of many women. She also fought hard in the campaign to abolish child marriage. People would criticize my grandmother saying, 'Tainu ki?' Why are you bothered? But Bibiji would stand her ground.

∞

While Bibiji was occupied with her social activism, politics, and the myriad aspects of raising her family and running a large household, Bauji was doing exceptionally well for himself as a leading criminal lawyer of Punjab. He would greet his clients at the thhada, which would forever be flooded with Jats from Haryana and Punjab, people who'd come from faraway villages to be represented by Pandit Gyan Chand Sharma, Vaqeel.

In those days, my grandfather owned a blue Morris Oxford. He had bought the car in 1933 when there were no more than ten to fifteen cars in all of Amritsar. The driver was a Sardarji called Kaala Singh. Bauji would go to the kachehri at the end of Court Road in great style and return home in similar fashion. My father told me, 'When the car drove through Hall Bazaar, people would rush to the doors and windows to witness its passage. As the sky-blue elegance rolled through the gully in a cocoon of dust and approached the house, the big phaatak would be flung open. The car would glide in, and be parked exactly where the cowshed is now. It was the second Morris Oxford in town.'

∞

The most vivid image I have of my grandfather is that of a turbaned man walking home through the phaatak holding a bag full of melons. He would be dressed in a suit and tie but always had a pagdi on his head. From time to time, I'd make my way to his study, where he would allow me to play quietly with my golliwog as he continued with his work. His worktable was made of Burma teak with a green velvet top. There was a brass table lamp on the right, next to a black telephone. Once, I skipped into his study, trilling a silly rhyme, 'Bauji namaste . . . chhole khao

khaste . . . . . paani piyo thanda . . . sir-ch maaro danda . . .' 'No!' said Bauji.
'No, Beta, don't say that. It's impolite.' It was the only time I remember
Bauji did not smile back at me and used the word *don't*. I kept looking at
him not knowing what I had done to upset him. I wanted to amuse him,
but had he not liked my singing?

∞

To my utter delight, I discovered quite recently from one of my uncles
that my formidable Bauji was a passionate moviegoer.

'Your grandfather had another side to him,' said Bindu Uncle. 'He
loved Hindi cinema and watched a film every day.'

'Every . . . what? Every *day*?' I was stupefied.

'You see, that was the only entertainment those days . . . After a hard
day's work at the courts, your Bauji would make it a point to go to
the cinema hall, and watch a little bit of the movie showing there, for
relaxation, and then walk back home. He'd go either with a chap called
Dauleya or with Moolchand, his munshi, with whom he would chat on
the way back home, discussing the plot of the film.'

In Amritsar those days, as I have mentioned, there were three cinema
halls in the vicinity—Chitra Talkies, Regent Talkies, known as Kanhaiya
Lal da Mandua, and Amrit Talkies—and Bindu Uncle told me Bauji had
a box reserved in all the three cinema halls, throughout the year.

'*Throughout* the year?'

My image of my grandfather with his pagdi on his head, and a
walking stick, holding a bag full of melons, did a somersault.

∞

The Partition of India was a tumultuous and exceedingly violent time. In
1947, hundreds of thousands of people were massacred on both sides of
the border in Lahore and Amritsar. News filtered in that Lahore would
be in India and Amritsar was going to become part of Pakistan. So,
the Muslims around the walled city started throwing the Hindus out,
burnt their homes, and killed them. Our house, too, was set on fire
by the maulvis next door. But then, in the month of June when it
was announced that Amritsar was going to remain in India, the Hindus
mobilized and started killing the Muslims. This time, too, our house

was set aflame—the Hindus had slathered our gate with green paint, designating it 'Mussalman Property'.

In Pitaji's words . . .

'One night, jadon aggaan lagiyaan . . . our house too was torched. It was the third attempt, but Bauji was warned in time and we fled. When we'd peep out into the bazaar, we'd see a house burning near Regent Talkies—another house in the bazaar was aflame somewhere—and we were holding our breaths. It was a pitch-dark summer night; there was no breeze at all. Mataji, my blind grandmother, now very old, was in the tonga with the rest of the family, and I was on a bicycle following behind. I remember a group of six Muslims who were looking at us. Our hearts were pounding. As the tonga started to ascend Bhandari Bridge, the jattha of Muslim men wearing pattaas on their foreheads came towards us, brandishing chhuraas. It was a petrifying moment. We thought we are all going to be killed now . . . the end has come! But just then, a turn of fate—a bus drove in from Lahore carrying Hindu refugees, and the jattha dropped the idea of chasing our tonga and instead ran towards the bus. As we sped away, I looked back. The clock of Hall Gate struck four. The eerie silence of the night was broken suddenly by the heart-wrenching screams of men, women, and children.'

'No story in Punjab is complete without the tragedy of Partition,' my father used to say. 'Bauji's village, Jalalabad, suffered immense tragedy. It was a dark, sad chapter in the history of Partition. On the fateful night of 8 August, all the Hindus living in the village were rounded up on the banks of river Beas and butchered by the Muslims.

'There was no rationale at that time. Since they were having to give up their homes and go to Pakistan, they decided, *let's kill them all before we leave!* Hindus being massacred *after* it's been declared that the territory will remain in India—such a massacre is not known throughout the history of Partition. To date the horror of Jalalabad remains unknown as there was no one left to tell the tale.

'When it got dark, around eight or nine in the evening, they started brandishing their daggers. "Niklo! Haramzado!" They went to each and every khola and hauled all the Hindus out of their homes, including women and children. Around three hundred people, the entire Hindu population of Jalalabad, were killed and thrown into the Beas River.

Jalalabad had become a graveyard. The moonlit night had turned to a dark *amavas di raat*. They had slain every single Hindu. Only a few young girls were spared, but were abducted and taken to Pakistan. A cousin, Dharam Chand's sister, dark, but young, thirteen or fourteen years old was one of the girls who'd been taken. Bauji lost every single person that he'd ever known since his childhood. The Jalalabad massacre left a deep wound in his heart. For days, he sat on the terrace of the house looking at the mosque, saying not a word.'

My father hadn't mentioned one gory detail. It was my Shashi bhua who reluctantly revealed it when I brought up the topic.

'Two girls from our family ... they fell to their fate ...'

'Abducted?' I knew about the dark girl.

'No, killed ... brutally ... nobody in the family talks about them.'

Pitaji's words came back to me: 'It was a dark *amavas di raat*.'

∾

We heard stories from Jeet and the others of Muslims being cruel—stories that left a deep impact on our young minds. But it was Raj Aunty who one day sat me down in her room and told me the truth—how the Hindus and Sikhs had committed the same atrocities against the Muslims. It wasn't just one way. The cruelty during Partition, both ways, was insane.

Bauji's role during those troubled times has always intrigued me. After the bloodbath of Partition many criminal charges were filed against the Hindus who had been involved in the massacres. Pandit Gyan Chand Sharma fought many of those cases and won them. He saved hundreds of Hindus from languishing in jails. In his mind, though, especially in the aftermath of the Jalalabad massacre, his actions were justified. He saw his fight to save Hindus as a fight to save his people.

For instance, one of the cases he took on involved the murder of four Muslims by Hindus. Pandit Gyan Chand Sharma got the accused off on the sheer strength of his arguments. 'Kalai kamzore hai, my lord! Chaar Pathan, te tin munde ... four Pathans and three boys ... they are just young lads, my lord! How could they possibly have killed the Pathans?' he argued. Family lore has it that even the Viceroy at the time was surprised by the accomplishments of this 'dynamic young lawyer' who never lost a case. People would swear by him. 'Haar hotay thhey gale mein, har roz!'

(He would be garlanded daily), the neighbours of Chandraavali recall even today. There was a saying in Amritsar those days—Hire Pandit Gyan Chand Sharma as your lawyer first, then go commit a murder!

Really? Was *that* my grandfather? It was a fact that had disturbed me. But then something within him changed. It was this very saying that drew a chasm between Pandit Gyan Chand Sharma's glory and the voice of his conscience.

Once the frenzy of Partition ebbed, Bauji's inner voice started to bother him. He was constantly tormented by thoughts of good and bad, right and wrong. It was during those days that Bauji began to seriously question his life and work. His conscience started to hound him. He started to feel that the profession of law was immoral. All his life up till now, he'd been fighting in courts to save his clients, twisting things around in order to win an argument, but was that right? Now, he began to doubt his own deeds. 'What am I doing?' he asked himself in great anguish. 'I'm turning truth into fiction and fiction into truth—just to win a case?' His heart implored him to undo the wrongs he had committed in the name of patriotism, and in the name of justice for Hindus. He needed redemption.

In the last years of his life, Bauji became highly spiritual and started studying the Vedas. Every evening he would visit the scriptures and spend endless nights bent over his green velvet tabletop, making notes on the Bhagavad Gita. He became a scholar of the Gita, and, in time, began to give discourses on the Upanishads, the Gita, and other Hindu scriptures. His notes on Vedanta were handwritten. That compilation remained on the mantelpiece of our hall kamra for most of my early years. Even today people recall the time when Bauji would walk all the way from Amritsar to Lahore, reciting shlokas. He became a true pandit, a scholar of the soul. He would now fight only for the truth, and nothing but the truth.

In 1955, my grandfather gave up practice as a criminal lawyer. Towards the end of that year, when he was asked to join the High Court in the newly built city of Chandigarh, Bauji decided to leave Amritsar forever.

While my grandparents were in the process of moving, Bauji met with a bad accident. As he was driving from Chandigarh to Amritsar, the driver at the wheel fell asleep and the car veered off the road at speed, crashed into a tree, and flipped over. A piece of sharp metal deeply gashed his left thigh. Bauji was bedridden for months.

I remember those days with clarity. A haqeem would come home every evening to nurse the wound, while Bauji sat on the wicker chair in the vehra, looking thoughtful and mulling over the various forms of injustice in the world. Once, while poring over the newspaper Bauji looked up pensively and said, 'Another stove bursts killing a young bahu. Wonder why stoves burst *only* when daughters-in-law are working in the kitchen? Have you ever heard of a stove killing a *daughter*?'

༄

Bauji died in Chandigarh on 4 December 1958. I was six years old. At first, all we were told was that Bauji was unwell and that my father should come to Chandigarh right away. It was quickly followed by a telegram saying he was critical. Mama packed whatever she could quickly, and we all got on a bus. I guess my parents had sensed the looming tragedy. When we arrived in Chandigarh, Bauji was already gone. It had been a massive heart attack. I don't have any clear memory of Bauji's death, except that I remember my father being in a state of shock. He could not speak.

Apparently, Bauji would, from time to time, get angina pain while he was out for a walk, but he never really did anything about it. The pain would come and go and it never occurred to him to go in for a serious check-up. And then, abruptly, the pillar of the Chandraavali house was gone. The family was shaken. In his own quiet, dignified way, the man who had lived a hard life but lived it to the fullest, left this world young, at age sixty. An Ambassador car brought us back to the house adjoining the mosque. Bibiji was with us. It was natural that my grandmother would now live with us. But it wasn't meant to be.

After Bauji died, a deep sense of loss and gloom permeated the Chandraavali house, where he had created a haven for the family. The darkness persisted for days ... an uncanny stillness prevailed in the house, perhaps an indication of things to come. Bauji's room was kept closed most of the time, but once, Pitaji saw his mother sitting quietly at the table where Bauji used to work at his files. She hadn't wept since the day of her husband's death. There was no trace of emotion on her face; it had simply turned white.

My grandmother had a premonition about her death. It was a little over a month after Bauji had gone. The night before she passed away, she had a dream in which she saw Bauji on a train that was slowly pulling out of the station, looking back and asking her, *'How long are you going to be? Aren't you coming?'*

That evening Bibiji had been sitting in the veranda. The sky was overcast but it hadn't rained. She felt uneasy with angina pain and asked for her medicine, but nevertheless remained in discomfort. She then said, 'Gayatri Mantar da jaap karo!' (Recite the Gayatri Mantra for me!) A few moments after the chanting began, Bibiji closed her eyes and was gone. Before the forty days of mourning were over, on a cold January night, my grandmother, like a true soulmate, quietly followed her husband to the other world . . .

I remember the night Bibiji died. We were in the Green Room upstairs with Mai Sardi, when shrieks were heard from downstairs. Women started wailing and crying . . . it was eerie, the atmosphere. Didi and I weren't allowed to step down, where Bibiji's body was placed on the floor, cold and still. They said she could not bear the shock of her husband's death. That night Mama cried inconsolably and I, a baffled and terrified six-year-old, was a mute spectator to her grief.

Bibiji and Mama.

∽

There's a story about Bibiji's death that I often heard Mama narrate.

In Mama's voice . . .

'Accounts had to be sorted, payments had to be made, monies had to be collected from various people, but neither your father nor I had any clue as to who owed us what. All I knew was that Bauji would keep a little red diary in which he'd note all financial transactions. I searched everywhere in the house for that diary, but nothing. I was exhausted and devastated. It was the second night after your grandmother's cremation, when I was woken up with a start very early in the morning—I had a sense of someone having just got up from my bedside after whispering to me, "Open the cupboard in the wall, and look under the old files." I got up sweating. I could almost smell Bibiji's presence in the room. Frightened but determined, I got out of bed and walked to the room that Bibiji had pointed to, opened the wooden cupboard set in the wall, lifted the heap of files, and there was the little red diary in frayed leather—with all the hisaab written in Bauji's hand. I stood trembling. I could not believe that Bibiji had come to me in person and rescued me. I broke down.'

Though at that small age I never realized what my grandparents meant to me, it was only many, many years later that I would begin to understand who these two people really were, and what they would mean to me in my life. How I'd be impacted by them, and how unknowingly, in many ways, I would imbibe and claim from them my true genes.

7

Mama

Hush-a-bye, baby, on the tree top,
When the wind blows the cradle will rock
When the bough breaks the cradle will fall
Down will come baby, cradle and all . . .

What a lullaby to sing to put a one-year-old to sleep. But my mother had grown up in British India, and this was the only lori she knew. Another one was simply—'*So jaa . . . aaaa . . . so jaa . . . aaaa . . .*' in her very melodious voice. I loved the feel of her fingers on my forehead and my hair as she sang me to sleep.

My mother was a beautiful woman, the quintessence of good looks, beauty, and grace. Even today when people see her black and white photograph atop the piano in my home, they ask:

'Which old film star is this?'

'That's my Mama,' I say.

'Wow! She looks like a celebrity!'

I look deep into that beautiful serene face and my entire childhood floats in front of my eyes.

'Yes, she *was* a celebrity . . . she was the *star* in my life!'

Without question, Mama was my idol: soft-spoken, sophisticated, well-read, loving, and forever caressing me. At heart, my mother was a simple woman. I never saw her crave saris, jewellery, or other material things. She always lived with grace. In fact she was the most graceful lady I'd known during my entire childhood. She was fiercely devoted to my father, something I secretly admired her for. All told, I felt Mama was flawless, someone who was cut out for the finer things in life.

She was always busy with something or the other—work, and when she wasn't busy around the house, sketching at the dining table or painting at her easel in the veranda, for my mother loved art, and was a wonderful painter. I so loved her painting of the old park at Connaught Circle, its autumn foliage, a riot of russet and gold.

At other times she would read, mostly books on psychology, a subject that was of great interest to her. Two things she was especially fond of were knitting and sewing. She made a lot of our dresses by hand, and all through the winter months, she'd knit, usually copying patterns from *Woman & Home*. For the longest time, each member of the family got a new sweater every year.

With her skill in needlework, Mama even indulged us when we needed to get ready for the stage at school, sometimes sewing our outfits herself. She always took extra care to see that our costumes were properly organized and that we had all the right accessories.

My mother also organized our birthday parties with great enthusiasm. All my school friends were invited home. She'd set up a treasure hunt and a game of musical chairs, both of which we girls thoroughly enjoyed. At the end of the party, she'd bring out the raffle, where you dug your hand into a glass jar full of small, iridescent packages and pulled out a silver-wrapped bundle with a little surprise inside.

I was a Mama's girl. I would cling to her at the slightest excuse. Every day, when I returned from school at three in the afternoon, there was a ritual that I religiously followed. As soon as I entered the house, I would fling my schoolbag on the wicker chair and run to the bathroom where Mama would be squatting on the floor washing clothes. I'd cling to her from behind, putting my arms around her, and start kissing her back where her skin showed between the sari and the blouse. Mama would laugh and pull me to her with hands full of frothy, soapy water; then there would be a long cuddling, smooching session between mother and daughter. By the time my daily quota of cuddling was over I'd be covered in soapsuds!

'Go, change your frock!' she'd say, pinching my nose so hard it would instantly turn red.

Sadly, this daily ritual wouldn't last forever. As years went by, Mama took up a teaching job, and would no longer be there in the afternoons when I returned home from school.

∽

Another little memory when I'm three ...

I'm upset with Mama. She has scolded me over something and I've been crying. Mai Sardi brings me some food in a plate, but I refuse to eat. Then Mama comes and sits next to me on my bed, trying to cajole me but I still don't smile. She then tries the old sing-a-song trick—

'*Laddu ... pedhe ... dud ... malai ...*' walking her fingers up my arm, '*Maano ... billi ... ayi ...*' and as her fingers reach my armpits, '*Kha-gai-kha-gai-kha-gai-kha-gai!!!*' and I shriek and roll over in bed, bursting into hysterical giggles!

Every time Mama scolded me she'd come and sit by my bedside and run her fingers on my forehead ... and that's how I'd go to sleep.

∽

A Russian ballet was performing in town, and Mama and Piti had gone to catch a show. Mai Sardi was cleaning the kitchen. Over at the maseet, the pigeons had settled in for the night. In Mochistan, the nightly singing with the dholki and manjira had begun. The neighbourhood cat, after having had its fill of milk from the katori outside our kitchen, was sauntering across the wall into Munni's house. It was late.

All of five, I'm standing in front of Mama's huge wardrobe mirror, entwined in her soft chiffon sari. It puddles around my feet on the mosaic

Mama's girl.

floor, six yards of sheer bliss. I glimpse my image in the mirror, wrapped in folds of burgundy. I can smell Mama on me. My hair, cropped across my forehead, is just long enough to slip behind my ears. There is no one around. The fragrance of raat ki rani that Mama loves so much fills the house. Tonight is my first ever go at Mama's wardrobe. Slowly and carefully, I start to wind the soft slippery fabric around me. The folds of the sari turn out uneven and zig-zaggy, not the way they fall on Mama. But I'm thrilled to see my little sari-clad form in the mirror, entangled in the delicate layers. Moving back a little, I lift my feet. It's not easy to climb up on to the stool by Mama's bed, but I somehow manage to reach the brass handle of the drawer and see inside the lipstick, the comb, and the tin of Yardley powder, the one she uses after her bath, patting it around her cleavage.

I draw out a glazed lipstick, and smear it on. I am fascinated by what I see: bright red lipstick, smudged around the edges of my mouth. Perfect! I am doing everything exactly as Mama would—drape her sari, winding the pleats to a count of six, always a count of six, throw the pallu across her chest, pin it at the left shoulder, and then stand in front of the mirror and put on her lipstick. I have watched her doing it a

million times. She starts with the upper lip, from the centre of the mouth
down to the left corner; then from the centre again to the right corner.
Then she goes at the lower lip in one sweeping motion, side to side,
filling up the entire lip. She then smacks her lips to get a blended finish.
Before the lipstick rolls back into the gold case, Mama places it in the
centre of her forehead, turning it round and round, to get that perfect
bindi. My mother looks heavenly, and I want to grow up to be just like
her one day. That's all I want at age five.

∞

Mama's father, my Bade Daddy, was a man from the hills. He was a Dogri,
hailing from the Kangra district in Himachal Pradesh, at the foothills of
the Himalayas, and later settled in Dharamshala. When Lily Aunty, my
youngest maasi, told me about the hill origins of my mother's side of the
family, I grew very excited and told Didi about it.

'Do you know we have Pahadi roots?'

'How come?'

'Bade Daddy was a Dogri, he was from the hills, from Kangra. So,
that makes us half-Pahadi.'

'Quarter,' she corrected me.

'You may be a quarter, but I am more Pahadi than anything else!
I was this girl, remember, who fantasized about growing up to be a
shepherdess?'

How come my mother had never mentioned this? I took a closer look
at a picture of my Nana—his East Asiatic features, the high cheekbones, the
broad, flat planes of his face clearly showed his origins in the mountains.

My childhood desire to be a shepherdess was linked to a fantasy I'd
had about my Nana being a carefree shepherd in the hills, wandering
about with his herds of sheep. This notion of him being a wanderer
greatly appealed to me, it was something I also fancied being...And,
while he wasn't a shepherd but had studied to become an accountant, I
quite enjoyed fantasizing.

Jagan Nath Kashi Ram Gangahar, Bade Daddy, was born in Datarpur,
a small pre-colonial Indian hill state in the lower Himalayas. His parents
were Dogras from Gurdaspur in Punjab, who settled in the Gangaraan da
Mohalla in Mukerian, then just a village in the foothills of the Kangra

valley. He went to school there, and later studied at the DAV College in Hoshiarpur where he passed his FA, and acquired a degree in accountancy. Jagan Nath had one elder sister, Harkaur, a child widow, and a younger brother, Vishwanath.

After completing his education, Jagan Nath was betrothed to a girl

from the neighbouring Misraan da Mohalla, a girl named Sarasvati Parashar. The matchmaking was done by the local women of the village. Sarasvati had attended a madrasa in her village, but other than that was not educated. Although she didn't go beyond the fourth grade in the local school, she was trained by her parents in the art of farming. Her parents owned land in Pind Mukerian, and Sarasvati's heart felt close to the soil.

Some evenings, when she walked through the neighbourhood where she grew up, she'd encounter Jagan Nath who would usually be seen with a group of boys, all

Bade Daddy and Badi Mummy.

fifteen-year-olds, hanging around the bicycle shop playing marbles. On seeing her, he'd loudly say to his friends, 'Oh dekho, meri vautti ja rai! Meri vautti ja rai!' (Look! There goes my wife!) Upon hearing this, Sarasvati would be so embarrassed she'd run all the way home. She did not speak to Jagan Nath until the day they got married.

Jagan Nath had a cousin who migrated to Burma. Her husband was a postmaster in Myitkyina who persuaded Jagan Nath to come over, as there were plenty of job opportunities in that country. Two months after their wedding, the young couple migrated to Burma where Jagan Nath worked for the Public Works Department as Chief Accountant. His younger brother, Vishwanath, and his widowed sister, Harkaur, came along. This was the woman my Mama called Bhuaji, whom she loved dearly. She was very pretty, fair, and delicate, a typical Paharan.

Gangahar family in Burma.

Bade Daddy settled his family in Mandalay, where his children grew up under the care of his brother Vishwanath. Bade Daddy's job kept him constantly on the move and he was forever travelling to towns like Lashio, Kyaukse, Myitkyina, Sandoway, and Akyab—wherever his work took him. My mother and her seven siblings grew up in Mandalay in Chacha Vishwanath's home.

The oldest child, born in 1914, was a girl called Gayatri. She was ten years older than my Mama. Then came a boy, Anirudh, then another girl, Savitri. Himadri, my mother, was fourth. After my mother came Mahinder, then a girl, Bhanu, then another boy, Virendra, and the eighth child was Dinesh. All the children went to St Joseph's Convent, and as the British nuns could not pronounce their Indian names, they conveniently changed them to English names. So Gayatri became Gertie, Savitri became Sarah, Himadri, my Mama, was called Winnie, and the youngest girl, Bhanu, was named Lily. Among the boys, the oldest boy Anirudh was called Andrew, Mahinder became Malcolm, and Virendra became Brian. Dinesh, the youngest, was the only one who managed to retain his original name, as he was just a child when the family returned to India during the Second World War.

∞

Badi Mummy and Bade Daddy later in life.

Bade Daddy would experience tremendous loss in his life. He'd put all his heart into making his dream house in Meiktila, as he liked being there, a house he wanted to retire to. It was a beautiful three-storey stone structure in the middle of an open field. He said to Badi Mummy, 'Sarasvati, all my life I've been running around, one city to another ... one house to another house ... each time you've set up your garden I've uprooted you ... but not any more ... I'm building a house for you where no one will take away your garden from you ... I want to stop running now and come to rest in this house which I want to make a home for us. Once the children go away, it'll be just you and me ... and then we will live quietly looking at flowers and your tulips.'

Sadly, that was never destined to happen. Bade Daddy had to move with the family again, and this time forever out of Burma.

The Japanese invasion of Burma in 1942 during the Second World War had left Indian families no choice but to abandon their homes and flee to India. Half a million Indians fled the country. Thousands of Indian families walked for weeks through the jungles of Manipur and Assam to cross over to India. As it became impossible for Bade Daddy to keep his family safe in Burma, he decided to join the great exodus that was taking place at the time. Bade Daddy had to leave Burma, migrate with eight children back to India, lay down his roots all over again, not knowing where to begin at this late age. Little did he know that this was only the beginning of his 'unsettling' ...

Post his return to India and after putting his children through schools and colleges in Jalandhar, Lahore was the place where he finally chose to settle down, least suspecting that there'd be yet another exodus awaiting the family a few years down the line. This time, it would be the Hindu–Muslim riots during the Partition of India.

The season in Lahore was beginning to change. Jagan Nath could

sense a dark period of doom. Riots had
erupted. He had to make sure his young
daughters were safe. The sense of home
was lost long back, and now there was
only a desperate bid to save life and
honour. On a night of horror, when
thuggish mobs were stalking the dark,
deserted streets of the city looking for
people to slaughter, Bade Daddy and
the remaining members of his family
managed to escape Lahore and came
hurtling back to Mukerian.

Twice a refugee now, Bade Daddy
opened up the old house in Misraan da
Mohalla, and looked at the walls. This
was where he was going to live now till
the end of his life—Pind Mukerian, Zila

Bade Daddy

Hoshiarpur, Tehsil Sisaiyaan. It was where he'd finally lay his old bones
to rest, surrounded by memories of his beloved Burma.

One of my favourite photographs of Bade Daddy from that time is a
faded sepia image in which he is looking like a true refugee—a broken
man, unsure of his destiny, burdened by responsibility, weak and lost. I
hold that image very close to my heart. In that one image I can see
Bade Daddy's entire life's journey. A gentle soul, he was God's good man.

∞

Winnie, my mother, was born Himadri Gangahar on 15 October,
the autumn of 1924, in Meiktila, a small town in central Burma. She
studied at St Joseph's Convent till class five, and later went to the Wesley
Methodist School, where she acquired her high school degree.

In the year 1940, just before the Japanese invaded Burma, Winnie
was sent to India. She came to Calcutta on a steamer, escorted by her
older brother, Andrew, who left her in Mukerian where she lived with
her maternal grandmother, Paro. From there, she went to Lahore to
study for her JAV (Junior Anglo Vernacular) teachers training at the Rai
Bahadur Sohanlal Training College for Women. When the rest of the

Himadri Gangahar

Himadri Gangahar with her friends at Wesley.

family returned from Burma in 1942, and
moved to Jalandhar, she joined the Kanya
Maha Vidyalaya as a teacher. Her sister,
Sarah, was already teaching there. Along
with her job, Winnie acquired her FA
and BA (diploma and Bachelor's) degrees.
Acharyaji, the principal of the institute,
was extremely fond of the Gangahar
sisters and would proudly show them
off to visiting academics.

I know how aesthetically particular
my mother was during her young days.
She could be most innovative when it
came to the smallest of things, even her
chappals. This is when she was studying
for her bachelor's qualification. During
exam days, she would take old voile
saris, cut out strips, and get them dyed

The Gangahar sisters—Sarah and Winnie.

in different colours. She'd turn the strips into bands by twisting them,
one flap to the right, one to the left, like Roman sandals. Each day she'd
match her slippers to the colour of her sari—bright orange, turquoise
blue, royal purple. In the examination hall, the girls would be surprised—
what is Winnie wearing today?

∾

In 1945, the Gangahar family moved from Jalandhar to Lahore. This was
intended to be their final move.

Mama loved her life in Lahore and spoke very fondly of those days:
the Victoria Gardens, the trees, the tongas, the art studio on Mall Road.
It was here at Sanyal Studio that she joined an art class to study painting
with the master painter B. C. Sanyal, who had set up the Lahore School
of Fine Arts, a studio on the upper floor of Regal Cinema. This was the
time my mother was the happiest; she had finally found her bearings
in India, her true calling as an artist. Dressed in a sari, she would go
every day to the studio riding a bicycle. Live models would come there,
and Mama got immersed in sketching, drawing, and painting in this

invigorating environment. The Sanyal Studio was not only an iconic and energetic space, a hub for artists, but also a place where people met, interacted, and contributed to the national movement. At times, there'd be exhibitions: Amrita Sher-Gil had her first exhibition at the Sanyal Studio. It was, in those times, quite revolutionary to have a space that was this creatively open.

My mother worked closely with Snehlata Sanyal, and painters such as Pran Nath Mago, Satish Gujral, and sculptor-painter Amar Nath Sehgal—all promising artists of the time. She would attend group meetings with the likes of veteran actress Achala Sachdev, Freda Bedi (actor Kabir Bedi's mother, and the first Western female monk in Lahore), and theatre personality, Sheila Bhatia. Along with some girls who were communists, Winnie would go into different mohallas in Lahore singing ekta de gaane, songs of unity. Those were very charged times. But this period of her life wasn't meant to last long.

The very next year, in 1947, the riots in Lahore during Partition uprooted her life yet once again.

My mother describes the time:

'I remember the day the riots first started in Lahore, the day Master Tara Singh came galloping on horseback through Mall Road, brandishing his sword. It was 4 March 1947, when the Akali leader stormed the

Winnie (fourth from left), and other girls, doing charity shows.

Assembly Building with his jathha of Nihangs. He was so close to our studio I could see him standing right up there, talwar in hand, raising slogans. Rumour spread like wildfire—Tara Singh had torn down the Muslim League flag. There was a big juloos of Sikhs and Hindus against the Muslims. We were very scared. With great difficulty we girls managed to come out of Mall Road and reach our homes.

'The inevitable had happened—a line had been drawn between Lahore and Amritsar. From this point on things only got worse in the city. Soon after, houses were torched and the killings started. We were in Mozang, a predominantly Muslim locality. I remember the last night we tried to get out of there. There were slogans echoing from everywhere: Hindu naare and Muslim naare. Mummy (Badi) was scared. "We have to take the girls and leave," she said. So, the family moved to Mason Road and then to Ichchara Mohalla, again a dense Muslim area on the Grand Trunk Road. Through the curfewed nights and the rioting mobs of Muslims and Sikhs, we somehow managed to escape to a camp and finally made it back to India.'

∽

Stories about Partition were disturbing, yes, but also awe-inspiring. As a young child I was most fascinated by the story of an old Mussalman tangewallah in Lahore—how he hid three Hindu girls in his tonga under gunny bags, pulled them out of the riot-torn mohalla in the middle of the pitch-dark night, and brought them to the safety of the refugee camp. One of the three girls was my mother. 'He risked his own life to save us girls, you know . . . Raaton-raat border cross karvaaya!' (He got us across the border) she'd say, and remained forever indebted to the old Mussalman tangewallah.

Once she came across to India and settled at her Uncle Bowrie's house in Amritsar, in Amritsar, my mother immersed herself in all art forms—dance, music, drama—performing on stage along with other girls, doing charity shows in order to help raise funds for the refugees pouring in from across the newly formed border of India and Pakistan.

∽

My childhood was full of stories. These had nothing to do with Indian mythology or stories drawn from the scriptures. There was no Ram for me,

Winnie at fifteen.

no Sita, no Ramayan, no Mahabharat. My mythology was stories of Burma narrated to me by my mother, the nostalgic recreation of her childhood days in the country of her birth.

She would often pull out a photograph to illustrate her stories, picked from a collection she kept safely in a tin box; my favourite photograph of Mama shows her on a bicycle, wearing a georgette sari, twice entwined around her waist. Her hair is in two long plaits, and her eyes are covered by black goggles, but she is looking into the camera.

She is fifteen in this picture, and surely beginning to dream about life.

A born storyteller, my mother's stories entranced me, and brought alive the country she so loved. Mama's Burma stories formed my mental makeup as a child. Every night before going to sleep we would cuddle up to her in bed, Didi and I, waiting for her to narrate the same incidents from her life, over and over again.

Each story fascinated me, firing up my imagination. Even today, I can recall practically every incident of my mother's Burma days in the minutest of detail: her schooldays in Mandalay, the moat around Mandalay Palace, her summer vacations in Lashio, the strawberry sellers of Maymyo, and the Baingi men carrying water buckets hanging from bamboo sticks across their shoulders. She'd speak fondly of Gertie Aunty, her eldest sister, from whom she learnt the art of sewing, knitting, cooking; she felt immensely indebted to her Gertie Bahenji. I loved to hear about the gramophone that Bade Daddy brought home one day and the music that filled the house every evening.

'Oh Lashio! Lashio!' she'd sigh ever so often, referring to a small hilly town in Burma that her father was posted to—a place that had clearly enchanted her, a place she most remembered with yearning and a sense of great loss.

The Burma stories were such a formative part of my childhood, that I feel the best way to weave them into the story of my life is to let my mother speak for herself, tell some of her stories in her own charming way. Some of the stories are simple, sweet ones, that revolve around the small pleasures of life in bucolic country towns, others are built on clear, sharp shards of memory, recreating images of such lucidity, images so vivid in my mind even today, that I feel they are part of my own reality, a reality which is my mother's, but also belongs to me. I'm reproducing just a few here to bring to life a very important part of my childhood.

In Mama's words . . .

'I was born in Meiktila, a most beautiful little town in Burma. Ours was a bamboo house built in front of the jail. Meiktila was a lake city built around a huge artificial lake. My brothers would go swimming in it and I'd sit on the shore watching them. You couldn't see the other bank, it was just a large sheet of water. Trees grew all around it but no leaves ever fell into the water. It was a religious thing.'

Winnie and her siblings with Uncle Vishwanath.

'We first came to Mandalay when I was very young. In Mandalay we lived in Uncle Vishwanath's house. He was Daddy's younger brother, our Chachaji. When we had to leave Burma during the Japanese invasion, he drove his car into the river. He was terribly distraught. "I'm not going to leave my car for the Burmese," he said, "nor will I let the Japanese have it!" When Uncle Vishwanath pushed his car into the river, it was a very sad scene. He stood at the bank of the Irrawaddy River and watched his car go down slowly into the water. And then he finally broke down.

'He came to India during the exodus, but after the war was over, his wife refused to go back with him, so he left for Burma on his own and never came back.'

∽

During my baby days I'd heard so much about the Pwes, the little festivals of light at the Shwe Oo Min Pagoda, the bamboo stage, the oil lamps on both sides of the lane and gorgeously dressed dancers performing comic skits—all visible from Mama's house where the family would spread durries and watch the show from their balconies.

'Mummy would be very fond of eating paan. So three-four Burmese ladies would sit down and have paan with Mummy. There would be a paan box in every Burmese home.

'One day, when I was four years old, Daddy announced that a photographer was arriving to take a family portrait. Everybody got excited

Mama (extreme right) wearing a sari at four.

and began dressing up. Mummy gave saris to Gertie and Sarah—voile saris with chikan work. I remember those saris so well. One was a white voile embroidered with big orange flowers, and the other had red or blue motifs. I too wanted to wear a sari and to be just like my sisters! Mummy was in a quandary, where was she to find a sari for her four-year-old? She did something very ingenious, pulled out a striped piece of fabric, about a yard long and said: "Here, let's drape this around her, this can be her sari." My sisters managed to wind that piece of cloth around me, tuck it into my waist and get me to pose for the picture.'

In Mama's tin box of photographs from Burma, I see the family portrait where my four-year-old mother is standing beside Badi Mummy, wearing her very first sari.

∽

'When I was in the first grade I hated going to school. That year a boy called Ribeiro used to bully me. He would get hold of an insect that we called an itchi-butchi, it was like a caterpillar, a very slow and creepy insect. He would pick it up with a stick and put it on my shoulder. I'd cry, "Itchi-butchi on my back! . . . itchi-butchi on my back!" Sister Pacific would then make him stand in a corner of the classroom. Later, when we were a bit older, he once spoke to me. "You used to get the teacher to punish me, make me stand in a corner."

'"You used to put an itchi-butchi on my back," I replied quietly.'

∽

'I remember a town called Kyaukse very vividly, a memory that dates back to when I was in the third grade or so. Mummy was very fond of going for long walks, and I'd accompany her. I love birds, as you know, and I love trees and flowers. Mummy, Gertie Behanji, and Sarah would be walking along the road with Andrew. Being the youngest in the group, I'd always be lagging behind. And guess why. I'd be looking at the electric wires, with all the lovely coloured birds sitting there, you know, twittering away . . . ! And I'd be entranced by their colours, and their melodic twittering. "Winnie, come on! Winnie, come on!" someone would shout and I'd run and catch up with them.'

∽

'I was in the third grade, I think, when I saw the Cutex advertisement, in the *Rangoon Gazette*. I remember the day when I got my first Cutex kit. I'm sitting there one afternoon watching all this cutting of the hay. Suddenly, this mailman comes in with a parcel. I ask, "Whose is it?" He says, "Winnie Devi." I say I'm Winnie Devi. "There's a parcel for you," he says. I take the parcel, and run inside with it, yelling, "Mummy! Mera parcel aaya! I got a parcel!" Opened the packet, read the directions: you have to have a basin of water, wash your hands very carefully, your fingers should be clean. It was a pink-coloured cutex.'

∽

'I loved my school, especially the third grade. My teachers there were Miss Varden and Miss Emily but Sister Pacific loved me the most. When I'd cry, she would say, "Come on Winnie, hold my rosary, come," and I would hold her rosary and walk along with her, distributing pencils in class. I remember all my school friends, my closest companions in those years, some of the names are etched in my memory: Emma U Tin, Dorothy Furgasson, Shireen Shirazi, Peggy Nation.'

∽

I loved Mama's story about Florence Nightingale, a strong image in my head even now.

'I was in the tenth grade at Wesley School when I took part in a play about Florence Nightingale.'

'Did you play Nightingale, Mama?'

'No, I played the wounded soldier, who gets up from the floor and kisses her shadow on the wall as she passes by in the night, holding a lantern.'

∽

'In those days, we rode around in what were called hackney carriages. In Mandalay, the hackney carriages were grand. Two horses in the front, and the coachman would be sitting right at the top and you had windows and two doors in the middle. You could open and shut the windows, and they had shutters. When it rained you could pull down the shutter. Everybody would use them. It was like public transport. The hackney drivers had addas, their resting places. You would see them standing under the trees and the drivers sleeping in them—just like the tonga stand here in Amritsar. We used a carriage driven by a man called Nasir. Every day, Nasir would take us to school and bring us back.'

∽

'One evening we were all sitting on the veranda—Mummy was busy working on her dance drama for the evening with some Burmese ladies— when what did I see? A man had climbed all the way to the top of the pagoda across the house. "Look here, men! What is that fella doing there? Clinging to the pagoda like a monkey? Come see!" I said out aloud. Everyone in the house came out on to the veranda and began speculating about what was going on. He must be a mad chap, climbed up there and now doesn't know how to get down ... Mummy sent Deepat, our servant, to go over to the pagoda to see what that fellow was up to. Deepat returned scandalized but amused. "He is scraping gold leaf off the pagoda!" he told us. We were horrified. Stealing gold? From the pagoda? We saw a crowd begin to gather around the pagoda. People began shouting at the man, asking him to come down, but he would not budge. Finally, the police made an appearance and managed to get him down.'

∽

'My love of gardens and flowers comes from my Mummy. We stayed with Uncle Vishwanath, as you know, and went home to our parents for our holidays. Mummy's message to me from Lashio would read, "The garden is ready. Lots of flowers are blooming and they are waiting for you, Winnie!" As soon as I reached home, the first thing I would do is run into the garden and be among the flowers. Even if we reached there at night-time, I would take the lantern and look all around what kind of flowers Mummy had in her garden. Once, I stepped into a huge bed of cannas and posed in front of those. "Take my picture, Bahenji, take my picture!" I said, and Gertie Bahenji clicked my photograph!'

∞

'I was very fond of being photographed. There was a Fuji shop behind the house and I used to go there with one rupee in my hand. I would sneak back to the shop and get three portraits of mine taken for a rupee. We'd  also get photographed with other Burmese girls, my friends, you know, in school; girls wearing longyis and flowers in their hair, long hair coiled into elegant buns, chappals and short blouses called eingyis, sitting coyly on the floor with both legs on one side. So enamoured was I seeing myself in photographs I even tried to buy the Brownie Co's Box Camera that I'd see in the shop's window. It cost ten rupees. "I can only give you five rupees," I'd say, but the shop owner would not agree and I could never buy the camera.'

∞

'I would listen to Juthika Roy's songs, all bhajans. She was a Bengali. We had many of her records at home. I would sing along with them. Daddy would say, "Come on, Winnie, sing a bhajan," and I would start to sing:

 *Sooli upar sej sajai, kis bid bole . . .*

Because of my childhood fascination with Juthika Roy, I thought that all Bengali girls were good singers. But it was not just the voice, I adored them for their wheat complexion, beautiful features, lovely eyes, and beautiful singing voices . . . I loved Bengali girls, so I used to say, "I am Bengali too . . . I'm the Beauty Queen of Bengal!"'

∞

'I had my share of fixations. I loved Kanan Bala, Devika Rani, and Bette Davis. I filled out coupons from the *Rangoon Gazette* and even enrolled for Sitara Devi's correspondence dance course. I would stand on top of the table and dance. My younger cousins would be my audience. I would

tell them I'm going to become an actress! Whenever Uncle Vishwanath would hear that, he would right away refute the idea. "Do you know what they do if you can't dance properly? They hit you on the legs with sticks!" and I would get disenchanted and immediately drop the idea!'

∞

'The Burmese people are simple, trustworthy, honest and God-fearing. We lived in a Buddhist atmosphere; it's different, you know. Early in the morning, four o'clock, you see monks out on their rounds . . . and you see them in the drizzle, filing down the street . . . It is such a lovely sight, and it makes you think—God is first—you think of God first. Only once, I remember, there was a huge agitation.

'In 1936, when I was in the eighth grade, violence broke out in the city. It was started by the Buddhist monks who objected to women wearing thin organdie blouses, the eingyis, through which their bras could be seen. The monks didn't like it. They found it very distracting. Burmese women had worn eingyis made of voile for years and years, but when they began wearing organdie ones, which were rather transparent, hard-line Buddhist monks started to protest. Very violently. They used knives to slash the blouses of women they encountered on the street. Ma U Thin's sister had been pushed off her bicycle, but she got away. Emma U Tin's mother came back home with her arms bruised. It was bad. So, the Burmese women started to wear their organdie eingyis only at home. When they went out, they wore thick, homespun cloth, like khadi. It came in grey, blue, brown colours, and you couldn't see anything through it.'

❧

'We loved to go to the movies, but whenever we did so we had to be chaperoned by Uncle Vishwanath and Aunty. We would tell him, "Chachaji, a beautiful movie is playing in the theatres, we want to go see it." Chachaji would say, "I'll go see it first. If the film is good then we can all go." So he would go, and when he came back, we would look at his face for his reaction, whether it was a "good" film or a "bad" film. Finally, he'd say, "Achcha, achcha, let's go." We didn't see too many films with Uncle, just four or five.

'We mostly saw Hindi films. Uncle never used to take us to see English movies, which we only saw on school excursions. There was no TV those days. *Tarzan*, the American film was the earliest. I was in the fourth or fifth grade then. I liked the actresses Savita Devi and Devika Rani. They would be wearing ghaghras and half saris—that was the custom, Gujarati style. I used to copy them. Devika Rani was my favourite.'

It is such a delightful coincidence that my very first award for Best Actress (*Ek Baar Phir*) was presented to me on stage by Devika Rani, the First Lady of Indian Cinema, my mother's favourite actress.

❧

Mama continues . . .

'In our home, the evenings were for music. We had a gramophone at home, sitting together, that Mummy and Daddy would listen to. My brothers would go boating in the moat across the house, hanging on the bridge over the water, singing:

Daisy, Daisy, give me your answer, do . . . I'm half crazy, all for the love of you! . . . It won't be a stylish marriage . . . I can't afford a carriage . . . but you'll look sweet, upon the seat, of a bicycle made for two . . .

'We sisters would be in the house, helping Mummy with the cooking and the sewing. Once dinner would be ready, I'd run to the window and call out to the boys, "Brian . . . Mahinder . . . Androooo . . . Come back hoooome . . . Dinner is Readyyy!"

'Andrew my brother . . . O, how I miss him! I would say, Andrew, play the mouth organ, and he would sit down and play the mouth organ for me; he played beautifully!'

∽

But my mother's enchanted Burmese idyll was coming to an end. As war clouds loomed, her father sent her back to India.

'None of us had thought we'd have to ever leave Burma.'

'What happened then, Mama? Why did Bade Daddy send you to India?'

Mama is quiet for a long moment. 'I don't know ... I could never understand that ... why Daddy decided to send me to India ... all by myself.'

'Were you scared, Mama?'

'Yes, I cried a lot. Andrew came with me to Rangoon, to accompany me on the ship that brought us to Calcutta. We travelled by train and bus before we eventually arrived in Mukerian.'

'Then?'

'Then he left me in Mukerian and went back.'

'He went back?'

'Yes, he returned to Burma. He had come just to escort me to India. This was my first visit to India and it was so new

Andrew

to me. I had been born in Meiktila, and I loved my Burma ... I never wanted to leave ...'

∽

'What about Bade Daddy's dream house, Mama? Maybe it's still there ...'
'It's gone,' Mama told me. 'When the Japanese captured Meiktila, they made this very house their headquarters. Then, when the Americans came and gutted out the Japanese, that was the first building they bombed. After the war when Andrew returned to Burma, he wrote back to us: "Daddy's dream house lies razed to the ground ... there is nothing left there but rubble and smoke emanating from grey stones," ... and he turned back.'

∽

At this point, Mama would always go back to remembering her house in Mandalay, the house she so loved.

'Our home in Burma was a huge house across the moat around Mandalay Palace. In the moat, you could see pink lotuses growing all over, and young boys and girls would sit in little boats and go boating through the flowers—singing, and playing the banjo. At times, we would see Burmese boys sitting on the bridge in front of our house. There are four bridges across the moat of the Palace. The Palace had a huge red brick wall all around it. We went there many times. An Indian emperor Bahadur Shah Zafar was imprisoned there, the one who wrote the lines, *"Do gaz zameen bhi na mili"* . . . we saw the room in which he'd been kept. The Palace was carved in red wood, a lovely deep shade, with high decorated pillars. It was a gorgeous palace, and once, the queens, the kings, the princesses—they all lived there. We'd often go up to Mandalay Hill, full of tropical plants. The view from there was beautiful!'

⁂

Sometimes, on storytelling nights, I'd lay awake in my bed imagining myself meeting Mama amidst the golden pagodas of Burma around the Mandalay Hill.

I can see myself in my blue frock and booties. In my left arm I'm holding my doll. I walk through a long winding towpath, open green earth on both sides. I amble along, humming happily. Then, the road begins to ascend. From a distance I can see a green hill covered with exotic plants. On top of this hill is an enormously beautiful castle, its magnificent golden edifice glowing in the wet rainforest.

I walk along the narrow path, the palace now standing majestic before my eyes. From behind the red wall appears a beautiful young woman. She is wearing a Burmese longyi and a white embroidered blouse. Her long hair falls to her waist and in her hands, she carries a bunch of flowers. This beautiful woman continues walking towards me from the castle. When she comes close enough, she stops to see me looking up at her with awestruck eyes. The woman does not recognize me, but I know her, she is my Mama. She bends down and hands me a flower from her bouquet of white lilies. I take it, never once moving my gaze away from her face. The young woman smiles.

'Who are you?' she looks into my eyes.

'Where did you get those eyes?'

'From you . . .' I whisper.

Startled, the young woman takes a step back. She does not understand my response. She smiles at me once again and walks away down the hill. Still holding my doll in one hand, and in the other, a white lily, I watch her disappear into the distance. The rainforest thickens and darkens. The vast green plain spreads out like a simbal quilt.

Such images were part of my imaginary world and they lived with me alongside my real world.

8

Exodus from Burma

My mother's experiences in Burma, and especially her family's traumatic escape in 1942, made such an impression on me that I could still recall the details many years after I first heard them from her. I'd been asked to write an essay in my English class in college in New York, and I based it on my grandmother's harrowing flight from Burma during the Second World War. Later, using my college essay as a foundation I created a quasi-fictional account of my family's escape from Burma that is reproduced here.

Little Woman and the Gramophone

'Oh Lashio! Lashio!'

Little Woman turned to look back longingly one last time at the land she was going to leave behind forever, the land she so loved, the land she would always call home, the land she would never stop yearning for ... Clad in a white cotton sari, a gramophone perched on her back, she stood at the precipice of the Tamu Pass, the last checkpost that marked the border between Burma and India. The sun was going down behind the hills. As she began to walk along the path to Pallel, the golden trumpet on her back, the horn of the gramophone, shone in the setting sun.

These were times of trouble. The year was 1942. The world was at war for the second time. Eighty thousand troops in Singapore had surrendered on 15 February; eight days later, the British–Indian brigades in Burma were crushed in the Battle of Sittang Bridge, a defeat that effectively left the path to Rangoon open to the Japanese advance.

Little Woman prepared for her family to leave before it was too late. They would go to Rangoon, and from there board the steamer that would take them safely to Calcutta. But her oldest son, Andrew, had brought news that the last boat packed with refugees heading for the Bay of Bengal had already sailed out, and the Rangoon harbour had closed down. It was now too dangerous to stay in Rangoon. Refugees were advised to move up to Mandalay and register for evacuation where the British government had organized treks to India by road.

Rangoon became the target of heavy air raids. On 7 March, the British forces started to evacuate Rangoon. The next day, Rangoon fell to the Japanese forces. The Burmese Indian families were left with no choice but to abandon their homes and flee to India. Of the over 500,000 Indians who fled Burma in the first half of 1942, only 70,000 were among the lucky few to evacuate Burma by sea. Some 4,000 were evacuated by plane. The rest were left with no option but to walk to India. The most direct route would have been from east to west; from Myitkyina to Manipur, then to Dhaka, finally reaching Calcutta. But in early May, the aerodrome at Myitkyina, the northernmost point of evacuation for the refugees as well as the armed forces, was bombed. The evacuees were left with no choice but to pursue seemingly impossible routes leading to different points of entry on the Indo–Burmese frontier.

Little Woman clung to the walls of her bamboo house and wept bitterly. It was time to go, leave everything behind—all her possessions: her home, her belongings, her vegetable garden, the creepers in the veranda, everything. Only the gramophone, she would not leave behind. The gramophone she insisted on carrying with her, on her back.

'Mummy, we cannot possibly carry *this*!' Andrew looked aghast at his mother as she stood stubbornly next to the old-fashioned instrument with its outsized, horn-shaped speaker.

'You can't. I can!' she said, pulling a white cotton cloth out of a cupboard and tying it around her waist.

'Help me with it, Andrew. Just make a pouch of this cloth on my back and stick the trumpet in.'

'On your BACK?' Andrew stood horrified, gaping at his mother.

'How *can* you? How can I *let* you do this?' The boy was at a total loss for words. But there was no time left to argue. The sun was quickly sliding down. The trucks were ready to go on the other side of the river; the elephants had lined up for more evacuees. Andrew could hardly walk, his own luggage weighing him down. He had little option left but to lift the gramophone and slide it into the cloth pouch tied to his mother's back.

For days, they walked over the hills, cutting through dense forests, camping at night and trudging through the near impenetrable jungles by day, their troubles heightened by the toughest of monsoons that month of March. Places high up in the mountains were infested with screeching monkeys and all around the dark forest they could hear the deafening sound of crickets. Drinking water was scarce and so, rationed. Since it was chlorinated because of germs and disease, it tasted more like medicine. Fever swept through the ranks of the fleeing refugees.

At night in the jungle, crickets would chirp and the moon, a pale sinking ball of yellow cadmium, would hang low in the sky. The air would be still and the jungle would breathe heavy. On nights like this, the women would huddle together and light fires while the men kept vigil.

After days of slogging through the jungle Little Woman was now fraught with exhaustion. She felt she could go on no longer. If the jungle and the night were to get the better of her, so be it. But not one more step could she take hereon. Her party had moved forward, her family members were among the people who would have crossed over to India by now. The people who were a couple of furlongs behind her on the narrow dust trail were taking time to catch up. Her back throbbed from carrying the weight of the heavy gramophone. The party that was carrying the foodstuff had been left way behind. She decided to take a breather, give her feet a rest.

She pulled the gramophone off her back, slowly swinging its weight to the front and untying the knot around her waist. She then placed it carefully on the stone mound and sat down beside it. There was no one around and it was quickly getting dark. She was certain that she was lost, but decided she couldn't go looking for the others as she wouldn't know where to find them. Best to wait on the trail for someone to catch up. And her feet were killing her. She decided to wait, sit for a while, calm her nerves.

She took a long breath, stretching her body. With both her hands she pulled the hair back from her sweaty forehead knotting the long tresses into a bun at the nape of her neck. She looked at her sari, the pale white now almost brown from days and nights of plodding through the jungle. The maroon velvet Parsi border, handwoven, had frayed along the edges, the delicate mal-mal giving in to thorny shrubs and undergrowth through the trackless jungle.

As darkness fell, she tried once more to call out to the other members of her family, her voice frail and quivery.

'Andreeeeewwww ...!'

'Briiiiiaaaaannn ...!'

'Saraaaaaahhh ...!'

Not one human sound came back. All was silent. She was probably not going to make it after all. Her family must be thinking that she was up ahead with the other women and children from the last camp, so no one would even come back looking for her. She was lost for certain.

She looked at the gramophone, her only prized possession in the world, her eyes brimming. Gently, she ran her fingers over the glazed wooden base, the brass plate shining with the engraved lettering 'His Master's Voice'. How could she have ever left this behind? How could she possibly have thrown it away in the jungle, a thing of such beauty? Slowly she unwrapped the arm and the needle. Her shan bag, which held the last of her records, lay next to her on the ground. She dug her hand into it, pulling out a shiny black disc. With the pallu of her sari, she carefully wiped its black surface, her hand moving over the HMV logo, His Master's Voice, a painting created in 1899 by Francis Barraud, of the dog Nipper listening to a cylinder phonograph.

∞

She remembered the time her husband had brought the gramophone home. Jagan Nath had purchased it from the old Indian shop in the market. It was a genuine German piece. Ah, how could she ever forget that evening! They were in the Meiktila house then. It was early evening and she had been planting rhododendrons in her garden when her husband walked into the house with a large carton in his arms. As the cardboard box was unpacked, Little Woman ran into the house exulting at the sight that greeted her: a gramophone! A gramophone in her house!

Jagan Nath had opened the box, revealing the beauty slowly, and carefully placed the glazed oak wood plateau on the table against the window beside Gertie's sewing machine. Little Woman stood next to her husband, watching as he connected the tone arm and slid it into position. Finally came the magical horn, hand-hammered from brass, a shimmering gold trumpet which, by itself, was a thing of great beauty.

Little Woman's joy was boundless. Jagan Nath was a good man, she mused, a good man she had married, as she watched him pull out from another cardboard box a bunch of records and place them alongside the gramophone. Then he asked his wife to shut her eyes and pick from the bunch, any one record. Eyes closed, Little Woman ran her fingers gently over the glazed black discs lined up on the table. Then she held one out and handed it to her husband. Jagan Nath smiled and placed the HMV disc on the turntable. He then cranked up the machine until it was ready to play.

Little Woman moved back and sat on the edge of the sofa, fixing her blue voile sari, straightening it slightly over her left shoulder. Her hair was pulled back and the floral Parsi border framed her lean brown face. Jagan Nath lowered the needle gently, just enough to let it rest on the rotating disc. Little Woman held her breath. The first sound was the unexpected crackle of the needle on the ungrooved edge of the record. Almost unbearable, she felt, the emptiness of that crackle, and then . . . a melody started.

The first stray notes of a clarinet, then the woodwind set, and, finally, the sweet voice of Kanan Bala rising high and melodious, filling the small house, its dark bamboo walls and their lives, with joy!

Ghoonghat ke pat khol re . . . tohe piya milenge . . .

As the music rose, Little Woman sprang to her feet clasping her hands with joy and danced around on the bare floor, the pallu of her sari swirling around her petite, fragile frame. The sound of music emanating from the hall brought all the eight children running back inside the house to gather around this new addition to the family, the gramophone.

Every evening thereafter, the husband and wife would sit around the gramophone and play records. Little Woman loved playing her favourite songs: Kanan Bala's voice in a high octave, 'Duniya yeh duniya ... ye toofan mail ... duniya yeh ...' the bhajans sung by Juthika Roy and Kundan Lal, the songs of Uma Devi, Ashok Kumar, and Devika Rani. She especially loved the song 'Gaiya', adored the melodious voice of the singing beauty, Suraiya—'Dil le gaya ji koi dil le gaya, dil le gaya'—and the evergreen K. L. Sehgal's 'Ek bangala bane nyaara ...'

'His Master's Voice' had taken over their lives in the little bamboo house in Meiktila. Besides the songs, drama recordings were added to the collection. Those included dramatizations of the Krishna Leela and parts of the legend of the Ramayan. The family would sit around the gramophone in the evenings, with Little Woman in the centre, listening to these renditions.

Gradually the record collection grew and built to a hundred. Little Woman's favourite, though, remained the Mirabai bhajans, the ones sung by Juthika Roy: 'Ae ri main to prem diwaani ... mera dard na jaane koye'. She would play them over and over again as she went about doing her household chores—the cooking, the washing, the gardening—singing along, 'Mere to giridhar gopal ... doosaro na koi ...'

∽

Little Woman, lost and footsore, had given up all hope of making it to the Indian border, even be rescued by her family. Having footslogged for days and now separated from her family, Little Woman was tired and full of despair. She needed music to lift her spirits. Without really thinking, she knelt down and began to crank up the gramophone so she could play a record. Slowly, she rotated the crank, once, twice, and then again. Then, she stopped, transfixed by the terrible sight of the animal that stood barely twenty feet from her, its eyes following her every move. All sounds of the jungle vanished. The breeze stopped. Beads of sweat erupted on her skin. Her small fragile frame shook with fright.

She stood frozen to the ground, only the low growl of the tiger reverberating through the pin-drop silence of the night. Slowly, she began to straighten up, unable to get her eyes away from the tiger. This was the moment then, she thought, her heart pounding in her chest. *This* was the death people dreaded—being eaten alive by a wild tiger.

The tiger looked at Little Woman straight in the eye, its gaze unwavering. Little Woman couldn't tear her eyes away from the tiger, and stood there petrified, trapped in a terrifying fatal moment. She then shut her eyes tight, as if she was going to die, but she could not bear to see herself being mauled by the animal.

All at once there was an unexpected movement within the frozen tableau. The metal handle of the gramophone began to turn anti-clockwise; as that happened the disc on the machine began to revolve, the needle lowered on to the vinyl's glazed edge, an unbearable empty crackle ... then incredibly, music began to sound through the dying light: the notes from a cello, the bass starting up, an accordion. And then, cutting through the terror and tension of the death valley, clear and high pitched rose the voice of Juthika Roy.

'*Bhed jiya ke khol, man re, kahe na mujhse bol . . .*'

Little Woman stood motionless. She thought, if death is to be this moment, let it be accompanied by music. There was no other sound in the wild forest, only the melodious voice of Juthika Roy:

'*Kaahe na mujhse bol . . .*'

Little Woman slowly opened her eyes. The tiger hadn't moved. Then, even as she watched, it turned its head slowly, took a lazy step to its left and melted into the jungle.

∞

Back on the Pallel checkpost, after waiting all night, as the little group of Indian refugees turned around dejected and started to make their weary way towards the landscape of India, a child in the group turned around and shouted: 'She's here ... look ... Little Woman is here!' The figure of a petite woman emerged from behind the hill; Little Woman looked up, and then began to make her way, step by step to safety, the golden horn of the gramophone tied to her back ablaze in the light of the rising sun.

∞

The story of my grandmother and her gramophone which I memorialized in my college essay was the image that lingered in my mind the longest about my mother's family's exodus from Burma, but there were other aspects about this traumatic period that my mother would often talk to me about.

Here are her words:

'In 1942, during the Japanese invasion, there were air raids on Rangoon. On Christmas day, the first of these raids started a general exodus of Burmese and Indians from the city. News came in that students in Rangoon University had been captured and tortured by Japanese soldiers. Indians were asked to flee if they wanted to save themselves from the torture camps. So, Daddy and Mummy decided to return with the family to the country of their birth, before it was too late. There were several members in the family and they could not afford to send everyone by plane. The only option was to go by ship. Daddy planned for the family to go to Rangoon, and from there, board the steamer that would safely take them to the Bay of Bengal. Andrew was sent

Andrew Uncle

up ahead to Rangoon to buy tickets for the ship to Calcutta. But they soon learned there was no hope of getting out that way. Andrew returned from Rangoon with the news that the last ship packed with refugees heading for the Bay of Bengal had been torpedoed by the Japanese, and the Rangoon harbour had been closed down.

'Daddy knew there were no options left. His family would have to get across to India on foot. Eight people crossed over—the four boys—Andrew, Mahinder, Brian, and Dechho along with the women, Badi Mummy, Bhuaji, and Sarah. Uncle Vishwanath also crossed over with his wife and two sons. But your Bade Daddy could not accompany them. He was on the verge of retirement and could not run away without permission. In order to qualify for his pension back in India, he would need to stay in Burma. He came afterwards, a month later, on a cycle, along with Deepat, the servant.

'The family had to leave most of their possessions behind. But Mummy would not be parted from her gramophone and her hundred HMV long play records. Mummy was ready to leave every single thing behind in Burma, but not her music.

'When they started on the trek through the jungle, they came upon a sign that read: "INDIANS NOT ALLOWED". The British had erected the sign. There were two routes that could be taken. One was a bit more organized, and had dak bungalows every ten miles or so. You would walk for those ten miles, stop at a dak bungalow to rest and eat, and resume your journey the next day. But this route was reserved for the British, Indians were not allowed there. On the other route, the Tamu–Pallel route, there was nothing. No arrangements at all. You travelled at your own risk, no paved roads, only kachche raste. But there was no other option so they set off. It took them over two months to cross over. They had with them a huge dhurrie. Whenever night fell, they would spread that dhurrie on the ground and break journey.

'In the night, when they walked through the jungles, there was constant guard from wild animals. So, they had to light torches, mashaals, to keep the animals away! The boys would stay up and keep vigil all night, in shifts, while the rest of the party slept. When the mashaals ran out, they burnt whatever clothes they could spare. Mummy had been collecting saris for her daughters' trousseaus. She had to pull out all the beautiful Banarasi silks and the georgettes with Parsi borders, douse them with kerosene, and set them aflame. One by one, all our trousseau saris went up in flames along the ravaged passage to India!'

∽

The most heart-wrenching part of the exodus story for me has always been the moment when Badi Mummy had to throw away her records. I'd insist on hearing that bit over and over again, and each time Mama narrated the details, I'd start to picture the entire scene as if I was watching it in a film.

'Due to excess luggage, the coolies refused to carry the weight any further. Everyone said, "Throw away the gramophone, Mummy! Throw the records." Mummy started crying. Her heart was broken, but she finally resigned, and threw away her most prized possession down the hill. She kept throwing them away, and kept weeping ... one by one, she flung into the dark valley, all hundred long play records, sobbing like a baby ...'

This scene would break my heart every time I would hear it.

'But, Mama, she saved the gramophone, didn't she?'

'Yes, the gramophone ... that she brought back with her to India.'

*

It was on 12 Feb 1942 that the exodus began, and the Gangahar family reached Mukerian on 5 April, after a harrowing two months. It is from Brian Uncle's first-hand account of the trek that we get more details of the walk from Burma to India.

In Brian Uncle's words:

'We left from Kyaukse for Monywa by truck along with Uncle Bowrie's family who lived down south in Tavoy. From Monywa to Kalewa we travelled by boat. Our next destination was the border town of Tamu, also known as Tamu Pass. We had to go from Kalewa to Tamu on bullock cart; three or four bullock carts were hired to carry

Brian Uncle

the members of the family and all our stuff. I am not too sure how long this journey took us. We stayed in Tamu a few days, readying ourselves to cross the border into India, but no transport of any kind was available. Finally, we gave up and took off from Tamu to Imphal in Manipur on foot, walking along the Kachin hills. Phuaji was really old and could not tackle the hazardous terrain. So, palanquins were hired to carry Phuaji and sister Sarah; Dinesh and I took short rides now and then. There were thousands of people fleeing, mostly Indians.

'There were no provisions made by the government of the day—no water, no food, no toilets, nothing! We had to carry our own provisions, camp at night in the open. Fires would be lit around the campsites to keep the wild animals away. We could hear all kinds of sounds from the jungle—buffalos, wild bears, tigers. There was also death and disease and we saw decomposed human bodies lying around; it was a really sickening sight. I nearly passed out on seeing some of those bodies. Andrew had to pick me up and carry me a short distance. Sarah was in tears. This bit was perhaps the worst part of the journey.

'We were on the road for days, walking ten or twelve miles daily through that treacherous mountainous region, until we reached Imphal. Here for the first time we came across some officials who directed us towards some makeshift bamboo huts where we were to spend the next day or two awaiting coaches to take us to the railhead town of Dimapur. These coaches were provided by the British Indian Government. I remember the first night we spent in those bamboo huts. A guy came around late at night, poked his head through the door and shouted, "Keep the doors closed at night, there are tigers around!" That put the fear of God into everyone, especially because the doors were so flimsy and there were no locks! I don't think anyone slept that night.

'The coaches arrived the next morning and took us all to Dimapur, from where the Indian Railways took over and we boarded a train to reach Jalandhar. It was a great relief. Finally, we arrived in Jalandhar where the families split up. The Bowries headed for Amritsar and the Gangahars took a train to Mukerian, about forty-five miles away.'

∽

Though the stories that my mother told me about the exodus were deeply impactful, the one that left an indelible mark on my young mind was the story of her cousin Roland. The thirteen-year-old Indian boy had been captured by Japanese soldiers and kept for months in their torture camps as an interpreter. Burmese people were subjected to inhuman torture and Roland was made to sit, watch, and translate. The saga went on for weeks. By the time the war came to an end, Roland had lost his mind. He couldn't get the images of the torture camp out of his head. He would wake up in the middle of the night with knotted fists, shrieking and wailing.

∽

My mother's yearning to go back to Burma affected me greatly. She remembered the 'beautiful life' she had there and it was always with a sense of regret that she'd recall those memories. I could see the pangs she felt remembering her homeland—it was a feeling of great loss. I had promised myself that, someday, I would take my mother back to the country of her birth. And I did. She was like a little girl, excited beyond belief, seeing all those places from her childhood. I took her back to Mandalay in the winter of 2001—sixty years after she'd left her homeland.

Back in America my mother continued to be a teacher till the time she retired; she loved teaching little children. And she continued to paint till the end of her life. Mama's landscapes and portraits in pastels had the most amazing quality—at once soft and strong, traits that marked her own personality. The gentlest of souls, deeply passionate, unbelievably tender and compassionate with a remarkable sense of self-esteem—these are qualities I attribute to my very special mother.

Whenever I would go back to visit my family in Long Island, I'd be excited to see Mama's latest works. Each time I entered her room overlooking the garden, I always found my mother sitting at her easel against the light, painting . . .

That's how I remember Mama.

9

Piti

'Piti' is what I would call my father, short for Pitaji, because as a baby I could never say that right, so it has always remained Piti.

'Goodman di Laltain!' (Goodman's lantern) was his takiya qalaam, his favourite expression when he was particularly tickled about something. Originally, this phrase was used by army officers to praise their juniors; but at some point, it passed into local parlance. I can picture my father typing away at his desk on the veranda when suddenly the wind begins to howl and it starts to rain. He gets up and sprints through the drizzle in the courtyard towards the kitchen and says to Mama, 'Winnie, perfect time isn't it, darling, for a steaming hot cup of tea?'

And when Mama says, 'It's ready, darling!'

'Goodman di Laltain!' he exclaims, rubbing his hands together to warm them. Every time I'd hear that phrase, I knew my father was in a cheerful mood.

∽

My earliest memory of Piti is when I am three years old, sleeping on the wicker chair in the vehra of our house in Amritsar. Mama is winding up the kitchen. I hear her voice, 'Look! Deepi has gone off to sleep on the moodha.' Then someone gently picks me up, puts me on their shoulder, and carries me up two flights of stairs to the terrace and tucks me into bed. That's my father. I pretend to be fast asleep. This is my first memory of my father, being lovingly carried on his shoulder.

As a young child I remember he would play the harmonium to wake us up. It is a cold winter morning in Amritsar. My sister and I are fast asleep under our quilts. Piti quietly stands in one corner of the room and begins to play the harmonium, the instrument perched on a stool. How beautifully he played . . . Gently we turn, stretch, and wake up to the sound of music.

∽

Another undimmed memory dates back to when I was around twelve years old. At this stage of my life Piti and I would sometimes go for a long walk in the morning. One Sunday we walked all the way up to the Jandiaale-waali nehar, the canal on the outskirts of the city amidst the green fields. We were both quite surprised at how far we'd come. I remember we didn't talk much, just silently walked alongside each other, enjoying the morning sounds. Our communication through that walk had been wordless. That was often his way.

The fact that my father didn't say much meant that his antecedents always remained a bit of a mystery to my young as well as adolescent mind. He didn't speak much about his childhood, his family, not the way Mama did. It was only much later in New York, when he surprisingly started to open up a little, that I began to understand who my father really was.

∽

My father was born on 8 April 1921, in a small village in Punjab called Nava Shehar, in Vaidaan da Mohalla, Bibiji's ancestral home. He arrived at the stroke of 4 a.m. As the little creature began to make his first thin, squeaky sounds, Manorama Devi, my Bibiji, knew what she was going to call her son. 'Uday', the baby boy would be named, representing the rising of the sun, the break of a new day.

Piti grew up in Katra Kanhaiya, in the old walled quarter of Amritsar. In 1933, the family moved to the Chandraavali house, our ancestral home next to the mosque in Hall Bazaar. 'It was a very quiet street,' said Piti. 'There were just a couple of shops in the entire length. Two cycles would pass in the street and we'd think, Ajj bazaar vich raunak hai!' Today the bazaar is abuzz!

My father was a very quiet, shy adolescent. The only son in the family, he grew up with five sisters. In a household teeming with girls, he gradually turned into a loner. From time to time his male cousins from  Africa, Bibiji's brother's children, would come to visit. Doli, Kirki, Bindu were all strapping young boys, tall and statuesque. Compared to them my father felt small and insignificant. In his later years, he told me that as an adolescent, he grew up with a complex—about his looks and his physique—though when I look at his portrait as a young man from his Lahore days, I feel that he had rather nice features. But it had been ingrained in his mind that because he wasn't tall and fair complexioned like other Punjabi boys, he was not good looking. It wouldn't be until he was thirteen that young Uday would come into his own. In fact, before that, my father went quite unnoticed in his own home.

∽

After matriculating from Pandit Baijnath High School, Amritsar, in 1935, Father went to Hindu College to do his intermediate for two years. He then went to Lahore and joined the Government College to study English Literature. Here, Professor Eric C. Dickenson became his favourite teacher; the English professor was also very fond of young Uday. It was under his guidance that Father was drawn to the world of art. The years 1936 to 1941 were very productive for him in many ways.

The Lahore of my parents' time was a splendid city, a lively, vibrant place. Government College was like the Harvard of North India. Culturally rich with its Mughal architecture, its elite society, the Victoria Gardens, the city was a hub of the performing arts. It had a thriving theatre community, cinema houses: Regal and Plaza on Mall Road and art galleries—all things that young Uday was hugely drawn to. He said to me, 'I have very, very fond memories of Lahore. I think even now I would say that it is the best city I ever lived in. They say na, "Lhaur Lhaur hi hai!" There was lots of cultural activity with something going on at all times. Art exhibitions, debates, declamation contests . . . Everything was accessible. You could go on a bicycle everywhere. There was the Government School of Art and the Mayo School of Art. Because I was such an art enthusiast, I would go there frequently and made many friends!'

Piti, Lahore days.

Little did my father know at the time that the famous Sanyal Studio in Lahore was where my mother, the girl he'd finally marry, would come to study painting. It intrigues me that both my parents were in Lahore around the same time, had similar interests, but hadn't met. And they were not going to meet, not until the Partition of India was to happen in 1947.

In 1941, after Uday acquired his Master's in English Honours, he returned to Amritsar. With his newly acquired sophistication and appreciation of the arts, he decided he didn't want to be another Sharmaji on the streets of Amritsar. So, he decided to give himself a new name. Naval, is what he chose, meaning 'New'. Henceforth, he'd be known as Uday Chandra Naval.

∽

In 1948, my father Uday Chandra Naval married my mother, Himadri Gangahar. The matchmaker had told Bibiji, Manorama Devi, that there was a certain Gangahar family in Mukerian who'd migrated back from Burma and had eligible girls of marriageable age. This happened around the time, just after Partition, when my mother, along with other girls, was performing stage shows to raise funds for the refugees coming from Pakistan. Sneh Aunty, my father's sister, who'd met my mother at a women's conference in Hyderabad, was full of praise for this beautiful girl from Burma who had great grace—a lovely voice, impressive demeanour, and considerable charm. When it was learnt that she was Punjabi and from the same caste as my father's family her stock went up further. Bade Daddy's friend, Des Raj Sood who was in Amritsar became a facilitator. As Mama danced on the stage at Chitra Talkies at one of the fundraising programs, Piti, I believe, watched the show and instantly fell in love with her. The next day, he took his parents along to see the girl.

Their first meeting was at Chitra Talkies where they sat together in a box and watched a film. They spoke perhaps a sentence or two here and there, but nothing much. Before my mother knew it, she was walking in the Company Gardens of Amritsar with my would-be father. Mama had asked her younger sister, Lily, to walk a few steps behind to make sure he wasn't shorter than her. My father apparently told my mother, 'I don't want a woman who is a decoration piece in my drawing room. I want to marry someone who can be my support system in my life, my equal in every aspect.'

Three meetings took place before the final decision was made. It was at their third meeting—at Mr Sood's kothi on Lawrence Road, when Mama showed Piti her sketches from Lahore—that my father, totally charmed by her artistic sensibility and talent, decided that this was the girl he was going to marry. This was my father's version.

When I asked Mama about her courtship and wedding, all she said was, 'On our wedding night, your father gave me a book, "Read this," he said. "We'll discuss it in the next couple of days." Imagine! I looked at my mother aghast, then we both burst out laughing. She continued: 'Your father was an atheist and a communist, hugely influenced by Karl Marx. He never believed in God all those early years of our marriage. During the havans at home, he would quietly slip out of the house.'

Piti and Mama as a young couple.

A significant little detail about my family history has always made me very proud. My father had taken just one rupee as token dowry in marriage with my mother; he was strictly against the concept of dahej.

∞

When my parents got married, Piti was still struggling to make a livelihood. When he described to me his days of struggle the details intrigued me: 'After coming back from Lahore, my struggle to make a living started. It was an ugly phase in my life—I was cut off from myself, I was cut off from the family, cut off from everybody.'

His first venture was a pencil factory, which was a complete failure. Says my father, 'I set up a pencil factory on GT Road. We found premises, set up machines but by the time the pencils got made they were so defective, not a single one was sold. The factory was shut down. We lost 18,000 rupees. I was distraught. What was I doing with my life? Besides the enormous financial loss, I was stricken by the fact that after acquiring a degree in literature from a top college in Lahore and having developed a keen interest in art, I'd been able to do no better than start a pencil factory to make a living. I thought it was a big tragedy but it was my own decision, no one forced me to do it, and I don't remember where the idea came from.'

He next tried his hand at the utensils business, under the name of India Metal Works, but this, too, turned out to be a disaster. Sultanwind Gate was the place where the India Metal Works factory was located and they made brass katoris. The company headquarters were located in Calcutta. There wasn't enough capital to invest in the venture, so my father's partner suspended dealings with him, and he lost out on the business.

As I write this, my heart sinks. A student of English literature, making katoris . . . how on earth was that going to work?

Through all this, Mama gave Pitaji her full support. She not only supported him, but worked along with her husband in running the business—keeping accounts, dealing with the workers, visiting the factory, and so on.

A few years down the line, my father made yet one last attempt at business. He set up a factory in the gully next to Ajit Bookbinder. It

was so close Didi and I would just skip across to the factory. In it was installed a huge machine called the Hammer which made cycle de purze—cranks for bicycle pedals. I remember the day the Hammer was set up and we all went for the inauguration. There's a photograph in which both Didi and I are standing next to Pitaji in front of the larger-than-life machine. But the giant contraption was not destined to last for long. Mrs Kunti Pal,

Opening of the Hammer factory.

Mama's co-worker at the Women's Conference office, brought the Hammer to a standstill. 'Dhamak paendi hai!' she said to my father. 'My whole house shakes with the impact of the damn machine!' Finally, the Hammer was grounded to a halt. The factory had to be shut down and the machine was shifted back to Sultanwind Gate. India Metal Works was finished.

All three factories that my father started had failed. It would be an

understatement to say that the first few years of marriage were rough
for my parents. It was during these difficult times that both Didi and I
were born.

∽

My father, clearly not cut out for business, finally turned to something
that was his calling. In 1955, he joined the Hindu College as a professor
of English literature. Gyaniji, our family friend and an extremely learned
man, was instrumental in convincing my father to take the job. He came
to know there was an opening in Hindu College and knew that Pitaji
had been struggling for years with his business. However, when Gyaniji
initially approached him, my father was unconvinced 'What would I
do with a three-hundred rupee salary?' he would argue. But Gyaniji
eventually managed to convince him.

∽

Being a professor in a college may not have been very lucrative, but my
father loved to teach. Even on days when he didn't have to go to college,
he could not resist the opportunity to impart knowledge. For many years

Piti (third from right, front row) at Hindu College.

Piti speaking at an event.

during my childhood, Sundays were days reserved for Piti's seminars. He would round us all up in the veranda and chalk out in white script on a blackboard all the points he intended to drive home into our little heads. Sunday evenings were meant for lessons in self-improvement, etiquette, civic sense, and more. The seminars would discuss moral issues, the importance of being disciplined and hard-working in life—a place for everything and everything in its place—there was huge emphasis on good manners and duties. Books and studying were the big focus all through my childhood years.

'Come for the seminar! It's five o'clock everyone!' I'd hear my father's sprightly cry as he emerged from the hall kamra into the veranda taking his position in front of the blackboard placed on Mama's painting easel.

'Here we go again,' I'd grumble as I stopped whatever I was doing, preparatory to attending Piti's seminar.

'What's the topic for today?' I'd ask.

'I don't know,' Didi would look at me as if I'd asked an outrageous question.

Mama would quickly put away her knitting needles. 'Just grab your notebook and go sit there!'

She supported Pitaji in whatever he did. If we ever said anything unkind about our father or complained about how strict he was and how we could never really relax with him around, Mama would snap at us—'Not a word against your father, understand? I won't have it.'

At the blackboard Piti always spoke with a slight twitch of his left shoulder, a habit he wasn't aware of. This happened when his mind was racing with points he was determined not to miss out on while teaching. We'd rapidly make notes as he spoke—one side of the page was marked 'Pros', and the other 'Cons'—and then we would fill up each column as he discussed the topic of the day.

'One must set goals in life,' he'd say. 'You should not go about life in a wishy-washy manner. Be target-oriented. Set high aspirations for yourselves. Don't think that you cannot do something just because you are girls,' Piti would emphasize. This was an oft-repeated lesson he wanted engraved in our minds. 'Value for Time' and 'Time Management' were other favourite topics. Piti always spoke passionately and with considerable amount of wit.

Once the seminars were underway, I quite enjoyed them. My main grouse with Piti's seminars was that they were too student–teacher like for my comfort. I grew up feeling that my father treated us less like his children and more like students. The only way he could communicate with us was by standing at the blackboard.

It was only much later that I was able to see things in the right perspective. Once in New York when Piti asked me what his shortcomings were as a father, I mentioned the seminars. I felt the seminars were responsible for creating a chasm between us—children and father. Piti was surprised. After a bit he asked:

'So, were the seminars a good thing or a bad thing?'

'They were a good thing,' I said, 'but you never patted me with love, or held me close or put me on your lap.'

Piti was thoughtful at first, then spoke carefully.

'It was the way of our generation, beta. In our time, fathers seldom mollycoddled their children. They just did the work, were the providers, guided them, and left it to the mothers to cuddle the kids.'

It was in that moment that I began to see the whole thing in a completely different light. In a flash I realized that the seminars were perhaps the best thing that Piti could have done for us. I felt sheepish to have held them against him; so much of the values I hold on to were rooted in them. Today I can only say, thank God for Pitaji's seminars.

∞

Art was the only thing Piti loved more than scholarship and teaching. Such was his love for art that, as a young man studying literature under the guidance of Professor Dickenson, he published a small booklet called *Joy of Art* which had a long essay by the Russian painter Nicholas Roerich, with whom he shared a fond association up to the time of the painter's demise in 1947. One of my favourite stories from my childhood is my father's account of his first meeting with Roerich, who was living in India at the time. He had settled down in a tiny village in the Himalayas called Naggar, which overlooked the river Beas as it gushed through Kullu valley.

Many years later, when I was doing my research for this book, my father who was eighty-eight then, retold the story (which I will put down here, lightly edited) he had narrated to us as children.

In Pitaji's words . . .

'I had first gone to Manali at Christmas time in 1940 with my friend Harbhajan Singh Dogra, who used to visit the Kullu valley very often. We were together in Government College, Lahore, studying English literature, and were both passionate about art. I wrote to Bauji seeking his permission to go to Manali. My father wrote back, surprised, "Manali? In this severe winter?"

'When I reached Manali I found that a Russian artist called Nicholas Roerich lived there in a small hamlet called Naggar. How unusual, I thought, for a painter from Russia to come all the way from his country to find sanctuary in a small Himalayan village.

'I wrote to Roerich, requesting a meeting. Those days I was preparing to publish a small journal called *Joy of Art* and I thought it would be most exciting to have the Russian painter's views on art for our first issue. Roerich's answer came in the form of a handwritten note delivered by a Pahadi man. I read the letter over and over again.

Dear Uday,

I would be delighted to receive you at my home. Please do come to Naggar. Next Friday seems appropriate. You are likely to reach the valley by noon. Once you arrive at Patlikuhal, there will be a mule waiting by the bridge to carry you up to the cottage. It's quite a steep climb . . . and don't forget to carry your overcoat. Me and my family shall be waiting for you to join us for lunch.

'The end of the yellow inland was signed in blue ink:
Nicholas Roerich.
'The Lahore air felt crisp around my ears. The road outside the hostel

was awashed with fresh drizzle. A few tongas trotted past, the tick-tock of the horses' hooves in sync with my own sprightly gait.

'A mule? Why, I certainly would not need a mule to carry me up the hill. I should well manage to walk the incline on my own two feet. I should politely refuse this very gracious offer. It would be most unaesthetic, and certainly not poetic, to arrive at the house of the great Russian painter sitting on a mule. After all, we were going to discuss Art!

'I wrote back. "Please don't send a mule, I will get there on foot."

'The old clock tower of Government College struck four. It would be Mr Burn's class next. I would have to skip it, and also the next one on English literature. I should actually be packing to leave, almost right away; take the Punjab Roadways bus all the way up to Kullu via Pathankot. If I remember correctly, Patlikuhal should be a little way up after the beautiful wide valley of Katrain I'd been so enchanted with on my earlier trip. In 1940, there had been no roads; we boys had traversed the untouched, pristine Himalayan mountain trails on foot.

'I took a bus that night and reached Katrain. At the house of a fisheries inspector I found lodging for the night—a friend of my friend Harbhajan Singh. The inspector was surprised that the very reclusive Roerich had invited me over to his house.

'When I reached Patlikuhal, I realized the incline was pretty steep. It was 2 January 1941. The cold was severe. I stood on the bridge at Patlikuhal and gazed at the mountains around. The river Beas, one of the five rivers of Punjab, gushed beneath my feet.

'All around me the mountains stood tall and mysterious, glistening with white snow. Naggar was this quaint little village perched fairly high on the slope of a mountain. The incline up to the house of the Russian painter was steeper and much longer than I had imagined. Even though I was nineteen, sprightly, fit, and light-footed, I had not reckoned with the intensity of the climb. Two hours after I started climbing, there was still no sign of the Russian painter's cottage.

'A couple of Pahadi men in pattoos walked past me, going downhill. I paused my climb to ask them about the cottage.

'Bas, ithhe, agge-ee hai!'

'This was the fourth time someone had said, "It's just there . . . a little ahead!" That's how hill people keep going, I guessed, going up and down these steep slopes all their lives, with a "just a little ahead" attitude. Not a bad example to follow. I kept going.

'As I turned each curve on the track, I would see an even more enthralling view of the river Beas. The higher I went, the more enchanting the sight of the river became. After a while I paused on a precipice to catch my breath. The air was scented with the smell of pines, dry needles crunching beneath my feet. The sun was right overhead now. I worried that I'd be late; the painter had written, "Please reach by noon." But this climb seemed endless. How I wished I had accepted the offer of the mule.

'I felt I'd been walking all day when I finally saw two beautiful old huts on the mountainside, local Pahadi houses. There were women on the rooftops spreading orange corn to dry on the black slate tiles. A few round-faced, red-cheeked children ran around, giggling. I paused to take in this pleasing sight and catch my breath.

'Naggar finally seemed near. An old man at the only dhaba in sight pointed towards an entrancing stone and wood structure jutting out from the edge of the mountain right in front of where I was standing.

'"Is that the Russian painter's house?" I asked getting excited.

'"No, that is the old castle . . . Roerich Saab is just beyond."

'A small, steep path wound around the Naggar Castle, an enchanting little fortress overlooking a breathtaking view of the Kullu valley.

"Roerich Saab is over there," said a hill man pointing to a cottage just a little further ahead. The distance from the old castle to the Roerich cottage was barely a few yards, a level walk on a very narrow dirt track. It was already late in the afternoon. I kept walking, brisker now than before.

'The Roerichs were aristocrats. When the Russian Revolution took place in 1917, Tsar Nicholas managed to escape to New York, although many members of his immediate and extended family were killed. A good proportion of the aristocracy lost their lives as well, but many of the lesser nobility got away. I had heard that Mrs Helena Roerich was the niece of the empress Tsarina. The Roerichs fled their country and after much wandering about finally chose Naggar to make their home in exile.

'By the time I reached my destination, it was almost three in the afternoon. The Roerichs had waited and waited and finally given up on me. When I arrived at their house the family was already at the dining table having their lunch.

'I rang the doorbell. Roerich's older son, George Yuri, came to the door and welcomed me in. "Would you like to wash your hands?" he asked an unusual question.

'"Yes," I said, with prompt surprise.

'I washed up and sat down with the family for a meal. Mrs Roerich was dressed very aristocratically. She wore a long flowing garment, I remember. I wanted to stare at her, the manner in which she sat and ate, but I dared not. There were three or four bearers around, serving the meal—someone would come and place a dish on the table, another would wait to pick up the empty plates after we were done. I was very impressed with the whole scene. The food was not Indian at all; it was strictly European. That was the first time I was required to eat with a fork and knife, which I'd never done before, and I made some goof-ups, dropping this thing and that thing . . . I used the wrong spoon to eat my soup with, and Mrs Roerich broke into giggles, but she controlled herself at once.

'Roerich must have been sixty or sixty-five at the time, very distinguished-looking, with a flowing white beard. He did not speak very good English. I remember his accent was odd. At one point he used the word "thoughts" and I did not understand what he was saying. He repeated the word four times. He was referring to a painting whose title was *Thoughts* but his accent was such, I could not make out what he was trying to say.

'After lunch, we retired to Roerich's study upstairs. I browsed through his books. Then we sat and chatted. We spoke about Tagore, Shantiniketan, etc.

'I was wonderstruck by everything about the house. I found the interiors to be very beautiful. There were wooden railings all around the house and wooden beams and columns

Nicholas Roerich

supported the roof. There were many artefacts all over the rooms and Tibetan art everywhere on the walls, the colours, chrome and deep red. It was the first time I was exposed to such a lifestyle. It was a unique experience for me.

'Sitting upstairs on the balcony overlooking the hillside speckled with lights and the Beas River, we talked mostly of art. Then I told Roerich that I would have to leave now, as I would need to take the bus back from Naggar to Manali.

'"You don't have to go," he said, "you can stay overnight." I was very pleased to hear this.

'"But, sir, I have not brought any night clothes," I said.

'"Don't worry," he said, "you can wear my pyjamas."

'I floated in Roerich's white pyjamas, the pyjama bottoms trailing all over the wooden floor. It was so cold in that house that I shivered all night. Even though they gave me three or four blankets, yet I kept shivering through the night. But I wouldn't have missed that experience for anything, it was completely memorable. We discussed art till late in the night. Roerich had travelled extensively through the Himalayas and had spent a number of years exploring Tibet, and I was fascinated by the experiences he shared with me. The next morning his orderly woke me up at five as I had to take the 8 a.m. bus from Manali. I rode a horse on the return journey.

'Following my visit to Naggar, Roerich and I corresponded for many years. I proposed that Roerich write a piece for me on art. He sent me a long manuscript. I condensed it and decided to publish it with the title 'Joy of Art'. I wrote to Rabindranath Tagore asking him to write an introduction. He agreed. But it took six months for the publication to come out. In the meantime, Gurudev passed away. I was disheartened. However, when I wrote to Rathindranath Tagore, the poet's son, saying his father had very kindly agreed to write the introduction to *Joy of Art*, he told me, to my surprise and delight, that Gurudev had written the introduction before he passed away.

'I then decided to ask Dr S. Radhakrishnan, who later became President of India, to write the foreword to the volume. I went to Banaras to meet him. He was ill and in bed but nevertheless agreed to meet me. He told me that he was not the right person to write the foreword but suggested

I ask the painter Abanindranath Tagore to do so. But I insisted that he write it himself and fortunately he agreed. After that I reached out to Abdur Rahman Chughtai, who made the sketch for the book.'

∞

Many years later, when I returned to India to sell the ancestral house in Amritsar and was going through all our things to decide what to keep and what to discard, I came across a small booklet made out of brown handmade paper. I turned a leaf and found my father's name on it: UDAY CHANDRA NAVAL. My eyes welled up. In my hands I was holding one of his great achievements as a young man, a small khaki-coloured booklet called *Joy of Art*.

∞

Pitaji was a unique personality in many ways. He broke with family tradition often, and was unafraid to follow his own path once he was convinced he was doing the right thing. For instance, he refused to take any dowry when he married my mother and changed his name to Naval. Sometimes, his desire to follow his instincts led to disaster, as with all the business ventures he undertook. But undeterred, my father would plough on. He was happy when he secured a job as a college professor. However, he dreamt of a wider horizon and sought better opportunities for his family. He felt no hesitation, late in life, about emigrating to the US in order to give his family the quality of life he felt they deserved— no sacrifice was too high a price to pay to achieve that objective. He emigrated at the age of forty-eight and completed a PhD in Linguistics at the advanced age of sixty-four—not an ordinary feat to achieve. I have always been tremendously impressed by my father's grit and resolve.

My father's uniqueness was also evident in his experimental nature. He was always trying new things—for example, playing the harmonium to wake up his daughters. This trait was also evident in him towards the end of his life in America when he was very taken up with life after death and he'd talk about it to us at great length. At this time, he turned

to Christ—forgiveness, he believed, was the greatest virtue of all. He spent
the last fifteen years of his life, expounding on the theory of karma and
the concept of reincarnation. I find it quite extraordinary that he never
lost his questing, curious nature throughout, whether as a young man, or
later in his life. During my childhood, I remember he once got fascinated
by a book he'd read—*Life After Death*—and was very intrigued by the
spirit world. It was a time I like to recall as 'The Planchette Nights'.

∽

Every evening Sunderlalji, a family friend, would arrive at the house and
the two men would sit in séance at the dining table in the hall kamra,
with their fingers placed on a coin, waiting for a spirit to appear. Mama
wasn't too keen on her husband's latest obsession but was unable to
persuade him to give it up. One night, Mama, Didi, and I were in the
Green Room upstairs, getting ready to retire for the day. Mama waited a
long time for my father to come up and when there was no sign of him
she decided to practise auto-suggestion, another of my father's passionate
teachings that he had 'imparted' to his family during the seminars. Mama
sat up in bed, her eyes closed, and whispered under her breath,

'Tonight the spirit is NOT going to come! The spirit will NOT
come tonight . . . NO spirit will come tonight.'

Strong, clear, and prescient, she continued the chanting as Didi and I
looked at each other surprised. When Piti finally came upstairs to sleep,
Mama casually asked him, 'So, how was it? Did your spirit come?'

'No, not tonight, it didn't . . .' said Piti ruefully.

Mama looked at us. Didi and I threw the quilt over our faces and
broke into giggles.

Such incidents were typical of my father. Adventurous, smart,
enterprising, artistic, passionate, and deeply protective of his family, it
was difficult to pigeonhole him. He was, however, happiest when he was
writing. His literary lineage can be traced back to his grandfather, the
Urdu poet of Jalalabad, Pandit Shiv Ram Khaaki. When I was growing
up, I'd see him clanking away at his typewriter, a huge old Remington
on his desk in the veranda, every chance he got.

To me, my father was an academic luminary. He wrote several short
stories in his youth, and if they'd been published and had given him a

measure of success, I'm sure he would have persevered in his efforts to be a writer much earlier in his life. He then wrote a book on work study called *Karya Jaanch: Kyoon Aur Kaise*. Later, following his PhD, he started the most important academic work of his lifetime, as the writer in him resurfaced. After years of research, he produced a huge volume called *Striped Zebra: The Immigrant Psyche*. The book was a major study of the psychological impact of migration on immigrants across the globe, and was likely one of the first books to focus on this subject.

Piti and Mama.

So much of my life today reflects my parents. They shaped my sense of the world, and instilled in us the deeper values of life. Though it was my mother who was the painter, the music lover, the performer, it was my father who was the aesthete. Mama taught me how to *feel* for little things, look for beauty in the ordinary, and to live in the essence, the micro.

Pitaji brought in the macro; a larger perspective on life, larger goals—to be productive at all times and to build a life of achievement. From Mama I learnt to stand alone and be strong. And Piti, he gave me the desire to grow, to be a student all my life, to stretch my limits, and instilled in me a sense of adventure, the ability to take chances in life, and to never say die.

That I continue to act, paint, write . . . is a legacy of my very special parents.

SECTION III

A COUNTRY CALLED CHILDHOOD

10

The Blue Frocks of Diwali

In all our lives, childhood is a vast country filled with adventure, emotional landscapes, a host of people, and a number of memorable experiences. If we are lucky, as I was, this country called childhood will shape you, nurture you, and remain with you, in some form or the other, for the rest of your life. Here's an impressionistic account of many encounters, incidents, escapades, people, and emotions, some happy, some sad, some poignant, and some bittersweet that have stayed with me for many decades.

Didi and I on Diwali.

Once, I remember going to the Gandhi Ground for a Dussehra mela. The festival takes place a few days before Diwali and celebrates the victory of good over evil, as Ram defeats the demon king Ravan. A tonga was arranged to take our group of little girls to watch the highlight of the festival, the burning of Ravan. Pemu in her new frock, hair nicely oiled, plaited, and pink-ribboned, Didi and I in our white frocks and sky-blue sweaters, Munni, Baby, Shobha—around eleven of us, out on a mission. Arriving at the ground, we saw huge crowds milling about.

Our tonga drove quite close to the huge effigy of Ravan. I still remember the dark looming figure of evil, painted in black, the devil man with ten heads. As we arrived, a group of men and boys were raising the effigy off the ground by pulling at the ropes, a huge black wooden figure glistening in the lights. People jostled each other to get a better view of the spectacle. Our tonga moved in closer. The stiff, toori-stuffed, ten-headed monstrosity seemed to jerk itself up. It began swaying at an angle of forty-five degrees, moving back and forth, the crowds scuttling back and forth along with it. My eyes widened in awe—the power of evil rising to the sky.

Then the loudspeakers announced the burning of Ravan and everyone was pushed away. The crowds moved back in waves, mouths agape. The effigy was now torched with mashaals. Flames began to rise from the legs of Ravan, and slowly move upwards. Sparks began to fly from his entire body. It was an astonishing, thrilling sight. The sky was now filled with the sparkle of firecrackers. Ten black heads decked in silver crowns dazzled in the floodlights. Just then, the neck of the effigy began to creak and as I watched, the ten ornamented heads slung over to one side. The crowds gasped. Then it happened! The heads began to slide down the body and fell to the ground amidst the din of human shrieks, then lay scattered in the dust. People stared at the ground, shocked. It was at this moment, just as it seemed the tamasha was over, that the patakha-stuffed heads started to burst.

Sparks meant to fly up in the air now sizzled across the ground, scorching the feet of the spectators. Everyone went berserk, hopping from one foot to the other. The spectacle grew even more colourful. From Ravan's neck, a jet of fire shot up into the sky, while on the ground his ten severed heads began spinning like jalebis, hurling circlets of sparks among the delighted crowds.

Not everyone was thrilled, though. Our pony grew skittish as the fireworks went off, and then, as the explosions gathered in intensity, it became uncontrollable. The tonga began swaying from side to side, and then tipped up as the pony suddenly leapt in the air, whinnying, trying to escape the sparks flying into its eyes. No amount of whipping had any impact on the poor creature. Finally, the tongawallah had to blindfold the pony and stuff rags into its ears to calm it down. It must have been quite a sight: the pony bucking in the same spot, struggling in its harness, the tonga tipping over, a spill of little girls, giggling, crying, tumbling out of it. I don't remember how we made our way out of the cacophonous crowd, but to date I retain the image in my head: the ten heads of Ravan, spark-spinning on the ground . . .

∞

Another Dussehra image that has been undimmed by time is that of an army of little boys all decked up in red and gold tinsel, with long tails and silver crowns on their heads, filing down the street to the accompaniment of the dhol. I watched them from Raj Aunty's balcony.

'They are called langurs,' Raj Aunty told me, 'Hanumanji's sena!'

These boys represented the monkey armies of Hanuman, who famously assisted Lord Ram in the battle against Ravan. My aunt explained that the langurs would take out processions for seven days until the grand finale of Dussehra, when the effigy of Ravan was burnt. The langurs would don their finery every morning after bathing at 5 a.m. They would then parade around the streets before making their way to the Sitla mandir. Having worshipped at the temple they would make their way home. In the evening, they'd do it all over again. As the little red jattha moved towards Regent Talkies, the sound of the dhol fading, Raj Aunty explained the significance of the langurs.

'It's a way of giving thanks for the fulfilment of a mannat,' she said. 'A wish. When a woman wants a son, she makes a mannat at the temple. When that wish is granted and a little boy is born to her, at around age two or three, he is to be dressed up as a monkey, and taken to pray at Hanumanji's temple.'

'Do all boys go, Aunty?' I asked.

'No, only the firstborns.'

∞

Right on the heels of Dussehra came Diwali, the grandest festival of the year. It was a time of not only firecrackers and sweets but also an occasion for new clothes for us girls. Mama would take great care in getting pretty frocks, identical ones, made for both Didi and me.

Lighting candles all over the house was the best part, especially on the terrace. I loved the feel of candles, tilting each one to let the melting wax drip on to the concrete edge and then placing the flat end of the candle carefully into the warm wax to hold it upright.

The mochis celebrated Diwali in their own special way. The little winding lane to the back of our house would be glimmering with lights. They would start singing early in the evening and play their dholak till late into the night. Their homes would be glowing with oil lamps, a beautiful sight from our terrace.

We'd play with firecrackers inside our compound while the little mochi boys would light up anaars just outside the phaatak. I don't remember being particularly fond of patakhas but I loved the sparkling phuljharis and anaars. At times the dazzling chakris would come whizzing right into the house from under the gate, making us shriek and jump with excitement as we kicked the little fireballs back with our feet.

The next morning, I'd run up to the terrace to collect all the melted wax. I'd scrape the lumps of varied colours and shapes from all the ledges and sort them into small wax chips and larger pieces. The chips I'd save in a glass jar and the rest would go into a yellow biscuit tin with pictures of the English countryside.

∽

One Diwali night was particularly eventful. I would later remember it as the 'Blue Frock Fiasco'. I must have been about seven years old then. In preparation for Diwali that year, Mama had cut out from *Woman & Home*, a beautiful picture of two little white girls wearing identical frocks. The frocks were a rich, deep blue with gathers at the waist. Dainty white lace frills hung off the edges of the collars and sleeves. Mama wanted the exact same blue frocks stitched for Didi and me for this Diwali.

She had a very fine piece of white muslin lying in the wooden almirah, which she decided to get dyed a brilliant blue. The muslin was pulled out from the cupboard one afternoon and taken to the rangwallah who'd dye it the same blue. Mama carried the magazine with her to show Colour Singh exactly what she desired.

'As blue as this,' she told him. 'Nothing less. It's called Prussian blue.'

'Yes, yes!' he assured her.

Then the old Sardar tailor from across our house was called in. 'I want the exact same pattern,' she said, placing the magazine in front of him. The old man got down to work immediately, Diwali being just a day away.

The day of Diwali, I was very excited. Every now and then, I'd run to the thhada to check if the frocks were ready. Day turned to evening and evening came to be night. But this Diwali night, the frocks did not get stitched on time, though the darzi stayed up till late, working on them, little blue strips scattered all around him. Both Didi and I waited. I remember we didn't light up patakhas that year. We simply waited on the thhada for the tailor to finish sewing on the hooks and buttons and hemming the sleeves and collars so that we could get to wear our new frocks before the night was over.

I walked up to the terrace and leaned over the edge looking down at the mochi dwellings—how beautiful their homes appeared, lit with oil lamps, the sound of their nightly dholak more rigorous, the singing more intense! The mud houses glowed with freshly coated walls and the white powder motifs painted on the thresholds and around windows. The scene looked like it was out of a picture book! Yet, despite the lamps and the rangoli and the music, there was something sad about this Diwali night.

On our terrace we had not lit the candles. As the night wore on, the festivity around us began to fade. The firecrackers that had lit up the sky a while ago creating a fantastic backdrop for the white minarets of the mosque had dwindled to a handful of flashes here and there. Children around the neighbourhood had finished bursting the last of their crackers for the night and were now going back inside their homes. This was the quietest Diwali for us girls. The thunder of explosions and dazzle of light had died down. Only one yellow bulb still glowed. The old Sardar darzi sitting on his wooden stool, working away in his modest establishment, giving the finishing touches to our frocks by hand. His was the last shop still open in the gully.

Both Didi and I were quiet. Mama stood at the thhada with us, sharing our disappointment. All the iron and wooden shutters of the shops on our street had clanged shut, a finale to the Diwali night. We came back inside the house—time now to change into our pyjamas and get into bed. This Diwali night was gone forever from our lives, uncelebrated.

Suddenly, there was a knock on the phaatak. Without pausing to think I ran to open the main gate. I perched on my toes to push up the iron latch so the small gate could be released open. In my heart I knew whoever was knocking on our door at this hour could only be a godsend.

Sure enough, there he was, the old Sardar darzi standing in the dark, his face frayed and tilted to one side, both his arms stretched out. My eyes lit up at what I saw. Our very own messiah, his grey beard and white turban glowing in the light of the street lamp. The Saviour, himself! In his hands he held two hangers on which hung frocks of the most brilliant blue I'd ever seen. The old tailor's face had a faint smile of regret and benediction at the same time. I looked at the frocks and then at him. Didi came up behind me; there we were, two little girls, misty-eyed, gaping at the old man who stood Jesus-like, blue colour dripping from his palms.

Mama quickly changed us back from the pyjamas into our new blue frocks. That Diwali night we were the last two girls up on a terrace, lighting firecrackers, invoking the gods, illuminating the dark skies.

∞

This takes me back to another festivity in Delhi when I was much smaller—a mela that didn't quite turn out the way I wanted it to, but I remember it still for a life lesson that I learnt.

The fair ground was huge and full of lights. The place was filled with bright fancy stalls and there were hordes of people around. Didi was with Pitaji and walked a little ahead of us, while I, holding Mama's hand, stood enthralled in front of a stall filled with dolls. My eyes fell upon a most beautiful looking doll and I instantly fell in love with her. She had on a frilly white net gown and wore pink booties. Her hair was long and golden and fell in curls around her waist, and she had the most amazing eyelashes I'd ever seen. I wanted this doll, and asked Mama if she could buy it for me. When Mama checked the price she politely put it back on the counter and tried to steer me towards other stalls, pointing at all the different toys. But I wouldn't budge, I wanted this doll. Mama looked at my face and she knew my little, five-year-old heart was set on it. She walked up to my father and brought him back to the doll stall. My parents tried to haggle with the shopkeeper to bring the price down, but he wouldn't relent. The doll turned out to be beyond our means. Mama tried one last time, she really wanted me to have the doll. She took my father aside, trying to convince him to buy it, but Piti quietly declined.

As my mother took my hand and we started to walk away from the stall, I began to cry. I felt immensely sorrowful that night. It was the first time I'd really wanted something *this* bad, the first time I'd asked my parents to get me something I'd set my heart on, and they had refused. I was too young to understand it then, that you don't always get something you really want, that there are times in life when you have to learn to do without.

ↄfl

Festivals, melas, birthday parties, in the rather uncomplicated times when I was a pre-teen, were our major occasions for celebration. Most of them were not particularly memorable and are not worth recounting but there was one I remember for it taught me another lesson for life just as the mela episode did.

A party was being thrown by a school friend who lived in the cantonment area on the outskirts of the city, a friend whose name I now forget. Moolchand Uncle was chosen to be my escort. And how was I to be escorted? Sitting on the front bar of his bicycle wearing a crocheted white frock, holding a small packet in my hand, a birthday gift for my friend. Moolchand Uncle pedalled all the way up to the cantonment area. Beautiful houses lined both sides of the road and were quite different from the houses and rooftops of the walled city I was used to on our side of the world. We reached a cottage with lots of cars parked outside. Someone said, 'This is the house.' I was very taken by the beauty of the house—a quaint cottage with ivy running up the red brick walls.

I waited outside while an orderly went in to fetch my friend. She appeared in a frosty pink frock, all net and lace, with ribbons in her hair, looking like a little fairy. She greeted me with a big smile, took me by my hand and led me inside her home. At the door, she glanced back at the man standing by the gate with a bicycle.

'Your father?' she asked me, smiling politely.

'NO!' I was horrified at the prospect.

I remember my embarrassment at being taken for some villager's offspring. Dark-skinned Moolchand Uncle, with buck teeth and a hooked nose, dressed simply in a white kurta pyjama, stood patiently by the gate, waiting to take me home when the revels were over.

'...Err...he's my Uncle...err, staff...he's my father's munshi,' I said sheepishly, as I gestured to Moolchand Uncle to wait there.

My friend smiled warmly and we turned to go inside.

There were a lot of people there. Everyone, children and elders alike, had gathered on the lawn where a large table stood set with food and drinks. A huge birthday cake was placed at the centre of the table, covered in lit candles. Everyone was doling out presents for the birthday girl and placing them on the table. The embroidered handkerchief set that Mama had carefully wrapped for me as a gift for my friend was still in my hands. I was hesitant handing it to her, the size of my gift seeming small compared to the large presents festooned with ribbons the other children had brought with them in their chauffeured cars.

We ate sweets and had lemonade, after which some games were played. I remember playing musical chairs. Prizes were distributed to the winners. Finally, the gifts were unwrapped amidst cheers and clapping. Books, games like Ludo and Snakes & Ladders, a set of candles, a large box of chocolates wrapped in silver, and a cashmere sweater. I was most fascinated by a doll that closed her eyes if you laid her down and opened them wide when you sat her up. My friend showed great delight when she unveiled my tiny gift and the dainty white and orange cross-stitched handkerchiefs tumbled into her hands. She showed them off, saying how pretty, how pretty, and that certainly made me feel good.

'My Mama made these.' I shyly told her.

She beamed at me. I noticed how polite and soft-spoken the girl was, and how well-behaved, qualities I hadn't noticed about her in school. It was one thing knowing her as a classmate in school, but in her home environment she seemed different.

As if for the first time, I took in the ambience of my friend's home, compared it to my own. Her home was small and quaint, a large garden all around, in this serene, quiet, and exclusive neighbourhood. I realized with some wonder that people I knew lived in parts of the city that were much nicer than my own, and that our large looming house next to the rough-and-tumble of Mochistan wasn't the only way of existence.

When it was time to leave, my friend came to say goodbye to me at the gate. Some of the other kids who were leaving as well got into their cars, others clambered on to scooters and were driven off. I made my way to where Moolchand Uncle was waiting with his bicycle. The embarrassment of Moolchand Uncle being taken for my father still weighed on my heart. How I wished Mama had come with me instead! Everyone would surely have been charmed by the way she spoke, her voice, her beauty, her grace and then they'd all have seen what my roots truly were and where I belonged. On the way home, I noticed that Moolchand Uncle had gone extremely quiet. He hardly spoke a word. I suspected he'd registered my embarrassment at him being taken for my father. That silence made me a feel a bit unworthy and ashamed of how I had behaved. Moolchand Uncle loved us dearly and would do anything any time to keep Didi and me happy. He belonged to the Chandraavali household. He was part of our family. How could I have made him feel otherwise?

That night when I went to sleep, I felt petty, and ridden with guilt.

That incident has remained fresh in my mind to this day, and has helped me correct myself from whenever I have shown signs of prejudice, discrimination, or bias.

∞

While there were the occasional festivals and parties to spice up our lives, for the most part, my sister and I hung out together, especially in our pre-teen years.

At home we'd perform our own little pwes in the veranda, just like the ones at the pagoda across Mama's home in Mandalay. The entrance for the dancers was from the hall kamra. We were eight or nine years old, performing just outside the fly screen door of the drawing room, singing and dancing for the kids from the neighbourhood. In school I'd learnt to dance to the song, '*Murli vaale murli bajaa, sun sun murli ko naache jiya*' showing off to our audience in the vehra and to the knot of dark bright faces peering at us from the small gate of the phaatak.

∞

The other major past time for us girls would be playing 'Ghar-Ghar', a little game Didi and I, along with Munni, played during the winter afternoons up on our terrace, in which we pretended to be grown-ups. The 'Ghar-Ghar' episode I am about to describe took place when Didi was nine and I was seven. One of the props we used was a miniature tea set on a tray that was placed on a stool.

The playing Ghar-Ghar days.

Here's the setting . . .

Mama sat nearby on the wicker chair reading Hemingway's *The Old Man and the Sea*. Outside the house, in the gully, skinny brown boys playing gullee-danda let out occasional shrieks. The sweeper woman had just cleaned the commodes and washed the toilet floors. The smell of phenyl lingered in the drain below the phaatak. Jeet was in the vehra drawing all the dry yellow leaves into one corner. Piti was at his desk in the veranda, typing away.

'Oh, I'm from Ambershire!' I said, tucking my little batua, my purse under my left arm as I sat down, crossing my legs the way Fleur Ezekiel, Miss India, did on the cover of a magazine.

'From where?' Didi sternly inquired.

'From Ambershire, you know? Ambershire!'

Ambershire was the anglicized word we convent-going girls had made up, taking our inspiration from the way rustic Punjabis pronounced Amritsar—they would always say Umbersar or Ambarsar, but never Amritsar. You might say that all we were doing was helping the process along, helping the name travel from the Punjabi heartland all the way to England.

Didi played along. 'But where is this *Ambershire*, bahenji?

'What? You haven't heard of Ambershire?

'I'm afraid I haven't stepped out of my village as yet.'

'Oh . . . Ambershire, you know? Like Yorkshire or Oxfordshire? Same way . . . Ambershire!'

'Oh, achha, achha . . . I heard that . . . like Delhi-shire and Bombay-shire . . . like that, Ambershire! You, sisterji, have come from Ing-laand, I suppose?' Didi rubs it in. 'Oh, please sit down. Let me get you something to drink. You must be thirsty.'

'Yes . . . yes . . .' I looked around the imaginary room of our make-believe house.

'Please, sit here. Here, have some tea. Would you like something to eat?'

'Ooh . . . excuse me, bahenji, but there are just tooo many flies here, you know flies? . . . I mean, makkhees . . .'

Didi snatched the empty teacup from my hand. 'Stop it. Give my tea back! I don't want you in my house any more.'

'Arre, but I'm only being funny!'

'What's so funny? You are criticizing everything in my home, I don't like it!'

Munni tried to calm things down. 'She's only being funny, Bobby!'

'Yes, she can be funny, but not hurt my feelings. She comes to my house, I give her tea, she doesn't like it. Too hot here. She wants a fan, there are too many makkhees—she can go back to her Yorkshire, Ambershire, wherever that is, I don't care! I don't want to play this game any more.'

'Okay, okay . . . I'll do it all over again, see? This time, I'll do it your way, all right?'

'Okay, come to my home if you have to, but don't come from England. Just come from Jandiala or Verka.'

This time round I take a chunni and cover my head to look like a lady from India, and not from England. Pretending that I'm holding a purse in my left hand and my veil over the left side of my face, I knock on the door of the imaginary living room again.

'Knock-knock.'

'Hello ji! Please come in. How come you haven't visited us in such a long time? Please come and sit.'

'You see, behanji, I was away in England . . .'

Didi glares, puts down the stool she was about to offer me.

'You were away *where*?' she emphasizes.

'Er . . . Jandiala, my hometown, you see . . .'

Didi is mollified. 'Achha, achha, sit down. The journey must have been very tiring, it's so hot. What can I offer you? Some tea or cold

sherbet? Will you have thanda or garam? Wait, let me give you a cold
drink, you must be boiling in the heat. Here, take this pakkhee!'

'Ooh, pakkhee! How sweet.'

I take the imaginary fan and begin fanning myself.

Didi passes me an imaginary glass of sherbet. Then, settling down,
she says unexpectedly, 'I'm sorry, behanji, these days there are so many
makkhees here.'

'Oh, not to worry. I don't mind at all, we have so many makkhees
in Jandiala. I just *l - o - v - e* makkhees!'

Munni rolls around, laughing.

Didi hides the smirk on her face. 'Oh, stop exaggerating and get
out! You're making fun of me. What the hell do you think of yourself,
telling me you love makkhees? Who in their right mind could love flies,
dumbo! Don't even know how to act!'

'No, no . . . really, we have lots of makkhees but we don't have such
pretty, frilly, yellow pakkhees,' I say.

'Fine, but when I will say we have lots of makkhees, don't say "I
love makkhees", that's stupid. Don't become stupid. Just say "Oh please,
don't worry about makkhees, behanji, they're all over." Just say that, okay?
Be normal.'

'But I'm *acting*! I must do *something* . . . '

'Abnormal?' says Didi.

'. . . Extraordinary!' I declare.

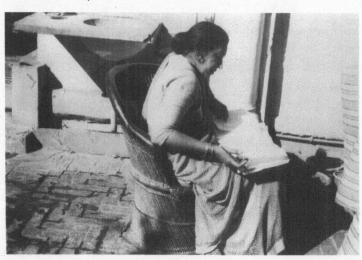

All this while, as our game careens along, Mama sits on her chair reading, a half-smile on her face, enjoying each and every word of our trying-to-be-grown-ups act.

⁓

Sundays were days when the entire family got together. Piti didn't have to go to work, we didn't have to rush off to school. Sundays were meant for lazing around the breakfast table pulled out in the sunlit vehra. Piti would be poring over the *Hindustan Times*, while Mama and Jeet would be in the kitchen organizing the family's Sunday lunch. The table would be laid out with the mauve crockery, my parents' favourite. Didi and I would shuffle the pages of *The Tribune* between us, laughing over Chic Young's Dagwood & Blondie comic strip. Jeet always made aloo–gobi parathas or saag and makki di roti for our Sunday lunch.

Often we girls were expected to help. 'So, which one of you is going to win the race today at laying the table?' Piti would say. Didi and I rushed to win. We were each given one half of the table to exhibit our skills at setting the plates, placing the napkins over the green cross-stitch mats—the ones Mama embroidered with pink and maroon threads—the spoons and forks, then the bowls right next to the plates. I always made it a point to hurry in last moment with the black ceramic salt and pepper crows with yellow beaks. My parents would clap for whoever won the competition.

⁓

'Goodman di Laltain!' exclaimed Piti one Sunday, and sprang up, newspaper in hand. 'Look at this!' he said, pointing to an article in the paper: 'Sardarji Spots Flying Saucer in Simla!'

'What?' We jumped up and gathered around Pitaji, trying to snatch away the paper and read the article for ourselves.

I remember everyone talking about the incident for days. So there *are* flying saucers…they are for *real*! Someone out there has actually seen them!

The little kids in the gully had their own version of the people from outer space.

'Their eyes are large magnified discs and they have no su-sus!'

'How do you know? You saw or what? How do you think they pee?'

'They don't need to pee, silly, They are not human like us. They are superhuman!'

'Super slow human! And they don't pee because they don't drink water. And they don't need to eat food either.'

'Don't they go to the potty?'

'No, stupid! There are not like us, na . . . they are from the moon, remember? They don't do potty or pee-pee!'

The excitement over the Sardarji's close encounter with the flying saucer lasted for a couple of weeks, possibly even longer. Mama and · Piti talked about it at length. Mama's reaction was of great awe, and for Piti, it was an intriguing phenomenon, one he was seriously inclined to explore further, given half a chance. For me it was an enthralling little joy of childhood, full of mystery and a sense of worlds just out of reach.

∽

Sundays were also days for crudely displayed tweeters, lodged on hand-pulled rickshaws, announcing the next release in town. Mastana Sangeet Party Band would make its enthusiastic entry into our street blaring the song:

Hansta hua nooraani chehra!

I remember *Parasmani* and *Lootera* being touted as the most entertaining films ever made.

Advertising those days was flexible though. The song being played needn't necessarily have to be the song from the film being released. The announcements bristled and crackled as the rickshaw carrying the tweeters wobbled along the potholed street towards Hall Bazaar, while the music played on:

O das, main ki piyaar vichon khateya . . .

∽

Some Sundays were more fun than others—they meant picnic time. Mama and Piti would say, 'Chalo bai, nair te chaliye!' The Jandiaale-waali nehar was always an exciting proposition. I loved the idea of going all the way out of the city into some village to spend the afternoon at the

Didi and my bhuas in the nehar.

nehar, the cool water canal flowing through lush green fields. We kids
would duck right into the water, splashing around for most of the hot
afternoon, while Mama and Piti, would sit on the bank along with Jeet.
Once we were out of the water, we'd sit under the kikar trees and open
our picnic basket, spreading the lunch boxes out on the dhurrie. Jeet
would have made gobi parathas and aloo sabzi, and there'd be raita to go
along with the spread. As we ate Piti would tell us stories about the canals
and waterways of Punjab, the land of five rivers. The main excitement of
these nehar outings was eating the delicious mangoes—the Dasheris and
the Maldas that my parents would stop to buy at the fruit market outside
Hall Gate on our way out of town. As soon we arrived at the picnic spot,
Piti would hammer a peg into the grassy earth, loop some rope around it,
tie a bucket to the rope and suspend it in the cool waters of the canal. Into
the bucket would go the golden yellow and green mangoes. All the while
that we were frolicking and eating, the mangoes would be cooling in the
water . . . And then would come the big moment—as we splashed about
in the canal, every once in a way, we'd wade across to the bucket and fish

out the season's best, tearing into the delicious fruit, juicy yellow streaks running down our elbows.

∞

Occasionally, the family would get together for a havan. Havans were performed on special occasions like birthdays, death-days, and Diwali. Ours was a Hindu Brahmin family that strictly followed the path of the Arya Samaj, which meant no idol worship, no going to the temple. There was nothing ostentatious about our havans. As there were no gods and goddesses to worship, there was no emotional blackmail, no wheeling-dealing with the idols—if you do this for me, I'll do that for you, the endless negotiations that render so much of religious observance far less than spiritual.

During the havans, Didi and I would sit cross-legged before the fire ceremony, reciting mantras, usually without a flaw. Except for one part in the text where the shlokas sounded so funny, 'Chhukra-mu-cha-rata pa-shame-sharda shatam . . .' We'd both sneak a look at each other and end up in soundless giggles. Each time that shloka came up, and we'd anticipate the word 'shame', the same giggle fit would ensue. Mama would give us a 'warning' look, Piti would avoid looking in our direction, but when she was still alive Bibiji would be more vocal and say, 'Beta, havan karte samay hanste nahin!' (You should not laugh during havan). Bauji, I remember, would have a slight smirk on his face but would remain solemn.

Of the shlokas I learnt to recite then, the Gayatri Mantra has continued to comfort me, especially in times of trouble when I find myself going back to it for inner strength and courage.

∞

In our home, the accent was on books. Both my parents were very fond of reading and our hall kamra was full of well-thumbed titles. Each time they bought a new book at the Book Lovers' Retreat, there'd be much excitement. They'd turn the first two pages of the book and write down their names in it, along with the date. My parents wanted to see us with books most of the time—each time we heard my father knock on the phaatak, we'd grab the first book at hand and pretend we'd been reading. But up in the Green Room, the scenario would be different. Didi would

Some of my Meena Kumari cuttings.

be mugging up her Chemistry chapters, while I'd spend my precious time cutting out pictures of film stars from magazines and sticking them on to the inside of my books closet.

Sometimes, the pigeons would be witness to what was my favourite past time and coo right into the Green Room, settling in the bay windows.

Those were the days I'd dream of Bombay and would look out for the latest editions of *Picturepost, Filmfare, Screen,* and the *Illustrated Weekly*, delivered regularly to our home. On the left shutter of my cupboard was Asha Parekh in a hat and jacket, from the film *Ziddi*, Sadhana of *Mere Mehboob* in a sharara, smiling in her French cut, and Nanda of *Hum Dono* with a beauty spot at the edge below her lower lip. On the right shutter were pictures of Meena Kumari—the ultimate! There was Waheeda Rehman from *Baat Ek Raat Ki*, and of Nutan as well, but most of the photos were of Meena Kumari, and those I have preserved till today.

Among all my collection of Meena Kumari cuttings, there's a picture of her in a blue blouse that's my favourite; I could look at that picture for hours.

One of the books Pitaji gave me to read was Dale Carnegie's *How to Win Friends and Influence People*. I was pretty taken up by that book and had decided I'd charm people the Dale Carnegie way. Mama would smile, seeing me engrossed in the book perhaps a little more than necessary. One day when I was lying in bed nursing a cold, and Mama saw me blowing my nose into a white handkerchief, she started laughing. 'How daintily you blow your nose! Does your Dale Carnegie show you how to do that as well?' she said teasingly.

Another magazine that sat demurely on top of the stash of books was *Reader's Digest*, our family's all-time favourite. It was *Reader's Digest* that opened my mind to a whole lot of things. I loved the stories it carried, stories with heart, stories about courage and humanity, about daring, selflessness, and about standing up for the right thing. Pitaji encouraged us to read *Reader's Digest*, as he himself would read it cover to cover. It was the *Reader's Digest* that provided us a vocabulary-forming environment. We also had *Reader's Digest World Atlas* in our home that I was especially fascinated by. It had, at the end, a double spread of a pictorial map that illustrated all the milestones of world events and marked the history of humankind, like the Mesopotamian and the Indus Valley civilizations, the rise of Christianity, the French Revolution, Spanish Civil War, the Great Wall of China, and the two World Wars. It even traced the origins of the Ramayan and Mahabharat—the chart showed everything that our usual schooling ignored.

When I tired of *Reader's Digest*, I'd skim through the Hindi language *Parag* and *Chandamama* for the famous Vikram and Betaal series.

∽

The memory of the Green Room takes me to another room in the house that became a significant part of my childhood—the music room. After the death of my grandparents, Bauji's daftar, opening to the street, was rented out to a music teacher. We called him Masterji. My parents happily let him have the room for just fifty rupees rent, as they were already planning to send Didi and me to a music class. Now our music class came right into our house.

Indu Bhaiya, who was living with us those days, also joined the class. So there were Kechhi and Shoki, Goel Uncle's daughters, Didi, Munni, and

Bauji's daftar turns into music class.

me. The fee for the class was fifteen rupees a month. We all sat around the harmonium and did riyaz together. Masterji would say,

'Chalo bachcho, ek sur mein gaao: *Sa—Re—Ga—Ma—Pa—Dha—Ni—Sa*' and we'd go trilling after him, '*Sa—Re—Ga—Ma—Pa—Dha—Ni—Sa ...*'

When I look at myself in one of the old photographs, at age five, sitting in the music class with that nasty expression on my face, I feel very strange. How could I have had such disinclination towards music, something I love so much? I'm sure it must have been the constant riyaz that irked me even at that early age, because the class never seemed to go beyond *Sa—Re—Ga—Ma—Pa—Dha—Ni—Sa*. But the singing lessons didn't end with that. I continued learning music day in and day out for five years. So did Didi, and so did Munni.

Later, our class shifted to Mrs Naiyyar's home, above the Bombay Photo House in one of the gullies off Hall Bazaar. It was during these later years that I learnt all the basic ragas: Raag Aasavari, Raag Bageshwari, Raag Bhairavi, Raag Malkauns, *Mukh mod mode muskaat jaat*, Raag Kalyaan, *Ari ae ri aali piya bin*. But all of that is now forgotten, though I still remember some of the paltaas I learnt back then. Sometimes I catch myself humming a notation that I'd learnt in the music class during the years 1956 to 1960.

At five I'm grumpy, but in another photo where I'm aged seven, I seem quite tickled with the idea of music. Skipping down the by-lanes of Hall Bazaar, the one thing that the music class taught me was 'sur ki samajh', an ear for music . . .

A thing once learnt can never be unlearnt.

11

The Madman of Manali

I was four years old when I first went up to Rohtang Pass. It was the summer of 1956. There were no roads beyond Manali at the time. Rough and ready roads were built the year after, when Pandit Nehru was to visit the valley.

Mama and Piti were very fond of the Kullu valley, so for our summer vacations we'd regularly go off to the mountains. Mama would make paintings of the rocks, huts, and pine trees, while Piti would be off exploring the landscape, egging us on to do the same. My parents' love

Didi, Piti, and I on a walk.

for the mountains and the outdoors was one of the greatest gifts they bestowed on me.

Every year, when our school closed for the summer, Piti's college also shut for vacations. My parents would pack us into a Punjab Roadways bus and we would all head for Kullu valley. We'd spend the two summer months in the mountains. Getting away from the sweltering heat of Amritsar, especially during the month of June, was a huge relief. Yet that was not the reason why I remember my Kullu holidays so fondly. It was the sheer beauty of the place, the glorious walks in the wilderness, on untouched, solitary mountain paths holding my father's hand, watching my mother paint, the house in the apple orchard, and encountering a delightful madman at the bridge over the Beas River. These are the things I recall the most.

I remember when I first set eyes on the Valley of the Gods, I found it to be a place of astounding beauty, the kind I'd seen only in picture postcards.

Back in the mid 50s, Manali was just a little mountain hamlet surrounded on all sides by snow peaks. Dark-roofed huts of old wood and stone stood amidst gushing white streams, and thick forests of pine

The Apple Cottage, Manali.

The apple orchard

and deodar. There was an old temple at a great height in the middle of a dense deodar forest, which could only be reached by a steep path all the way up the mountain. It was the temple of Goddess Hadimba.

My parents rented a house for fifty rupees a month. It stood in an apple orchard on the left bank of the river, some distance away from the main Manali village. It was a beautiful cottage with a gabled roof and a balcony around it, built in the old Pahadi style. There was no market around the place for us to go and buy vegetables or any sort of provisions. All we had around us were apples. So, Mama would serve us apples for breakfast, apples for lunch, and apples for dinner! For breakfast we'd find freshly cut slices of ripe golden apples, artistically served on white enamel plates with dark blue rims. For lunch we'd get to eat apple sabzi. For dinner, after a whole day's trek when we returned to the cottage Mama would quickly cut up an apple salad to be served along with apple soup. And, for dessert, there'd be the 'custard' apple waiting for us at the round table! Yes, she had a knack for cooking apples in many different ways. On some days we'd get apple stew for lunch, and at night we would eat apple pudding.

Lying in the khud at Kothi.

On days when we couldn't eat any more apples, Piti would go all the way to the tiny market in Manali to buy provisions, Didi and me in tow.

But mostly all we did was laze around the place. Piti would take his book and go lie down by the stream to read, while Mama sat on the rocks with her oilpaper and Camel tubes, painting huts and gushing water in the pristine Himalayan landscapes. She painted the most beautiful pictures on oilpaper, which I preserved with me for as long as I remember. There were hundreds of sketches and oil sheets depicting scenes of the Kullu valley. Later when we moved to America, I gave them away to my school friends.

I remember on my first holiday to the mountains, when I was no more than four years old, my father decided we were going to trek all the way to Rohtang Pass.

At an elevation of 3,900 metres, on the eastern end of the Pir Panjal range of the Himalayas, Rohtang La is also known as the Pass of the Dead, where, it is said, spirits pass over to the other world. Overlooking the Lahaul valley, the pass is situated on the watershed between the water basins of the Chenab and Beas rivers.

A bus ride from Manali took us to Palchan and then, after a brief hike, we reached Kothi. The little dark wooden bridge over the naala at Kothi was an ordeal to cross. I was carried across by my father while Didi crossed it on foot. She was petrified walking across that rickety wooden bridge that threatened to split and drop her all the way into the deep dark gorge. I remember Mama holding her hand and the pony following us across the 'Khooni Naala'.

My mother went into raptures seeing the landscape around Kothi. The scene was dramatic—green meadows swarmed by high rocky peaks all around. Mama always swore by the beauty of Kothi and remembered it as breathtaking!

The landscape at Kothi.

We rested at a little shack run by the forest department known as the Inspection Hut. Half the day was gone so we decided to stay the night there. Early next morning the family set off on a trek to Rohtang. I rode a sturdy mountain pony while the others walked. Ahead of us was a long ascent to our next destination, the Beas Kund, the source of the river Beas.

A photo taken during that trek shows the three of us at the Beas Kund—Mama wearing pants, jacket, and a muffler around her head, holding both Didi and me, dressed identically in little woollen pants and jackets, me in my short crop and fringe, clinging to Mama on her right and Didi, her hair braided, sitting on the snow, smiling, holding snowballs in both her hands.

Didi and I with Mama at Beas Kund.

At the bridge near Palchan.

When we reached Rohtang Pass it was already late in the day. The Pahadiya up there running a tiny tea counter in a tent, was taken aback seeing my parents walk all the way up with two little girls, and a pony in tow. 'Bauji, what have you done? You've brought children this small to a place like this? I've never seen kids this age come up here ever!' he said, looking at both of us, me slumped on to the pony's back. 'It is not safe. Cold hard winds start to blow after three o'clock. It can get difficult to breathe! You'd better take your family and start the climb down back quickly!'

We took the chaiwallah's advice and began our descent after a short tea break. As the evening began to set in, we made our cautious way along the pony trail that zig-zagged down the slope. All along the way I could hear Mama gushing over the stunning beauty of the mountains. She'd describe the colours as they changed on the ridge and how everything looked so different now in the evening light, so much more enigmatic. My first perceptions of nature came from my mother. The way she reacted to the landscape, the way she saw everything, the colours, the magic of the moment, the silence, all that, and more ... all came from her. Mama gave me the gift of aesthetic sensibility and a deep appreciation of nature.

Manali and the Apple Cottage were still a long way to go and it was already dark by the time we reached Kothi again. My parents decided to stay put in the Inspection Hut for the night. The chowkidar lit some

Summer holidays in the Valley of the Gods.

Top: With Moolchand Uncle and his son at Rohtang Pass.
Middle: Snow at Rohtang Pass.
Bottom: The meadows of Kothi.

firewood and made tea for us as we sat under the star-studded sky, warming ourselves around the crackling embers.

Now when I think of it, the trek to Rohtang Pass, back in the 50s was certainly one of the most magnificent spectacles of nature that I preserve in my heart.

∞

'WAAAH . . . JEEEE . . . WAAAH!'

Those were the only words he would ever utter, the madman of Manali, swaying over the bridge at Beas River.

My father was very fond of going for long walks. Both Didi and I would accompany him, trotting down the mud track along the left bank of the river, all the way from the house up to the bridge at Manali. And every time we'd cross the bridge, there he would be—the harmless lunatic of Manali. Burly, unkempt, with long, dishevelled hair, he'd suddenly spring up from nowhere, and greet us with a beaming smile, swaggering alongside our little party for a few yards saying:

'WAAAH . . . JEEEE . . . WAAAH!'

My father would humour him and greet him back though he'd chuckle nervously when he did so. Didi and I were scared of him, though we'd pretend we weren't.

He never harmed us or threatened us in any way, that madman of Manali! And in time we even began to look forward to running into him and hearing him intone the only three words he seemed to know:

'WAAAH . . . JEEEE . . . WAAAH!'

I don't know what became of the madman of Manali. No one was able to tell us anything though Piti did make a few attempts to trace him down in our later visits to the valley. We were told he wandered off into the high passes, never to be seen again.

I can effortlessly summon up his grin and carefree disposition even today . . . Much later in life I would find him once again, in another time, another era, this time as a mad Tibetan, in the winter in Ladakh, by the river at Choglamsar, living in a roofless tent, striking matchsticks in the wind! Both these souls came to epitomize, for me, freedom in the way that gypsies and vagabonds and other solitary wanderers experienced it. It was something that intrigued me and I responded to; I memorialized these madmen of the spirit in a short story I published a few years ago. Madness was also a subject I became deeply intrigued with as a school friend of mine slipped over to the other side. I write about this in a later chapter.

∞

The mountains gave me another enduring memory and a rather unexpected metaphor. When I was six or seven, all of us went to Mussoorie to visit Hiralal Uncle, the father of our cousins Indu Bhaiya and Ashu, who were then living with us in Amritsar. Hiralal Uncle was a naturalist, worked at the Amar Bharti khadi showroom, and bred honeybees. After reaching his home, Ashu and I (both the same age) ran through the house in great excitement, flinging open the doors and windows. As we flung open a long-shut window, a swarm of yellow bees suddenly assailed us and seized our necks. Terrified, we shrieked, slapping at ourselves with both hands, our eyes bulging in sheer fright. Our nerve-chilling screams brought Mama rushing into the room. Horrified by the sight before her, she leapt towards us, and violently started swishing around the pallu of her sari to get the bees away. She then grabbed my blouse and ripped it down to my waist, leaving me in my chemise with a ballooned-out red neck. I remained there shivering, more from fright than the cold mountain air. There wasn't any great damage done, and I recovered soon enough, but years later when I embarked on my acting career and was occasionally subjected to vicious, filthy gossip in film journals, I'd be reminded of the honeybee attack on me as a little girl in Mussoorie. Just as painful, just as unexpected, but fortunately unable to cause any permanent damage.

As the years went by our annual vacations to the mountains dwindled and then gradually fizzled out completely. My parents were trying to live within their means and by the time my sister and I were in our teens, and our little brother being a precious addition to the family, there was little money to spend on luxuries like family vacations in the mountains.

But I've never really been able to get over the beauty of those mountains and keep going back for one more glimpse at those pristine peaks. Even now as I continue going back to the Kullu valley, I find myself looking out for old structures, trying to somehow find the stone and wood house with the gabled roof, the Apple Cottage of my childhood days. So drawn am I to the mountains that I finally ended up making my little hideaway there, a little den I can get away to, and find some quiet time painting and writing.

12

The Frontier Mail

The lights across the railway track glowed like stars on earth, bluish-white, deep blue, hazy, smudged at the edges.

'Cobalt!' I said.

'Emerald,' Mama corrected.

I was leaning over the railing on Bhandari Bridge waiting for a train to pass. This I would do, night after night, during the after-dinner walks. From the bridge, I could see the railway platform, just a few yards in the distance. I would stand there, hanging on to the railing, all the way up on my toes, as tall as I could make myself, until a train chugged past beneath me. I always waited for at least one train to pass under the bridge before I left. Mama, Piti, and Didi would wait at the corner of the bridge and see two feet propped up on the iron bars, peering down at the railway track.

Me at four.

'Why is Deepi not coming?' My father would stop to turn back.

'She won't . . . her train hasn't passed yet.'

'Deepi, stop hanging over that edge! Come on now. Stuck forever on that bridge, this girl! Hurry up, we're leaving.'

'Wait, Mama, the signal is down, it's coming . . . please wait, 9.45. That's the time for the train to come.'

My eyes would be glued to the signals. Two tall poles on each side of the tracks with black stripes painted on them supported four signals each. Flat white metal plates shining in the dark from the headlights of the approaching train. It's from here that I could also see the yellow house, a quaint little dwelling down by the railway track, with trains rattling past every now and then.

Mesmerized, I'd watch the lights around the tracks, chimera-like, as the train approached full steam, the plume of grey smoke rising high up in the night sky. And with it, train sounds, an addiction for life. Nothing thrilled me more. Slowly at first, and in the distance, the train would snake its way up the glittering tracks, gaining speed, and finally whooshing past and away from my sight into the inky night. Later, I'd do anything to take a train journey. Life would be marked by train sounds, mile-stoned by train rhythms.

∞

Though our train trips were few and far between we'd occasionally go to Delhi to see my bhuaas—Sneh Aunty in Harding Bridge or Saroj Aunty across Golcha Cinema in Daryaganj. I don't remember much of the time we spent there but I do have a few distinct memories of the overnight Frontier Mail to Delhi. I can picture that time like I am living it right now . . .

After a long wait, the train steams into the platform. People shuffle their luggage in even before it has come to a halt. Once inside the train, we look for our seat numbers. 'First just sit down . . . sit anywhere, we'll sort it out!' Mama tells us. The vendor boys squeeze past the crowd bottlenecked at the door shouting their shrill cries of 'Soda—Soda' and 'moongphali—rioriyaan'.

Finally, some semblance of order prevails and we find ourselves the seats we have reserved. Without blinking an eyelid, I grab the window seat before Didi can slide into it. She looks at me begrudgingly; I smile. We are seated in the Mixed Compartment as Pitaji is travelling with us. For now we are sitting up, but as the lights on the train dim these seats will convert to sleeping berths. Mama is unbuckling the brown leather straps of the holdalls and unrolling them to spread on the top berth for Didi and me. I'm gazing out the window and eating aam papad. Once the bedding has been dealt with, Didi helps Mama unpack the tiffin boxes carrying dry jeera-aloo sabzi and parathas, dinner for our night on the train; my mother is particular about not eating food off the railway platform. Piti has got down on to the platform to fill our thermos with water. At the water tap there's a long queue of people waiting to fill their bottles and flasks.

'*Chai garam . . . chai garam . . . chai gara*,' the chaiwallah's cry comes cutting through the barred window. Suddenly the signal goes down and the train whistles, but there's no sign of Piti with the thermos. Slowly, the train starts to pull out. My feet begin to coil inward. Please let him not be left behind, doesn't matter if he can't manage to get the water, let him just get back on the train safely. Mama strains her neck to look for my father. Her anxiety is unnerving me. All our eyes are fixed on the door. The vendor boys jostle to make their way out, shouting:

'*Soda—Soda—Chanae lelo, Chanae . . .*' Piti manages to make it back just in time as the train leaves the station.

Once it picks up speed, I raise the window shutter and tilt my head on the bars to feel the wind on my face. Suddenly, a speck of coal dust flies into my eye and I wince. I recoil from the window squinting violently. 'Told you!' Mama says. 'Told you not to put your head out so much!' I've rubbed my eye so hard it is reddened and watering. My head is now on Mama's lap. She folds the edge of her sari several layers, then blows into it and places it on my eye. Her warm breath brings some relief to my watering eye. Didi, watching me from the berth above, simply shakes her head.

Now that the window is shut on me forever, I excuse myself to go and pee. There, at the open door of the bogey I stand looking at the landscape. The wind is on my face again as I stand there for a long time, watching the dark fields rush past my sight. As the train rounds a curve, I am able to glimpse the old locomotive, its great steel spine, the smoke spiralling, spreading across the winter landscape. How I love train journeys! I wish they'd go on forever . . .

'How long does it take you to pee?' Didi comes looking for me. 'Come back in! Mama is calling you!' Reluctantly I follow my sister, grumbling under my breath: 'I will *not* live inside a house . . . I will live *outside* of it, once I have a house of my own!'

∞

Another time I remember—we are a little older now—I am sleeping on the upper berth, head towards the window and feet close to the ladder.

Didi is lying next to me ulta, head towards the ladder and feet towards my face. We sort of coil in and make our own little spaces, when we notice a man hovering around our bogey looking to make room for himself.

Suddenly, the fellow jumps up and sits on our berth where Didi and I are sleeping. Didi's head jolts up as the guy almost lands on her shoulder. He stinks so bad he is obviously boozed out. Didi shrinks away from him. I wake up to my mother's voice cursing in her perfect convent English. 'Get down you scoundrel! How dare you! Can't you see young girls sleeping on the berth? GET DOWN this minute! or I'll PULL THE CHAIN!'

My mother's voice has people shuffling on other berths and waking up from their sleep. Piti rushes to our rescue. Soon, people crowd around the guy, grab his scrawny legs and yank him to the floor. The fellow stumbles down with a thud and quickly scrambles away into the dark end of the bogey. See? My Mama! She will take no nonsense from no one! The excitement over, everyone dozes off again, swaying in rhythm to the motion of the train.

∞

There is one more image that comes into focus and takes me back to the Frontier Mail days again. A little way down in our bogey there seems to be some commotion. Men are caught in a near-brawl situation, fighting for space in the overcrowded compartment. A lean, middle-aged man tries to pacify the crowd but no one is listening to him. A fat Lala in the crowd snaps at him, irritated by the calmness of his tone.

'So where should I put my luggage? On your head?'

'Yes, please ... put it on my head!' the slightly built man says and before anyone can comprehend what he has just uttered, the man picks up the Lala's leather suitcase and places it on his head. Silence falls in the bogey. The scuffling men look sheepishly at one another, but no one says a word. The lean man stands there in the middle of the passage holding another man's suitcase on his head. He won't sit down. People coil back into their seats. The minutes pass. Night falls. The train whistles past another railway station. Slowly I drift off to sleep. I have no idea how long I have slept, but when I wake up in the middle of the night the man is still standing there, his eyes now closed, the suitcase still on his head, wobbling in sync with the chugging of the train. And I wonder why the Lala hasn't taken the suitcase back from him all this while—is it embarrassment or stubbornness? I can't tell, but I hope the poor man doesn't have to carry the baksa on his head throughout the journey.

Very early in the morning I wake up and grapple my way to the toilet, only to find a long queue of people lined up outside it. The door of the bogey is banging in the wind. I stand by it for a long moment, spellbound by the frostiness of the misty landscape. Clusters of kikar trees stand in the fields like spirits from another world. A cold wind whips my face . . . Before I know it, the chill gets to me, and in slow, super slow motion I begin to slide in a faint to the floor.

The next thing I know I am being tucked into my berth in a warm woollen blanket by Mama. When she notices I am awake she says: 'Thank God you fell to your left. If you'd fallen to your right, you'd have slid right out of the running train!'

I look around the compartment. I notice that the man with the suitcase on his head is no longer on the train. Nor is the Lala, whom the suitcase belonged to.

Long after we return home, Piti continues to recall the pacifist who'd brought calm to the overcrowded compartment on the Frontier Mail to Delhi, the man with the suitcase on his head . . .

13

The Nuns of Sacred Heart Convent

My first day at school was pretty traumatic. I was four years old. Mama left me in the hands of a Sister, a nun at the convent school where Didi had been studying for a couple of years now. The nun was in a long white gown and on her head she wore a sort of white flowing cape. I remember thinking it was an unusual way to dress, all white, from head to toe. The strange new place full of stranger faces, especially the nuns with their long white robes, was terribly alienating. I was miserable. I spent the day mostly howling for Mama.

I was made to sit in a classroom next to a girl who was tiny like me and also looked lost. The Sister was writing something on the board while the other little girls around me were fidgety and inattentive. Then the Sister asked us to pull out our drawing books. My mind rushed back to Mama. She's the one who teaches me drawing, I thought. I want to learn drawing only from my Mama. I started to sob. I didn't want to be here. I got up from my desk, left the class, and ran up the corridor to where I knew Didi's class was and stood there crying. All I wanted was to go back to Mama. It didn't matter if I did not get an education; I did not want to be educated. I just wanted my Mama.

Sister Gabriel, my Didi's teacher, stopped her lesson and asked Smiti to leave the class to go see what was the matter with her little sister. Didi came out, trying to hush me into silence.

'Achcha, chup kar ja ... you're creating a scene out here!'

The two of us, a six-year-old trying to pacify a four-year-old, must've been a sight. 'Sister Rita,' whispered Didi, as an Indian nun passing by, took in the scene—Smiti with her smaller version. She tried to pacify me, but seeing how devastated I was, she took us both to the office of the Mother Superior.

'Mother,' she said, 'this is Smiti Naval, and this one is her little sister, admitted only today.'

'Oh, I remember her coming in just this morning? What's her name?'
Sister Rita turned towards Didi. 'What's her name?'

'Deepti, Sister . . . Deepti Naval.'

Then Didi said, 'Mother, she won't stop crying . . . she wants to go
back home.'

Mother Superior rose from her desk and came around to take a look
at me. She bent down and smiled.

'What is it my dear? You don't like it in school?'

My crying had now built into little hiccups.

'In three hours, you'll be able to go home, isn't that good?'

My hiccups intensified. I looked at Didi and broke into a fresh
round of sobs.

'It's not so bad here . . . see, your sister is here with you, isn't she?'

'Mama . . .' is all I finally managed in terms of words.

'Oh, my poor child . . .'

Mother Superior returned to her desk. 'Take her home, Smiti. Let
her go back today. She'll be all right by tomorrow morning.'

For days I sulked in school. Leaving my class and landing up crying
in front of my sister's class had become a common sight for the school.
Didi was quite rankled by now with this whole act of mine. She decided
that every time I came crying to her class, she'd harden her heart and
not give in to me. I'd have to learn to deal with school. Just like all the
other girls.

Such is life. You finally compromise. So that's what I did, and from
that point onwards things began to get better.

Sister Francis Teresa was my class teacher in kindergarten, a rather
nice nun. But the seniors made fun of her behind her back—they called
her Sister Nak-katti because she had a chipped nose. She was very fond
of both me, and Pemu, the chubby little girl who sat next to me that
first day in class.

A few months after I was admitted I found myself back in Mother
Superior's office.

'Let's see who we have here now? Smiti Naval's little sister!' said
Mother Superior and smiled. I smiled back.

'Ah, you are smiling! I can see you are beginning to get comfortable
here after all . . . do you like your class?'

I smiled again, shyly nodding.

'Who is your teacher?

I looked at Mother Superior. She had such white skin.

'Do you know her name?'

I coiled into myself, and said nervously, 'She is ... she is ... Sister Nak-katti!'

'Oh, *good lord!*' Mother Matilda's face fell. Scandalized, she threw her hands up and sank back in her chair.

'You should not be uttering such words, my dear child! Where on earth did you hear *that*? Her name is Sister Francis Teresa ... will you remember that, please? Sister Francis Teresa!'

I continued to smile without saying anything. I liked the Reverend Mother. She seemed kind and gentle. I also liked the dark looking Sister standing next to me, the one who'd brought me in, one with the big mole on her chin. She was even kinder. Her name I knew. She was Sister Rita.

∽

Established in 1937, the Sacred Heart Convent of Amritsar was started by Mother Matilda. Sardar Dharam Singh had built the school, a grand red brick structure on the outskirts of the city set amidst lush green fields. The magnificent British architecture was built along the lines of similar

establishments in England. Our school was by far the most impressive looking building in the city of Amritsar with the exception of Khalsa College and the Golden Temple.

The school had sprawling spaces, a church with a prominent bell tower in the centre, and a beautiful rose garden in front of it, a large assembly ground, and, of course, the striking main building with innumerable corridors, pillared verandas, a concert hall, and a grand stage with its wings hand-painted in autumnal colours to make it look like a thick, deep forest.

One of the most striking images that come to my mind when I think of my school is a painting of Jesus Christ, the Good Shepherd, bending down to pick up a little lamb, which hung in one of the corridors between the classrooms. Every time I passed by the painting, I would slow down, my eyes fixed on the Saviour. Other times, I'd just stand in the corridor and gaze at the image for a long time.

It was a thing of such beauty that it would send me off on wondrous flights of fancy. I would tell the girls in my class that my maternal grandfather was a shepherd, living in the hills, grazing sheep. I would get so carried away that I grew convinced that my grandfather was actually a shepherd—after all he was from the mountains so it wasn't such a stretch that he was a shepherd, something I also wanted to be ... Though that phase didn't last very long, I did visualize myself walking from one valley to another, herding sheep. I'd imagine myself in a Gaddi dress, the attire of the women from Kangra valley, with a scarf around my head, and a rope around my waist, surrounded by a flock of sheep, rambling over hills and meadows, looking for greener pastures.

∽

The Sisters of the Sacred Heart Convent were from the Belgian Congregation of 1803 set up after the French Revolution. There were hardly any Indian nuns in our school those days, most of the sisters were from different parts of Europe. All of them had a big impact on me during my growing years.

The first nun that I remember was Mother Matilda, the Principal of our school. She was English. Sister Francis Teresa, a Belgian nun, was my class teacher in Baby Class and Nursery. One of the nicest sisters in school was Sister Dunstan, a German nun, my class teacher in the fourth standard, who also taught us geography. Sister Giovanni was from Belgium. She was really tiny, and wore thick, black-framed glasses. Though she tried to be very strict, she was a very, very sweet person. In later school she'd teach me French. The little bit of French that I got to learn was from her. Sister Gabriel, a German nun, was my class teacher in the fifth standard and I liked her immensely. She was also the one who'd teach me painting in high school. Some years after I enrolled at the Sacred Heart Convent, Mother Stanislaus, arrived at the school from England. She was a beautiful soul. I was always a little bit in awe of her. I thought she had the kindest face on earth. She was extremely dignified and had this aura about her, the aura of saints.

Sister Rita Thomas was the only Indian nun in school at the time. All the girls, seniors, juniors, were extremely fond of her. Out of affection, I assume, and for some strange reason, they all called her 'Khoga', whatever that meant. She was the only nun who spoke Hindi and also sang Hindi songs. She wore thick dark spectacles, had a big mole on her face and a few long hairs on her chin. Because of that the girls would tease her—'Sister Rita has a beard!' Every time they saw her passing by, they'd break into a Mohammed Rafi song, *Banda parvar . . . thaam lo jigar.* She was very tolerant and never minded anything we said. On the rare occasions when we made life impossible for her, Sister Rita would storm out of the classroom saying, 'I leave you on your honour' and rush to the Mother Superior's office to report our misconduct.

∞

I loved the attire the nuns wore. Their clothes fascinated me no end. They wore sparkling white in the summers, perfectly ironed habits, rosary beads hanging to one side, crosses dangling from their necks, their distinctive headgear. I loved that. But what fascinated me more was their winter attire. As the leaves around Company Bagh started to fall, and fog filled the fields around the school, the nuns would come out wearing all black. I'd always wait for that day. I found that transformation extremely dramatic, their all-black look with the white showing just a wee bit on the inside of the veils. I was taken with the way they kept their hands from freezing by sliding them inside the long sleeves of their habits. The sound of their black boots clicking on the floors, and the way they walked, especially Sister Jacinta—svelte, sprightly, and sharp of movement, striding across corridors of the classroom blocks—all this impressed me no end and these images would become an integral part of my psyche. I'd be drawn to nunhood in a strange way and quite fancied the idea. At one point in my girly days, I seriously considered becoming a nun.

⁓

Besides the nuns, we had a few regular teachers in school. In our early years we had one class teacher who taught us all the subjects. Later, as we entered middle school, we'd have different teachers for different subjects. Mrs Mahindru taught us maths. She'd always be in a sari and a shawl and her grey hair made her appear most elegant. I couldn't ever imagine her not having had them. Mrs Philips, the one with the big bindi, taught us drama and singing. I was happy in her class as I loved to sing. The very first song I learnt from her in school was:

Row, row, row your boat, gently down the stream . . .
Merrily, merrily, merrily, merrily, life is but a dream . . .

Physics and chemistry were the domain of Miss Monica Sood. Mr Jacob Dean was our sports teacher, and then, of course, there was Mr Franklin who ran a tuck shop in the morning, where we'd buy copies and pencils, and in the afternoon, he ran the canteen inside the school premises. Outside we also had vendors lined up with little stalls selling aam papad, imli, and ice-lollipops that we were very fond of—these last, stained our teeth red and green. Then we'd have to endlessly rinse our mouths to get rid of the colour.

⁓

Our daily routine at school started with the prayers in the Assembly ground.

Our Father who art in heaven,
Hallowed be Thy name,
Thy kingdom come . . .

Standing in the Assembly line, we'd be minutely inspected. The Sisters made sure our shoes were polished, nails trimmed, and uniforms clean, each pleat of our frocks neatly ironed. If there was any little thing out of place, we'd get thrown out of line and made to stand aside. After the inspection, we did P. T., the rigorous exercise routine. Following P. T., we'd go to class.

∽

Saturdays would be our church days. I looked forward to these especially because, as I have said, I loved to sing, and couldn't wait to sing along with the choir. I was enamoured by everything about the church, the ringing of the church bell, Mother Superior's beautiful rose garden in front of it, the candles, the pews, the altar, the paintings on the walls from the life of Jesus Christ, and the large image of Mother Mary in a blue cloak, frozen, pietà-like, on the right wall. As with my interest in the faqir who came singing into our street during the winters, my attraction to the church and its art and rituals as a child didn't exactly have to do with the religion they were part of, but more to do with the fact that I was drawn to the aesthetic beauty and mystic elements of the faith.

∽

Though I was shy in making friends and would not open up that easily, the few friends that I made in school, stayed for life. The girl who sat next to me on my very first day in school was a lovely child. Her name was Prem Lata Goenka but we called her Pemu. She lived in a white kothi named Garden Bungalow on Egerton Road (later known as Madan Mohan Malvia Road), a house we frequented all the time. Although Pemu, and her sisters, belonged to a conservative Marwari family, their father seemed quite enthusiastic about his girls getting a proper education. During mango season we'd gorge ourselves on raw green mangoes in Pemu's bungalow. Pemu and her sisters came to school in their personal horse carriage, unlike us who clambered in Dharampal's tonga that ferried a bunch of girls to and from school. Pemu was very friendly and always helpful. Once I hadn't finished my homework and landed in school with my essay half written. But Pemu came to my rescue; she sat down and wrote the whole thing for me. She wrote essays for me, for other friends, and at times, she ended up writing for the entire class.

Besides her some of the other girls I became very friendly with were Madhu Sadana, a studious, very cute, chubby girl with thick, long plaits who lived on Race Course Road. She was one of the first friends I made in school. Then there was Neeran Mehra, another girl who became a close friend. Once, we took part in a concert, standing upfront on stage leading the chorus. There's a photograph of us, dressed in white net gowns with silver sashes around the waist—Neeran, Madhu, and I—all dressed up to look like *stars*. It's one of my favourite school pictures.

I was also very fond of Jyoti Kakar, a lovely girl, who came from an

affluent business family and lived in a huge kothi on Mall Road. I'd sometimes go over to her house. I also have another kind of memory of her. I stole her eraser once! One day, she sat down next to me and carefully placed a beautiful pink eraser (what we called a rubber those days) on her desk. When it went missing, she hunted all over for it, while I sat there, pretending I had no idea where it was. When she gave up looking for it, she looked terribly sad. I was really dismayed at how things had turned out. I felt really bad for Jyoti, but did not have the guts to tell her I'd stolen the rubber and that it was hidden away in the recesses of my bag. That was the first and the last time I ever stole anything. If I was going to feel so rotten about it, I figured, I was just not cut out for stealing.

Other girls I remember with a great deal of affection from my early years in school were Kiran Duggal, whom I became really close to, Shobha Mehra, Komal, and later Rita Dutta, Chand Kapoor, Daman, Harry Randhawa, and Nandini Puri, who became my close friend by the time we reached high school and whom we affectionately called Nonu.

∽

We went to school in a tonga. Dharampal, our tongawallah would pick up kids from various parts of the walled city—Thaap Khatikaan, Hathi Gate, Katra Jaimal Singh, Beri Gate, Katra Kanhaiya . . . and finally as he approached Katra Sher Singh, Didi and I would be standing prim and proper in our meticulously ironed uniforms and freshly polished shoes, ready with our bags at the corner of our gully at 7.30 a.m. sharp.

At the incline of Bhandari Bridge all the kids had to get down and frolic along Dharampal's horse. As the bridge began to descend and the tonga threatened to tip forward on to the horse, Dharampal would shout, 'Keep your weight in the back, keep it in the back!' and we'd all lunge back. Our tonga passed by the V. J. Hospital, wound around the red cement wall of Company Bagh and after crossing the sign pointing to Batala to our right, it would get on to Majitha Road and then jogtrot all the way to school, beyond the city limits and in the middle of the green fields. On the return journey, in the sweltering heat of the summer afternoon, when the tonga dropped us back home, all the kids would be thirsty and shout, 'Paani peena! Paani peena!'

They'd all come rushing in through our big phaatak. We had a refrigerator at home and Mama would insist that all the kids be given cold water from the fridge. Nonu, who rode in the tonga with me, would go home and tell her parents: 'There's a girl in our tonga who has a cold water machine!'

∽

Not only did we have to bear the wrath of Phaa living below the thhada, but during our early schooldays we also had to deal with a madwoman living in the lane across Hall Bazaar.

She didn't have a name. Not only did she not have a name, at a time when everyone knew about the origins of everyone else in town in great detail, no one knew who she was or where she'd come from. Some kids called her 'Soti' because she was sculpted like a stick. A stick-thin figure who ran feverishly every single morning after the rickety tongas brimming over with bottle green-blazered schoolgirls. The shopkeepers of Hall Bazaar called her Dhanni Mai. I now suspect that perhaps that *was* her real name, Mai Dhanni. Mochistan called her 'shudain', which simply means 'madwoman'. But we girls weren't as kind. We had coined our own name for her—'Mai Kodhkirli', 'kodhkirli' being Punjabi for 'lizard'.

Mai Kodhkirli lived in the corner house at the end of the narrow lane across Chitra Talkies, connecting Hall Bazaar to Ram Bagh. The dilapidated red brick structure she called home was not really a house, it was all of a courtyard with a small tin shed attached. She lived off the green wall of her shed, and ate moss to survive—so I'd imagine.

Whenever Dharampal's tonga passed by this narrow lane, Mai Kodhkirli would come hollering out of nowhere and chase us all the way till the end of the road, leaving us shouting and screaming with fright until we'd make another left at Ram Bagh towards Majitha Road.

Twice a day, we'd encounter her at close quarters—eerily close, fingertips-close, knee-close, ankle-close, hem-of-the-uniform close ... far too close for my liking. Although we'd be extremely alert and prepared for the madwoman to suddenly spring from somewhere and pounce upon us, yet every time the tonga did make that right turn, and Mai Kodhkirli sprang out of nowhere, she managed to scare the daylights out of us! Horrified, we'd screech, scrambling over each other as we sought to get away from her. The tongawallah would grumble out loud: 'Oye, stop it, you girls! That woman is never going to *do* anything, you know that! Still, you go jumping all over each other! If you fall off my tanga na, it will be my neck!'

Mai Kodhkirli would run barefoot, breathless, blabbering, chasing after shrieking schoolgirls, till she'd exhaust herself, or till the tonga turned left and finally jangled towards our school. Perhaps in her crazy mind, her exclusive, running-screaming territory was only up till the end of the back lane.

All through my first few years in school I was petrified of our daily encounters with her. In my imagination I could feel her scrawny hands around my knees ... long-nailed fingers trying to grab my frock, pulling at the sleeve of my dark green sweater. What if Mai Kodhkirli, for once, actually managed to pull me down by my legs? That was the stuff of nightmares.

14

My Greatest Influences

If I had to pinpoint the exact age when the desire to become an actress crystallized firmly in me, I'd probably settle on the age of eleven. I will write about that period a little later but even by the age of nine I knew I wanted to become an actress. I was inclined towards films. I was hooked on cinema, but I was not the only one in the family who was into it. My mother firstly, then my aunts, and not to forget my grandfather, who had a box reserved in all the three cinema halls around the house. In addition to all this I was quite a little drama queen as a child, not in the classical sense of the term, but in the sense of someone who loved to ham it up (remember my 'Choochi ban ja' days), and when I was a bit older, I was quite happy singing on stage and being part of the choir in school.

My family loved cinema but if there was one member of the family who actually loved to sing and dance, it was my mother. I have with me old black and white photos that are a visual record of this aspect in my Mama's life. She was especially fond of doing dramas; she would direct plays, and also act in them along with other young women. I have one distinct memory of a scene being enacted in our house. I'm standing beside the dark blue curtain in the hall kamra and watching Mama rehearse with other women. She is in a sari and her hair is tied in a loose bun. She is wearing high heels and is holding a purse. I recall her entering the room, dangling the batua in her hand. She walks in and there's some dialogue with the other two women, words that I no longer remember. I watch the scene being performed in front of me with fascination. The door opens and shuts as Mama walks in repeatedly from the thhada entrance, revealing street activity behind her. Light filters in as she stands backlit at the entrance, looking like a veritable star. I wish I could recollect details of the scene being enacted but that's as far as it goes, my memory of that rehearsal.

Once, some cine stars from Bombay came to our city for a cricket match. Among them were Shyama, Nirupa Roy, and Bhagwan Dada. They performed a show at the Chitra Talkies. That's the time my mother also performed along with them. When she made her entry on stage, Didi, sitting next to me in the hall started to shout, 'Mama! . . .That's my Mama!' All heads turned to look at us. It was a moment that embarrassed my mother but she'd recall it always with a lot of love.

I assume that my mother did some more plays during my baby years, but by the time I was old enough to properly appreciate her talents as an actress she had stopped. Years later, she told me that Bibiji had once said to her, 'The women at the Women's Conference say that your daughter-in-law does dramas!'

'After that day,' said Mama, 'I stopped. I never did another play. Never uttered a word to my mother-in-law. I just silently gave up everything.' I was not aware of the impact of that finale in my mother's life, for she never showed any bitterness. But I know what that sacrifice must have meant to her. This was the woman who dreamt of becoming an actress and called herself the Beauty Queen of Bengal. Today, as I live my life as an artiste, I realize the gravity of those words. 'I silently gave up everything . . .'

∽

It also made me think of Mama's cousin in Burma, Sunny Bowrie, who had run away from Rangoon to become a dancer in Bombay Talkies. Brian Uncle once told me that Sunny was seen among the group dancers in the song 'Ramaiya vasta vaiya' in Raj Kapoor's film *Shree 420*. I have since been looking hard at the screen, peering crazily at the dancers in the back rows, looking for Sunny Bowrie, the face in Mama's box of

photographs, to somehow be able to spot
him dancing in a movie, a dream that he'd
left his home for. But according to Mama,
Sunny Bowrie was lost to the family a
long time ago.

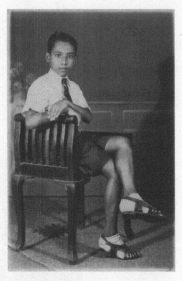

∽

Besides my mother, others in the family
who loved the world of acting, or more
properly Hindi movies, were my bhuas,
my father's sisters. Once a year, my bhuas
would come down from Delhi to Amritsar
along with their children. All of us
cousins—Manju, Babbu, Indu, Ashu, Alok,
Cheenu, Bunny, Didi, and me—would
be a quite handful for the elders. In the

Sunny Bowrie

afternoon, the women would put us kids to sleep and sneak out of the
house, to go and see the matinee show at Chitra Talkies.

On hot summer afternoons, all of us kids would lay down for an
hour on the terrazzo floor, its touch cool against the skin. The chicks

would be drawn in the veranda to keep
the sun out as we were all required to
take our afternoon nap. That's when
my bhuas would get up from the
floor, one by one, stand before the
hat stand mirror, brush their hair, put
on various shades of red lipstick, and
one by one, slip out of the house. That
was their ultimate getting-ready-real-
fast trick—comb your hair, apply red
lipstick, and off you go!

All the kids knew exactly what
was happening, but almost all the time

My bhuas.

we pretended to be asleep. Occasionally, we'd open our eyes, glance at
each other, and suppress giggles.

∽

With Indu Bhaiya, Bunny, and Ashu.

The biggest influence in my life as an actress perhaps was Indu Bhaiya, my older cousin. Indu Bhaiya, Santosh Bhua's older son, first came to live with us in the year 1958. I was six years old at the time and Bhaiya was probably in eighth class. He had not been doing well in school, so Pitaji suggested that Indu be sent to Amritsar so he could personally supervise his studies. I remember Didi, Indu Bhaiya, and me, playing with white plasticine balls, turning them into pigeons and buffaloes.

The second time that Indu Bhaiya came to Amritsar was in 1962. Bhaiya was by now eighteen, and I was ten. I sported the, then famous, Sadhana Cut, the much in vogue fringe those days, after the look in *Love in Simla*, and roamed around in my pinafore. Indu Bhaiya would every now and then tease me about looking like Sadhana, the star of those days. This was also the time I was just starting to become self-conscious as a girl.

Indu Bhaiya had told his family that he wanted to go to Bombay to become an actor. He would tell us all about Dev Anand; he seemed to be obsessed with the film star.

Asli Naqli, a Dev Anand–Sadhana starrer, had just been released in New Rialto and we had all gone to see the film. There was a scene where Moti Lal, holding sand in his palm says, 'Zindagi aisi hai, jitna aap usko zore se pakroge, utna hi aapke haath se nikal jayegi.' (Life is like these grains of sand. The more you try to hold them, the more they will slip out of your hand.) Then there was Dev Anand singing:

Asli kya hai, naqli kya hai, puchho dil se mere . . .
(What is real and what is false, ask my heart!)

That night when the cousins returned home with the women of the house after the show, Santosh Aunty decided to use the opportunity to pull Indu aside, and give him a piece of advice.

She took her son to the cowshed where for once the cows were tied, and there, sitting on the edge of the toori tub she took his *class*.

'So, what did you learn from the film?' she asked most hopefully.

Indu, lean and thin-featured, stood rigid in the yellow bathroom light. He spoke without hesitation.

'That a rich boy gets no love from his parents or people around him, so he leaves home and all his riches to go and live in the poor people's basti.'

Santosh Aunty shifted from one leg and alternately crossed it with the other. 'Yes, but what did you *learn* from the film?'

Chin low, eyes downcast. A flicker in the gusalkhaana light brought a sparkle to Arvind's eyes.

'A rich boy comes to find true love only among the poor people.'

Santosh Aunty flung her heavy right palm across Bhaiya's left cheek, dishevelling his immaculately styled, Brylcreemed Dev Anand-puff.

'So now you are saying that we don't love you? That you will run away from home, leave us all crying, to . . . to . . . become an *actor*? Have you not thought about your poor parents? All the love that we shower on you? About that, nothing you'll think? Oh God! Where have I gone wrong in bringing you up . . . I devoted my life to you both, and now you want to put mud on everything and go and join the film line?'

'But I want to be an actor,' Indu Bhaiya stood determined, the forelock on his brow quivering with ambition.

Santosh Aunty broke down completely in shaky sobs. All the other bhuas in the house, huddled together in the kitchen, could not comfort her broken heart. Her son, her older son wanted to become an actor! A worthless, useless, good for nothing *actor*! Shame! Shame! She was ruined! Finished! What would happen to the family name!

Indu Bhaiya stood silent after that with a mind of his own and a dismantled puff fallen over his eyebrows.

While this major scene was playing out in the dimly lit cowshed, in another part of the house, Jeet had her old wooden two-eyed radio groaning away with some sizzly broken voiced song—'*Leke pehla pehla pyaar, bhar ke aankhon mein . . .*' Jeet happily and sloppily sang along with the radio while chopping away at her onions and crying over them.

'*Jaadoo nagri se aaya hai koi . . .*' and she wiped a running nose on her

sleeve with a big *shroon . . . 'Jadugar!*'

'Shut that blessed thing off, will you!' Mama spoke in a hushed tone, walking into the kitchen. 'There's a crisis in the house . . . Santosh Bahenji is inconsolable and you are singing away!'

'What happened, Chamiji?' Manju rushed in behind her. 'Why is Maasi crying? Has someone died?'

'No', Mama shut the radio off. 'Arvind has decided to become an actor! Despite all the dissuading . . . he says he is going to leave home if he is not allowed to go to Bombay.'

'Oh my God! Run away?'

'Yes . . . now keep that tone down. Santosh Bahenji is already very upset . . . Here, take this food for Indu. He's in the cowshed. Go feed him there. He won't be coming inside the house. Not tonight!'

At the end of this episode, I also got the message loud and clear that it is one thing for our family to love movies and appreciate actors and actresses but quite another to dream of becoming one.

Some years down the line, Indu Bhaiya went to Bombay nevertheless and joined films. I was ecstatic—my Bhaiya was so handsome, he looked like Dev Anand, he'll surely make it. We heard that he'd already got work in a film produced by Rajshri Productions called *Dosti*. Though Bhaiya was in the supporting cast, for me this was exciting enough.

After his three-year stint in the film industry, and a few more roles, we were told that Bhaiya had given up on Bombay and come back home. When I saw him at Manju Didi's wedding after his return, I was a bit taken aback. Bhaiya seemed to be in a disturbed state of mind. He later confided in me and told me how he'd fallen in love with an actress in Bombay, but was left heartbroken. He'd lost his mental balance and had briefly undergone treatment as well. Luckily, for him and the family, things would later fall in place for Bhaiya as he put his dream behind, and decided to move on with his life.

But for me, Indu Bhaiya was and has always remained a hero.

∞

So, this is where it all gets connected, my passion for cinema ...

Imagine, I have spent the last forty years of my career as an actress thinking that I'm a misfit in the Bombay film industry, that I come from an academic background and have nothing to do with show business. But I had no idea that cinema has been in my blood! It is in my genes— between my grandfather's three little boxes reserved in three cinema halls, my Mama's stunning black and white photographs of Bette Davis and Devika Rani, and Indu Bhaiya's stint in the world of films, my destiny had been charted. I suddenly feel less responsible for having made the choices I made in my life. I'm a natural born here, and here I have my place in the sun!

∞

I have occasionally mentioned the movies I saw up to the age of ten or so in the preceding chapters but I would love to give you a proper idea of those movies and talk about the actresses and actors I adored that influenced me well before my teens.

1954: As I was taking my first baby steps and started walking all over the vehra, the radio with the yellow teeth perched on the hat stand sang:

'*Chali kaun se des gujariya tu ban-thhan ke*' from the newly released film *Boot Polish* and '*Nanhe munne bachche teri mutthi mein kya hai ...*'

Songs from films like *Nagin, Jagriti,* and *Boot Polish* were part of my psyche. During our childhood days we didn't realize how unknowingly these songs were impacting us as kids, transforming us. *Jagriti* released when I was only a toddler but it is not beyond the bounds of possibility that things seeped into my subconscious even as I was crawling around the veranda on all fours. It surprises me even today how I react to the famous patriotic song:

> *Hum laaye hain toofan se kashti nikaal ke, is desh ko rakhna mere bachcho sambhaal ke ...*

Even today my eyes well up at times when I listen to those words and to another song from the same film:

> *De di hamen azaadi bina khadak bina dhal ... Sabarmati ke sant tune kar diya kamaal ... raghupati raaghav raja ram ...*

Mama recalled having taken Didi and me along to see *Nagin* starring Vyjayanthimala, of whom she was quite fond. I, of course, have no memory of it, though the notes of the been, the flute, would have played on the radio all the time when the movie was at the height of its popularity. Later I remember dancing to the tune '*Man dole mera tan dole*' in order to entertain my sister. Mama would tell us that Vyjayanthimala's grandmother was so strict she never let her go to the studios alone, and would accompany her everywhere.

1955: Mama later told me that the film she had gone to see with my father on that dust-ridden night that I wrote about in the prologue, when I'd landed up at Regent Talkies Chowk, a few months shy of my fourth birthday, was *Jhanak Jhanak Payal Baaje*.

1956: A song filters into the landscape of my memory. I don't remember where I've heard it but it often surfaces into my conscious mind when I'm not really thinking of anything in particular. Though *Durgesh Nandini* at age four had been a fiasco for me, it must have left me with *something*. I later realized that my all-time favourite Lata Mangeshkar song '*Kahan le chale ho bata do musafir, sitaaron se aage yeh kaisa jahan hai ...*' was from that very film, though I have no memory of the song on the screen.

Another film that surfaces from my baby years is *Toofan Aur Deeya*. I can hardly recall the film but was very impacted by a song in it: '*Nirbal se ladai balwaan ki, yeh kahani hai diye ki aur toofan ki . . .*' I listened to the song very intently as it involved a sort of life and death situation.

Halaku, a Meena Kumari–Ajit starrer, as far as I was concerned, was only visible on banners carried on hand-pulled rickshaws, with Mastana loudspeakers trilling, '*Aji chale aao tumhe aankhon se dil ne pukaara*'. It seemed like a call to one and all within the walled city to come and watch the movie in City Light and Liberty Cinemas.

Then came the time both Mama and Piti saw the film *Jagte Raho*, and came back enthralled with the movie. They felt that we girls should certainly be taken to see the film as it had a great message, told in a very interesting way. But by the time I got ready to see my first Raj Kapoor film, it was already gone from the theatres. 'Jaago Mohan Pyaare' was the song that rang through the air at four o'clock in the morning from the Sitla Mandir—a wake-up call for one and all.

1957: After having missed out on a fun film like *Tumsa Nahin Dekha*, I decided to never ever lose another opportunity to watch a movie. I was about five years old when Piti took us to see a film called, *Ab Dilli Dur Nahin*, a much-planned excursion by my parents. I don't remember much about the film except that it was meant to be a children's film and was a poignant experience. I came back with the song '*Chun chun karti ayi chidiya*' on my lips. In my mother's recollections, I would skip about the veranda in my little frock to '*More bhi aaya, kaua bhi aaya, chooha bhi aaya, bandar bhi aaya . . .*'

When *Mother India* was released in Amritsar in the winter of that year, Mama and Piti made it a point to take us to New Rialto, to see the huge star of those days, Nargis, 'in the role of her lifetime'. We walked up the steps of the Railway Bridge crossing over the railway tracks to the other side. It seemed like an endless walk, almost out of town. It was a film of great pathos. There was a lot of sadness in the film and I came back remembering one scene in particular, the climactic one, in which Mother India kills her own son, a scene that left the audience startled, and me a bit confused.

1958: *Phagun* was the film in which I first saw Madhubala playing a gypsy, and recognized her as the same girl who stood smiling her slant smile at the door of the printing press. I remember her wearing fancy clothes and dancing to the song 'Ek Pardesi Mera Dil Le Gaya'.

Talaq was another film I have a hazy memory of as I quite liked the heroine in it. Years later, I came to know her name was Kamini Kadam. She played a schoolteacher in the film, and in one scene she sang to the girls in class, '*Hum pe badi zimmedaari, dekh rahi duniya saari, ghar ghar ko tum swarg banana, har aangan ko phulwaari . . .*' It seemed to me like she was saying something important to the girls, and I too wanted to follow her.

1959: I was seven when I saw the film *Chhoti Bahen* with Nanda singing '*Bhaiya mere rakhi ke bandhan ko nibhaana*' and ever so sweetly tying rakhis on her brothers. From that film onwards every single year during the Rakhi festival, the radio played the song the whole day and for days before and days after the festival, and I must confess, each time I heard that song, I felt a little filled with emotion. It was a sentimental thing with me, as that time Didi and I did not have a brother. We tied rakhis on Piti instead, proxy rakhis, one at a time, all the five rakhis that arrived in our letterbox in pretty little envelopes from all my five bhuas. Later, when Gugu, my brother Rohitaashv, came into our lives, naturally everything changed.

School Master was another film from that year that my father took us to see that I don't remember much of. I do recall seeing *Chirag Kahan Roshni Kahan* around that time and that film I remember clearly. It was my first Meena Kumari film, and it also starred the child artiste Honey Irani—I remember being awed by her. Both Didi and I were very taken by the lead pair, Meena Kumari and Rajendra Kumar, and decided the two were going to be our favourite on-screen couple.

Then came *Ben-Hur* and our outing to the majestic Chitra Talkies that I have written about earlier.

It would be a whole year before I, at age seven, would stumble into the theatre and happen to see my first somewhat adult film called *Dhool Ka Phool*. My parents probably thought it was a children's film as the posters on the rickshaws flaunted Daisy Irani, the child artiste, but it turned out to be a lesson for all *good girls*. It was touted as an extremely relevant film about a Hindu child being brought up by a Muslim, but turned out to be more than that. It told us about everything we were not supposed to know while growing up and had a huge impact. In that film Rajendra Kumar did not play such a nice guy, I remember. He got a girl pregnant and then went off and married someone else. How the hell that baby happened, no one knew! It seemed like if you stayed out with a guy in the rain, you were bound to get pregnant, and become an unwed mother whom society would then scorn. The theme of the film didn't really bother me, as I loved the drama in the film, and enjoyed watching Daisy Irani in the movie. I even came back with a song in my head, '*Dharakne lage dil ke taaron ki duniya . . . jo tum muskura do . . .*'

Sujata was the most memorable film from that year of my life. We had gone with Lily Aunty and Sneh Aunty in Delhi to see the film in Golcha Cinema in Daryaganj. Sunil Dutt falls in love with Nutan instead of Shashi Kala, but Nutan was just an orphan girl taken in by the family. I loved the song both the girls sing '*Bachpan ke din bhi kya din thhey*'. Then there was the sweetly melodic Asha Bhosle track '*Kaali ghata chaaye mora jiya tarsaaye*', that Lily Aunty would constantly sing. She loved Nutan. I thought Nutan was divine, but in those days, I had eyes only for Meena Kumari.

Lily Aunty and Sneh Aunty.

1960: There soon came a day the entire family, including Jeet, Teluram, and Gyanji, went to see Raj Kapoor's *Jis Desh Mein Ganga Behti Hai*. This was one film that caught my fancy in a big way; it seemed much grander than anything I had seen so far. It somewhat connected me to the land I belonged to and made me feel special about being a Hindustani. '*Hum us desh ke vaasi hain jis desh mein Ganga behti hai . . .*' was to get embedded in my heart for life. I was dazzled by the song and dance in '*Hum bhi hain, tum bhi ho, dono hain aamne saamne . . .*' Padmini as Kammoji had become all the rage with the uncles around me and so had her underwater song sequence, '*O maine pyaar kiya!*' I was amazed at how they could have taken the camera *under* the water! It was this film onwards that I started to become aware of the visual impact of black and white cinema. While life around me was in colour, I found black and white movies more sensuous, dramatic, and intriguing. I remember towards the end of the film when Raj Kapoor sings '*Aa abb laut chalain . . .*', Padmini is running across a strange rocky terrain. The boulders fascinated me; I hadn't seen such a dramatic landscape.

Another clear memory from that year is of the film *Kanoon*, which had Ashok Kumar, Rajendra Kumar, and Nanda in lead roles. What stood out for me in that film was a long-drawn-out court scene in which Rajendra Kumar spoke with considerable impact. In the very first scene when the accused accepts that he has committed the murder, I felt, O God! *Now* where's the plot going to go from here? My eight-year-old head retained the image of a ballerina with one chopped wing.

My parents somehow made it a point to take us to see all the films that had Daisy Irani or Honey Irani in them. One film I remember from the year 1960 was *Zameen Ke Taare* that had both sisters in it. The girls were around the same age as Didi and I, so we easily related to them. I loved the song '*O mere pyaaro, zameen ke taaro, jaane tumhe hai kahaan . . .*'

Great films like *Ganga Jamuna*, *Mughal-e-Azam*, *Madhumati*, *Naya Daur*, and *Pyaasa* were being shown in the theatres in the late fifties, but I didn't get to see any of those classics. In school the girls discussed the magic of all these movies in detail but I felt lost. *Mughal-e-Azam* was an especially big event in our town. People were fascinated by the grandeur of the film; they thronged the Nandan Theatre. There wasn't a soul who was not gushing over the film's Sheesh Mahal sequence where Madhubala sings '*Jab pyaar kiya toh darna kya*', the set for which had apparently taken two years to build, but all this was hearsay.

1961: Chitra Talkies, the grand cinema theatre, brings back the memory of another day when I'd gone with Pitaji and Didi to see *The Guns of Navarone*. It was a hot summer afternoon. There were hardly any people around; most of the seats were empty. Suddenly, in the middle of the movie, all the fans in the theatre turned off. But there was light in the projection room. The usher came up to my father and said it would take some time for the connection to be fixed. Piti looked at us. We hated the idea of not being able to see the film till the end.

'Bauji, the girls, if they wish, they can watch the film from the projection room.'

I remember being enthralled by the sloppy 'behind the scenes' scenario of the projection room. Two podgy looking projectors stood side by side in the middle of the tiny enclosure, fixed to the red cement floor on a high rectangular metal base. Several tubes and wires coiled in and out of the heavy black gadgets, with large spools attached to the front that went round and round in slow motion, making a loud rickety sound. The projectors appeared like strange creatures set against the half-green-half-yellow wall that displayed calendar images of Ram, Sita, and Hanumanji. The soundtrack in there was enormous. While Piti stood chatting with the projectionist adept at changing reels—ending of one spool and beginning of the next in perfect sync, I sat on a high stool, my legs jamming into the wall and head craned at an angle from where I could peer right into the square slot without obstructing the thick beam of light overhead carrying images from the spool to the big screen. I remember watching the rest of *The Guns of Navarone*, now gazing at the silver screen, and now at the magical white shaft of light emitting from the projector.

In 1962, when construction on the Nandan Talkies was finally complete, *Aashiq* was the first film to release there. The whole town went to the swanky theatre, first of its kind, built in contemporary architecture. People were thrilled seeing its frilly curtain automatically go up. I remember how badly I wanted to see that movie because it had amazing songs. But with a name like *Aashiq* I guess our parents discouraged us from seeing the film. Whenever I heard Mukesh's soulful voice singing, '*Laakhon taare, aasmaan mein, ek magar dhoondhe na mila . . .*' I'd drop everything and run to the radio with my copy and pencil. It was from as early as the *Aashiq* days that song lyrics started to engross me. I'd scribble away at feverish speed the words of the songs, skipping all the horizontal lines on the page to catch up with the next stanza.

∞

Possibly the greatest influence on me in childhood and those early girlhood years was Meena Kumari. By the time I was nine years old, I had a special place for her in my heart. I call this time my 'Meena Kumari phase'. Mama was very fond of her, so Didi and I got to watch most of

the Meena Kumari films. It was the Meena Kumari–Rajendra Kumar duo
that impacted me the most. I was taken with everything that the two felt
for each other on screen. To me all that was real. When *Zindagi Aur Khwab*
came to the theatre, I was convinced, at age nine, that if there was love,
it had to be as intense as the love between Meena Kumari and Rajendra
Kumar. I was horrified when Jayant reappeared in the movie. How could
life be so cruel as to bring this villain back into Meena Kumari's life when
she was already in love with a wonderful man like Rajendra Kumar?
It was perhaps the same year that I saw *Pyaar Ka Saagar*, again a film
starring Meena Kumari and Rajendra Kumar. Seeing the two together
was somehow reassuring. I felt they belonged together.

In the summer of 1962, I saw Meena Kumari in a lovely film called
Aarti. In December that year, I saw another outstanding film of hers
called *Sahib Bibi Aur Ghulam*. Mama, having a thing for Bengalis, was
keen to see it as Meena Kumari played a Bengali bahu. She loved the
song 'Na jaao saiyaan . . .' For days she discussed the scene where Chhoti
Bahu confronts her husband—a scene that had really got her. There was
something about that role of hers that didn't leave me for a long time.
No one could act better than her, I thought. It was a performance of
a lifetime! Then a year later I got to see *Dil Ek Mandir*, the last film
in which she and Rajendra Kumar would act together—again a movie
which created a lasting impact.

Meena Kumari to me was an enigma, there could be no one else like
her. There was so much depth in her persona, *and* she was beautiful too.
Mama told me that Meena Kumari had lost a finger in a car accident. I
was surprised. And yet she was an actress? I was enamoured by the fact
that though the little finger on Meena Kumari's left hand was missing,
she always managed to hide the fact. She'd hold her pallu in such a way
that the missing finger would never be visible. She even did an entire
dance sequence in *Chiraag Kahan Roshni Kahaan* in the song 'Andaaz
mera mastaana, maange dil ka nazrana . . .' with one hand; the other hand
forever being wrapped in her dupatta. In addition to the fact that I
worshipped her, I was bewitched by her ability to emote—she made me
believe every emotion she portrayed on screen.

Sitting in the movie theatre, I would cry easily. It was all so believable
for me, whatever was happening on the big screen. Each situation, each

emotion, was so God damn believable! I was convinced that everything that happens on the screen was for real, *that* was life, and the rest of what we lived, did not matter. I loved movies, and I *loved* Meena Kumari.

Once I even dreamt about her. I saw Meena Kumari holding a book in her hand, walking around the dome of our mosque and I watched her from my terrace—a young Meena Kumari wearing a black burqa, her head covered, walking slowly around the top part of

the dome. I woke up excited by that image and looked around but was disappointed when I discovered it was just a dream, and there was no Meena Kumari walking around the dome of the maseet.

∾

I did, however, realize there was cinema beyond Meena Kumari. Before I turned ten, I started to take a greater interest in all the big stars of the era. In *Jab Pyar Kisi Se Hota Hai* it was a delight to watch Dev Anand on top of a moving train, singing, *'Jiya o . . . jiya o jiya kuch bole do . . .'* to an Asha Parekh wearing a checked kameez, showing jhootha-jhootha gussa.

'*YAAAAAHOOOOOO*' roared Mastana's tweeters when *Junglee* first came to the streets of Amritsar, mounted on a rickshaw. All the kids ran after it, gyrating like crazy to Mohammed Rafi's '*Chahe koi mujhe junglee kahe!*' When Saira Banu sang '*Kashmir ki kali hoon main mujhse na rootho, Babuji*' it was the first time we were seeing a girl chasing a boy. Wow! The song, '*Ja ja ja mere bachpan . . .*' was so relatable as we were still kids but dying to grow up really fast.

The euphoria of *Junglee* died quickly when *Kabuliwala* was released in the winter of 1961 at Inder Palace Theatre, the area where Mama would go and distribute knitting needles to the girls at the Pingalwada. Pitaji, being a Tagore enthusiast, was particularly eager to show us the film, as it was based on one of his classic stories. Balraj Sahni, whom I'd earlier seen in *Chhoti Bahen* left a deep impression on my young mind. I'd sit real close to the radio each time I heard the song '*Eh mere pyaare watan . . .*' In *Kabuliwala*, Mini seemed to be me. Mini was nine and I was nine, and I loved Kabuliwala, he made me cry.

∾

Balraj Sahni

Little did I know that just two years down the line I'd be actually standing in front of Kabuliwala. It was an event, I now believe, that marked my life in a significant way—when the most incredible actor of Hindi cinema came to our city to perform a play.

The first star that shone on the screen of my real life was a tall, handsome, intense, and very polished man called Balraj Sahni. My encounter with him took place in the winter of 1963, on the third of November to be precise. A youth festival was in full swing in the city, and my father, knowing my fascination for the performing arts, brought home two tickets.

'There's a group here from Bombay called IPTA, staging a play, *Kanak di Balli*. I hear that the actor Balraj Sahni is performing tonight,' he said.

I lit up at once: *Kabuliwala?*

'Would you like to see it? But there is very little time, we'll have to rush!'

Piti was still speaking when I had already darted into my room. I had to quickly grab something warm to wear since it would to be cold out there in the open ... and my ... my autograph book! I rummaged through the Green Room. God! Where had I kept it? It was here in the drawer in my writing desk—and my socks, my socks—I leapt from my room on the terrace back to the gate, and before my father could finish saying what time the play would start ... I was all set, in my socks and shoes, and bottle green blazer over my frock, breathless, and ready to go!

The youth festival at the Gandhi Ground was the big event in Amritsar every winter and would last a good ten days. People thronged to it from all over Punjab, sitting out in the open-air auditorium during the fog-filled nights, munching peanuts and jaggery cakes as they watched a medley of music, dance, and drama competitions. The participants would perform on a makeshift wooden stage, displaying their talent before a raw, curious, non-judgmental audience.

When I finally encountered Balraj Sahni, it was love at first sight, a different kind of love, for this very gentle, well-groomed man who stood looming over me. And me, down there somewhere, holding out my autograph book, looking wide-eyed at this amazing creature—an actor! An actor who created magic on the big screen every time the lights in Adarsh Talkies dimmed for the matinee show—a face that ignited euphoria at first sight and then remained in your heart, forever!

I have little memory of the play though. Having reached the grounds late we could hardly see Balraj Sahni, even though Piti repeatedly showed the ushers the seat numbers printed on the tickets. But then, this was Punjab. There were no rules. First come, first seated.

I had imagined myself sitting in the front row watching Balraj Sahni perform at close quarters, but now I had to be content just listening to his voice over the loudspeaker. His voice was all that came across to me even though I stood on my toes for the whole hour on the seat, to get a clearer glimpse of the actor on stage.

But once the play was over, my father nudged his way through the crowd towards the back of the tented stage, holding on tightly to my hand. A crowd of rowdy boys had already thronged the backstage, wanting a one-to-one encounter with the star of the show, to speak to him, to touch him, to check if he was real, as he hurriedly stepped out of the makeshift green room. It was whispered that the actor was apparently in a great hurry to dash off to the railway station where he was to catch a train, the Frontier Mail, that left Amritsar at nine-thirty in the night. There was no time. Tearing through the crowd, Piti prodded me up ahead so I could at least get his autograph.

Tall Jats loomed all around me. My neck craned to get a glimpse of the star, to somehow draw his attention. It was difficult for me to find my way up to Balraj Sahni as he stood engulfed in the vociferous madness. My father and I managed to inch our way through the crowd and finally when we reached him, to my horror, I saw he was already turning around and rushing towards the exit.

'Can you give me an autograph, *please* ...'

I pleaded in a voice, which couldn't possibly have been heard by him above the din of the Punjabi language. I looked back at Piti. His expression, looking at my face, was one of great empathy. It was gone, my chance, I could see. The crowd had flowed between my dream man and me.

But then something altered; a turn of destiny. The loud voices around me dropped to a low drone. People started to look back to where I stood. Through the knot of human faces, I saw Balraj Sahni turn around and walk back towards me. I could not believe my eyes! He had heard me! He was actually coming back, for ME!

'Auto ... gra ... aff ...' I mustered something like a voice again. The star now stood before me, looking down, way below, where I stood, wide-eyed, gaping at him. Then slowly he lowered his arm, taking the autograph book from my hand, and without looking at me, said: 'If I keep signing autographs, my dear, I'll miss my train!' Then looking into my eyes, he smiled.

'My dear!' he had said, hadn't he? 'My dear'! See? I knew it! He was someone *my own*! He had spoken directly to *me*, singling me out in the entire crowd. He had addressed me, looked at me, signed my autograph book, with his *own* hand! I gazed at him, then at my notebook, where he'd written on the green page in blue-blue fountain pen ink, his name—

Balraj   Sahni

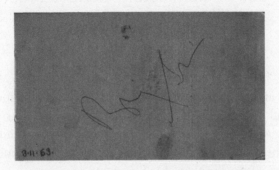

When I looked up at him again, the jostling crowd had already flooded in and torn us apart, the pandemonium of voices reaching a crescendo once again as the bright star disappeared into the winter night, the rabble at his heels. As for me, I remained trapped in that moment, when it had been just him and me.

I still have that blue plastic-covered autograph book. I was eleven then, an eleven-year-old who knew what she wanted to do with her life when she grew up. And I promised to myself . . . I'd be graceful like a Balraj Sahni . . . subtle like a Balraj Sahni, and no matter which role I played, I would be genuine like a Balraj Sahni, when I grew up to be an actress.

Yes, it was as early as age eleven that I had made a decision—I will be an actress. And if that doesn't happen, I'll become a nun.

15

Crack in the Picture-perfect Frame

Into every life a little rain will fall. If you are unlucky these will be major storms but no matter how fortunate, your childhood will have moments and phases of sadness, disappointment, and loss. The people dearest to me in early childhood were Mama, Piti, and Didi; they constituted the foundation on which my entire world was built. As long as everything was okay with them I felt reassured and happy.

My beloved parents.

When I think of my baby years, I can say that they were blissful, to say the least. I grew up believing that my parents had an ideal marriage and were a made-for-each-other couple. They always addressed each other as 'Darling'; it was somehow comforting. I admired their togetherness. Mama and Piti would often sit out in the sunlit veranda on Sunday afternoons, discussing Byron and Keats at the dining table, and sharing their views on life. I thought if there was companionship, it should be this! Any little displeasure we sisters showed towards Piti, Mama would at once retort, 'Don't you *dare* say a word against your father!' Their relationship epitomized the relationship I wanted for myself one day. I, too, would find someone, who I'd be able to *talk* to, share my life with, someone I could open my heart to; someone, who'd be my friend.

But I had memories, other memories ... There apparently was a crack in the picture-perfect glass frame.

The few times that I heard my parents in a heated argument are some of my saddest memories, ones that I cannot wash off no matter how hard I try.

∞

I was very small, when on a dim, yellow-lit night, Mai Sardi handed me a glass of milk and told me to go give it to my mother. The shadows in the courtyard loomed larger than on other nights. The air stood still and not a leaf had moved on the bougainvillea all evening. I held the hot glass of milk precariously with both my hands and began to walk one step at a time across the diagonal length of the vehra towards my parents' room.

As I took the two tricky steps up the veranda, I started to hear voices from the room, raised voices, of my father and mother. As I got closer to their room, I heard my father's voice over everything else. He was angry, very angry. I faltered a little, but held tight to the glass of milk, keeping it from falling. I couldn't exactly comprehend what was going on between my parents behind that closed door, but something made me afraid. The voices were now piercing.

I stood frightened at the door, my right foot turned inward, holding the steel glass, hot within my palms. Suddenly the door flung open. Mama charged out of the room in a rage and stood glaring at me. I looked up at my mother, petrified. Then I tried to smile faintly.

'Mama ... I got milk ... for you ...'

My mother swirled her hand right across my face in a great rage: 'GET AWAY from me, all of you! ... I DON'T want ANYTHING!'

Then came the sound of steel bouncing off the cement floor, and liquid splashing the yellow squares a milky white. I stood stunned, hot milk dripping down my frock into my rubber slippers. I burst into tears.

Mai Sardi dropped her kartari, her cutting knife, on the floor and ran across the vehra.

'Bibi, eh ki? Why hit the poor little girl?' She grabbed me in her arms and darted back towards the kitchen. The first sounds of the nightly dholak emerged from the gully. As I hiccupped in Mai Sardi's lap, the mochis began to sing in the unsettled night . . . This has been a big memory. Then the memory continues . . .

Later that night Mama sat quietly by my bedside, running her fingers across my forehead, as she would do while trying to put me to sleep. My eyes were closed but I heard her sobbing softly as she murmured:

'I'm sorry, beta, I didn't mean to hit you . . . I didn't mean to . . . '

∽

A painful memory of another such day has also never left my mind: I'm dressed in my freshly ironed uniform, polished boots, and laces tied into perfect knots, all set to go to school. As I hear the tonga in the gully, I run to the veranda to say bye to my parents, but stop outside their room. I hear voices inside, voices of my parents, fighting. Then, suddenly, there's the sound of something breaking, and I hear my Mama crying . . . Standing outside, I too start to cry.

At the corner of the gully the tongawallah calls out for Didi and me. Didi is at the gate with her books and her bag, looking back. 'Deepi, come!' But I refuse to go to school. My grandmother, who was alive then, tells Mai Sardi, 'Tell Dharampal to carry on without the girls, they won't go to school today.' Didi turns back from the gate. I crawl up the dark staircase in front of my parents' room that leads to nowhere, and crouch in the corner against the locked door, sobbing.

I remain there for a long time, my sobs turning to hiccups. Eventually it is Mai Sardi who rescues me from my hideout, carries me down and takes me to the kitchen where I cling to her for a long time. Finally, my grandmother puts my head in her lap and consoles me.

∽

There is yet another memory, from when I'm around six years old, which tarnishes my dream-like recollections of our summer holidays in the mountains. It's a memory of my father grinding his teeth while tying his shoelaces as he hisses the words, 'I'm leaving! I'm leaving!' Mama sits on the side of the bed in silence, looking vulnerable and distraught. Didi and I stand at the door watching, fearful of the expression on my father's face. I've never known a more intense feeling of insecurity than a man angrily putting on his shoes, wanting to leave. Here, memory fails me ... the frame freezes. I cannot recollect what happened next.

These hostile exchanges between my mother and father never let me feel completely secure in any relationship later in my life. These were the earliest cracks in my picture-perfect life; the image of something perfect, and yet not meant to last.

Although I had seen these few signs during my early childhood, it did still come as a shock when my parents eventually decided to separate, and that too, ironically, much later in their life. Their separation has been the biggest trauma for me. Two people who came together in their twenties to share a dream, and in their seventies realized it wasn't meant to be ... This is a fact that has been the biggest fiction of my life! I still haven't been able to come to terms with it, and still keep trying to bring them together ... even in death.

∽

Besides the few and far between disturbing encounters between my parents, the other most traumatic incidents of my pre-teen years both involved my mother. I remember the day I nearly lost her. When I returned from school that day, Mama was not at her easel as usual. She was inside her room, lying on the bed, looking frightfully shaken. The expression on her face was one I'd never seen before. She looked at Didi and I as though she had not expected to lay eyes on her girls again. We knew something terrible had happened.

It was late afternoon and Mama had a whole lot of things to get done. The papers for India Metal Works needed to be sent out by the end of the day. The women from the Women's Conference were to meet up at the Chandraavali house that evening and her clothes weren't ready. She scribbled a list of veggies that needed to be bought for meals that day on a piece of paper and handed it to Jeet. Then she pulled out a sari, switched on the iron, and spread a white sheet on the writing table, on which she intended to iron her sari. As soon as she picked up the iron, she was jolted back with a powerful electric current. She shrieked and fell to the ground, her entire body convulsing madly. It was the iron! She tried to throw the iron away but couldn't. It was crazy! She couldn't unclutch her fingers, the damn thing was stuck to her hand.

Jeet had but a minute ago stepped out with her thaela to buy vegetables. No one was around. The gully was empty, the mochi boys having gone to Hall Gate to shine shoes in the great June heat. Pigeons fluttered across the windows on the first floor. Piti was away at college; Didi and I were at school. Even the Sharmas on the first floor, who were forever peeping from their windows and keeping a tab on the goings-on in this household, had gone to Gurdaspur.

Fortunately, very fortunately, Jeet hadn't gone very far, when she heard shrieks from inside the house. It was her Phabiji! Horrified, she ran back home, scrambling through the phaatak which she'd once again left open despite Mama telling her a zillion times to lock it behind her when stepping out . . . and thank God for that!

The sight that met her eyes on the veranda freaked her out. Mama's whole body was twitching on the floor, the iron stuck to her hand, 350 volts of electricity passing through her.

'PHABIJI! PHABIJI!!!' Jeet shouted and ran towards Mama.

'NOOOOO!!!!' Somehow Mama managed to retain her presence of mind and waved Jeet back.

'TURN THE SWITCH OFF!' Mama's voice quavered.

In her panic, and given the tremulousness of Mama's voice, Jeet could hardly make out what Mama was trying to say.

'PULL the PLUG AAOOUUT!' Mama screeched. Jeet lunged towards Mama again in a state of panic.

'NO DOOON'T! . . . DON'T TOUCH MEEEE . . . STAY AWAAAY! THE CURRENT WILL GET YOOOU TOOOO . . .!

The words that came out of Mama's mouth were nothing more than a caterwaul.

'PHABIJI! . . . . PHABIJI!!!'

By now a few of the mochi women had gathered at the gate. They stood huddled together in utter shock—from where they stood they could see Jeet running around as if crazed, and my mother on the floor, thrashing her limbs, convulsing in seizure.

Her face streaked with tears, Jeet scurried around for leather, the one thing that could save her Phabiji, but in her confusion she couldn't find anything. Mama's whole body shivered crazily on the veranda floor, but she hadn't lost her presence of mind.

'THE PLUUUUG, FOR GOD'S SAKE!!!! PULL THE PLUG AAOOUT!' Mama's arm was jerkily pointing to the corner.

'PULL IT AAAOOOUT ... FROM THE WA ... AAA ... LLLL!!!!'

Jeet finally focused. She dropped the shoe she had picked up and dashed for the switchboard. Current or no current, she clutched at the black plug and with sudden manic force yanked it off the wall, and finally broke down. Drenched in sweat, Mama rolled on the floor, her head pulsating with pain. The iron toppled from her open palm and rolled over ...

When Didi and I returned from school that day Mama's eyes brimmed over with joy. She pulled us close to her on either side of the bed. She was too weak to lift herself up and hug us. Her head lay limp on the pillow. Jeet was at her feet, pressing her legs, still wheezing.

'I would have gone today,' my mother murmured as she held us tight, in a long, long hug.

'You may not have seen me alive ...' Her voice choked at the thought of losing all that she had in her life. Both Didi and I clung to her. Piti appeared at the door with a paper bag in his hands.

'Deepi, beta, take this ... feed your Mama some fruit, will you?' My father looked really shaken. That whole evening, I sat at my mother's bedside slowly feeding her grapes. If Jeet had not forgotten to bolt that door behind her ...

∽

The other incident that involved my mother wasn't one single incident but a traumatic time Mama went through after several of her children died just after childbirth. After Didi and I, my mother had given birth to three offspring, but none of them survived. The babies hardly made it out of hospital. They all died of the same thing—afaara—distension. There was Sunny, two years younger than me, who survived for eight months, but then surrendered to the condition and died at home, leaving my mother completely distraught. For days Mama continued to be unwell. She would remain depressed, sitting quietly by herself on the wicker chair in the veranda. Then came Baby, a girl, but she lived just a day or two. After that, a boy named Raju.

During Raju's birth, I remember my mother being taken to the hospital for her delivery. I was a little over five then. It was evening. I sat on the staircase outside Mama's room and watched my father, with the help of Mai Sardi and Raj Aunty, get Mama into an ambulance on the street. Then I remember some rejoicing when we heard of the arrival of a baby boy. My father returned home with a packet of mithai. Now my mother would return home any day, I was anxious. But very quickly it all became quiet again. I couldn't understand what was happening. Didi and I would huddle together a lot during this time. No one spoke much about the newborn baby. Piti would quietly return from the hospital and not say a word. It was at this time, that I wrote a note to my mother and asked Piti to give it to her in the hospital. I remember I sat on the dark staircase and wrote in my neatest handwriting:

'I miss you, Mama ... Please don't give all your love to the new baby ... Save forty kisses for me!'

We waited for Mama to come back home with our little brother, but little Raju never made it out of the hospital either. Mama returned home empty-handed. A gloom fell over the house once again. That night, when my mother retired to the terrace in her extremely frail condition, I sat looking at her without saying a word, waiting for her to hug me, unable at that age to fathom my mother's loss. I wanted to sleep next to her on the bed but Piti dissuaded me, saying that Mama was very weak and needed complete rest. Mama moved her head, and with a tired gesture of her hand, called me closer. Piti drew my cot next to hers. That whole night I slept with my two fingers placed on my Mama's bed. She lay that night on her bed under the open sky, her eyes full of fever. The moon shifted behind the dark clouds and stayed there a long time. A street lamp turned the dark dome of the mosque a dull yellow. The sound of dholak emanating from the gully faded into silence. How vivid is that night in my memory ...

∽

To my mind, of all the children she lost, Mama probably was most broken

Little Sunny in Mama's arms.

by the loss of Sunny as she was allowed to have him with her for a while before he was snatched away. It was Sunny's death that Mama would narrate to me for years after he was gone. My brother's tragic death played out in my mind over and over again until finally one day I sat down to write a quasi-fictional recreation of the great loss that had afflicted our family.

Those were days of scorching heat. The August air stood sweltering over a dry, parched chunk of earth. The park was flooded with people, fidgety, restless!

Mama had taken Sunny out for a stroll to the Company Bagh along with Mai Sardi. All of a sudden everything became still, the sounds in the park, the pace of people walking. Then something in the sky stirred. A sharp wind started blowing dust around. The sky changed colour; from a blue grey it suddenly turned a deep orange. A great swirl of dust rose from the earth, rising towards the sky.

'Nheri aayi! . . . Nheri aayi!'

People began running helter-skelter. My mother told Mai Sardi to watch over Sunny while she tried to hitch a tonga ride back home. The wind blew hard, then harder. Everywhere there was chaos! Mai Sardi was nowhere to be seen. When Mama turned back to look for Sunny, she saw a strange sight.

A strange woman was bent over the pram in which Sunny lay, making bizarre gestures, hissing words that were incoherent, her hair and fingers dangling over the baby boy. Mama ran towards Sunny and shooed the woman away just in time, but perhaps it was too late. The spell had already been cast.

'From that day onwards,' said Mama, 'Sunny was not able to breathe properly any more.' The doctors tried assiduously to keep the baby's abdomen from filling up with wind and getting bloated. The child would cry every night in his mother's arms while the mochis played their dholak and sang till late into the night, their music shrouding the baby's hissing cries of pain.

This was Sunny's last day with us. Mama paced the length of the veranda holding her baby in her arms, trying to put him back to sleep. 'Hush - a - by - b a b y ... on the tree top ... when the wind b l o w s ... the cradle will rock ... when the bough b r e a k s ... the cradle will drop! ... down come b a e ... ae ... be ... cradle and all,' she sang, her own voice a broken whisper.

Later, in the vehra, Piti held Sunny in his arms and pointed towards the terrace. 'Look beta, this is your house, you are at home with your parents ...'

Bauji hurriedly fixed his pagdi and reached for his walking stick. His foot tripped over the drain as he rushed out of the gate with the doctor's parchi in his hand. The mochi boys peering inside the house through the slit in the phaatak, dispersed quickly, then returned to peer in again. Bauji had not remembered to carry his umbrella and it had started to drizzle again.

Outside the gate he saw no rickshaw. It was dark and the shops had already closed down. He walked up to Hall Bazaar and stood in the middle of the chowk frantically looking all around, but saw nothing. Dr Bhandari had asked for medicines that were not going to be easy to find at this time.

Bauji thought of his little grandson in the house struggling for breath. His eyes filled up. He swallowed, looked at the slip of paper in his hand. Which shop will be open now? Where would he find the medicine that could save his grandson?

At the crossroad, he stood helpless ... and prayed to God: 'Rab, mainu das, main kehre raste jaavaan?' (Tell me, O God, in which direction should I go?)

An agonizing pain rose in his chest. 'Hey Prabhu!'

'That night Sunny died in my arms,' Mama recalled. 'His tiny limbs were burning with fever. His eyes had been looking up at me as if asking: "Can't you help me, Mama? Can't you save me?"

'That expression on his face I can never forget. It was like he knew— he knew he was going to die and he was scared. I couldn't bear it, that look of his. He was pleading with his eyes for his life. He could not speak; he was only eight months old ... and breathless! But his eyes were fixed on my face as the sun went down and night came. That look in his eyes haunts me till today: "Can't you help me, Mama? ... Can you not save me?"

'In the veranda, your father had closed his eyes—"Jaap karo ..." he said. I picked up the maala after Sunny's death, then I never gave up the Gayatri mantra da jaap. His death gave me a lot of strength. I came to know how much suffering I was capable of!'

∽

From this point in the narrative, every time I have tried to recreate Sunny's death in my mind, I have somehow only been able to see it from the other side.

It was 6.30 in the evening when Sunny's eyes finally closed to the world, his little soul rising ... rising above the shadowy pillars of the veranda, above the blue-green painted windows of the Green Room, above the open-to-the-sky fireplace on the first terrace.

Lightly it moved beyond the barsati, passing by the tin shed, wafting feather-like around the white dome of the mosque, its four minarets and beyond ...

Higher, higher above the gully, the mochi mohalla, where he could see the walled city speckled with lights, the sky engulfing it; the wet earth below turning to a mere shimmer ...

Sunny could see it all now with clarity—his mother and father turned into tiny specks on earth . . .

Eight months of breathlessness ... eight months of a beautiful woman's warm bosom to bury his tiny face into—all sensations he carries now through the enormous sky.

It was a night of shifting shadows. A bat flew low between the cowshed and the veranda. Mama touched her son's body. It was cold. The fever was gone. Life was gone out of him. The pain had ended. His face now appeared peaceful, calm.

Sunny felt lifted—swept through a white fog ... it's cool ... cool ... tingling! The wetness of the white poultice across his forehead no longer made him cry. He loved it, this new feeling of being tossed and thrown on this white foam. He danced about in the clouds, skidding on the unreal whiteness; a white mist that soothed and tingled him ... a breeze that drove the pores of his bodiless being wide open. The winds swept him sideways and upside down, drowning him in this blinding whiteness. Sunny giggled ... and a soundless ripple ran through the clouds. And then he was swept beyond! Beyond even the clouds ... He now saw a pitch-black expanse studded with bright sparkles of light. He was enchanted by the radiance, and he wanted it. He so wanted it. These were the very stars he had seen from the veranda looking up from his mother's arms. He'd seen these tiny flickering lights in the sky ... a sky endlessly fascinating, that had been far, far from his reach, but now it was here, so near to him, just fingertips away! It was all around him, as he was being swept away towards the brilliance!

Beneath him, a woman's heart-wrenching wail echoed in the universe. Mama stood in the vehra of the house, a shriek trapped within her. A shriek only her son could hear ...And he looked back, smiling.

'Don't cry for me, Mama, I'm happy now! Look, the pain is gone ... I'm HAPPY!'

Then her legs gave way. She buried her face in her son's cold, still body and sank to the floor.

Sunny laughed! By now he had moved beyond ... he had become part of the glow in the sky, was one with the brilliance, leaving behind on his last journey the echo of a woman who'd been, for eight good months, his mother on earth.

∽

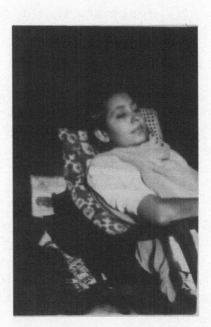

I also imagine an evening days after Sunny's death—I'm sitting at one end of the vehra, and Mama is on the swing, gently swaying. A bat flies low in the dimly lit cowshed, but Mama remains unmoved by it. She is softly singing under her breath:

> *Hush - a - bye - baby . . . up in the sky . . . on a soft*
> *cloud . . . it's easy to fly . . . when the clouds burst . . . the*
> *raindrops will fall . . . and down will come baby . . .*
> *to mother once more . . .*

Outside, in the empty street, little boys in red, dressed as langurs, pass by, beating on drums . . .

16

My Imaginary World

That which actually happens, is real, and that which happens only in the mind, what would we call it—reality, or fiction? How do we decide?

The line between the real and my imaginary world had always been blurred. It all started with my visualizing Sunny's death, but happier images soon surfaced—my imaginary world was coming alive. It was there, for real, for me to live in ...

If I was a timid child, I was unaware of it. In my mind I was having all kinds of adventures; stories I would weave around me and start to believe were part of my life. Like children anywhere in the world, I'd often fall prey to my fantasies. For instance, I believed that the little yellow house down by the railway signal, just ten feet away from the train tracks, was a house we once lived in. I knew that because Mama had told me as much.

Many seasons were spent imagining what my life had been in that house, with the trains passing by every now and then—pink trains that came whistling, puffing frosty white smoke clouds, the signals turning from yellow to red, red to green, just beyond our courtyard. I happily held on to this belief until one night, while crossing over Bhandari Bridge and gazing at the tracks, I casually said to Mama, 'That's the house na, Mama, where we used to live?' My mother looked at me, most astounded. 'Whatever gave you that idea, my dear?' Now I looked at her astonished. 'You did. Mama, *you* told me that we used to live in that little hut before we moved into the big house?'

'No ... when did I ever ... No, no, we *never* lived there, Beta, why would we live by the train track?' That evening I felt short-changed by life.

From that point onwards, my mother worried about me. She could never understand her younger daughter's mental environment. My sudden statements perplexed her. She did not know what to make of them. Was the girl dreaming? Did she not realize the difference between reality and dream? She would worry. I saw her catch up with my father. Piti looked back at me, a gesture that made me somewhat uncomfortable, and I felt my toes curling in.

Slowly, but surely, my splendid phantoms were clouding the real world around me. What was real and what was *all in my mind* was now creating confusion. But there was freedom in this fusion, and I let it be that way— as long as the powder pink trains, puffing frosty white clouds of smoke, went gliding by, feather-like, soundless on water tracks ... I was happy!

Later, as my world grew, I would go on to make Bebbe, an avatar of the real Bae, (Mohni's grandmother, living at the corner of our street) part of my life, owning her as much as I did the little yellow house besides the railway track. And Bebbe, to date, remains a part of me ... as the following story about this fictional character shows. This is how I always imagined her ...

Bebbe sat on the terrace of the Chandraavali house, at its outermost corner, from where she could see children playing on other terraces, rickshaws pulling in and out of the bazaar, and Shahni's buffaloes returning home at dusk. Once in a while she'd move her hands to fix the shawl over her head and take off her eyeglasses to wipe them with the corner of her dupatta. Until the sun went down and there was light enough to see, Bebbe sat and watched life beneath.

After dark when she couldn't see the world in the diminishing light, she would turn inwards and shift her gaze across the chhajja towards the yellow street lamps flickering in the deserted lanes of Katra Sher Singh. Once the electric bulbs lit up in the small, dingy shops, she'd then lift her legs off the ledge, one at a time, and step her way down to see life at close quarters.

Slowly she slipped inside her brown velvet quilt, dotted with yellow flowers. It had started to drizzle silently. Outside the wet square balcony of her room, she could see the empty street, where Phaa danced about his shadow under the yellow lamp post. The mochis in their labyrinthine world played on the dholak and manjira till late into the night. Short gusts of wind swept the dark terraces.

Bebbe in her sanctitude grew more and more clairvoyant. She could see things others could not, things beyond anyone else. That Bebbe, in her solitude, was growing stranger with every passing season, didn't seem to bother anyone around. They were too consumed with their own little lives. As long as she sat on top of the roof and kept a watch over the world, they felt safe and content.

I'd mostly see my Bebbe bundled up and perched on the edge of the roof where if she fell to her right, she'd probably drop into the water tub where the buffaloes drank and would most likely be rushed straight to the maseet to be purified. And if she fell to her left, the bazaarwallahs would hurl her towards Regent Talkies Chowk to put her on a handcart and be rushed to V. J. Hospital where she would, after exasperating everyone around, die before they could help. But she'd never leave the gully.

She would instead, turn into a dry autumn leaf, or spread out on a frayed yellow plot, and thus on stormy dusky evenings, when short gusts of wind began to howl, she would fly about the gully like a thin paper sheet, turning round and round in the wind like a song...

∽

Coming back to the real Bae . . .

It was wintertime, the winter of 1960, when Mohni's grandmother, Bae, met her tragic end.

'Bae dig pai! . . . Bae dig pai!' (Bae has fallen!)

A strange murmur started late one night at the far corner of the street. From our terrace we heard desperate, muffled voices from the gully below. Mama woke up first with some unease and looked over the ledge. It took her a while to figure out where the sounds were coming from. In the dark she saw a few people gathered around the street in front of the tabela; something unforeseen and unfortunate seemed to have happened. She woke up Pitaji. I remember waking up at that odd hour and seeing my parents standing at the chhajja considering the street below. A window opened in Raj Aunty's house and then her voice came from her silhouette.

'Bae-ji . . . Accident!'

That's all that comes to my memory of that fatal night. The rest of the details trickled in later.

The night was cold and wintry. The clock of Hall Gate struck 3 a.m.

In the Hammer-wali gully, Sardarilal woke up in the wee hours of the morning to give water to his buffaloes. His son Roopa also came along to the dairy. It was still dark and drizzling lightly. He milked the buffaloes, collected the fodder, and went off to sell the milk on his bicycle. Sardarilal saw in the dark, a figure sitting on the road beside the fallen body of Bae. He came closer to discover that she was dead. The man sitting next to her body was a faqir, a beggar who was passing by in the night. He heard the woman on the road crying for water. The woman lying on the street cried, 'I'm dying ... I'm dying ... give me water ...' He filled the karmandal, his black pot with water from outside Dogra's salon and poured it in her mouth. Then he kept sitting beside her. Sardarilal asked the faqir, 'What have you done? You have *killed* her?' The beggar saint looked up incredulously.

'She fell from the top ... in front of me ... I knocked endlessly on the door of this house, but no one came out.'

At 4 o'clock in the morning, Mohni's maternal uncle was called from Model Town. The family came down. The whole bazaar gathered. When Mohni's mother arrived on the scene, she was devastated seeing her mother lying dead on the road. Her shrieks muffled the notes of the first azaan.

No post-mortem was done. Bae was cremated at the Durgiana Mandir crematorium near Haathi Gate after being bathed in the passage at the entrance of her house below the staircase.

The story of Bae's fall quickly started doing the rounds. It was the day the Punjab University results came out. Sudhakar, Munni's older brother, had failed again while Mohni had passed with high merit. He came first in all of Punjab. Bae, his nani, went out in the bazaar bragging about her grandson's outstanding distinction and picked a fight with Sudhakar. 'You have failed for the *fifth* time, and look at my grandson!' She flew in his face. 'He has stood first in the *whole* of Punjab!'

Mohni was in the bazaar being congratulated by one and all when he came to know that Bae had humiliated Sudhakar badly. When he returned home, he confronted her. 'Bae, why did you insult Sudhakar?' Bae justified herself. A huge war of words broke out between Mohni and his grandmother. It turned into an ugly spat. Mohni lost control of himself. His anger was beyond him. 'I'm leaving! You are *never* going to see my face again!' he screamed and stormed out of the house.

There were several versions that floated around after this incident, and for months on end. No one knew anything for certain, it was all hearsay. Mohni never uttered a word about the circumstances of his grandmother's death.

For days I sat quietly on the terrace wondering if along with Bae, my Bebbe would also now be gone.

∽

In my mind, Bebbe's death happened a little differently.

Bebbe fell like gossamer, not a sound, just a faint, far echo. A muffled blob of old flesh and bones made a low thud—slowly, lightly, floating down like a white chiffon dupatta that slips off the clothesline. Feather-like, she fell in the empty street, wet from a night of rain. Tossed onto the ground, her brittle bones in a sack of old, shrivelled flesh, created a silent splash as the jute doll thudded, bounced lightly, and then lay still, forever.

Had Bebbe fallen from the rooftop and died in pain? Or had she met her end peacefully, in her sleep? I got up and looked over the edge; nothing there. Bebbe must be fast asleep or in a delirium. I knocked on her door. No answer. I banged again on that creaky wooden door when finally, with my pushing it slightly, something inside clicked and the bolt slipped open. Slowly I entered the room, and called for her.

'Bebbe . . .' I whispered.

Bebbe was lying among her chandeliers, still, and without life, wrapped in her pink and orange phulkari . . . and her eyes were open, forever.

Who was Bebbe in my mind, I've failed to analyse. In many ways, Bebbe is me, the writer, looking back at life, living in her inner world, keeping vigil over memories . . .

∽

Many years later, when I woke up in the middle of the night, and walked across the barsati in the drizzle, I saw her. There, standing at the edge of the rooftop was a figure of a young woman, clad in pale pink phulkari.

I stood, gazing . . .

'Bebbe . . .' I whispered.

Bebbe slowly turned her radiant face towards me and smiled. The night drizzled on . . .

17

My Brother Gugu

Unarguably, the biggest event of my pre-teen years was the arrival of my baby brother. It was September of 1960. I was eight, and Didi, ten. We received news from the hospital that Mama had given birth to a baby boy. After the loss of three of their offspring, my father was not taking any chances—Mama was taken to Delhi for her delivery. About a year earlier, Krishna Chachi next door persuaded my mother to go to Bawa Lalji's temple in Dhianpur to make a wish for a son. That mannat had finally been granted.

Tring! Tring!

The phone trilled. Someone picked it up, had a loud and ecstatic conversation, and then informed the rest of us that Mama was returning by the Flying Mail with our newborn baby brother, for whom Piti had chosen a Russian sounding name, 'Rohitaashv'. I loved the sound of the name and preferred spelling it with a double 'a', making it phonetically more appealing; Rohitaashv, meaning 'Bright Hope'. But we didn't call him by that name for long. We all ended up calling him Gugu, or at times, Gigi or Gigu, but seldom Rohitaashv. As I have grumbled earlier, this is an irritating cultural trait in the north of India, where a perfectly grand, majestic name is mangled and distorted until it eventually stands for nothing.

So Gugu, as we'd lovingly call him, was making his grand entry into our lives. Didi and I were excited beyond belief. Raj Aunty upstairs, along with her daughters Baby and Shobha, Munni, Shahni from the

dairy, Krishna Chachiji, all came over to the house. We girls got dressed in our best clothes, braided our hair in two plaits, threaded ribbons through them, and went to the railway station to receive Mama and her newborn.

As soon as I lay eyes on our little brother, I knew Rohitaashv was the most gorgeous looking baby in the whole world. When Mama walked through the phaatak into the house, she was delighted by the reception awaiting her. We girls had flowered the pathway which went right from the gate all the way up to her room on which she'd walk holding our little brother.

In the days and weeks that followed, our baby brother became the centre of our lives. So enamoured were we of him that during the hour-long recess in school, we'd cycle all the way back home just to catch a glimpse of him. After hurriedly gulping down whatever packed lunch we carried, both Didi and I would rush home. This became a sort of a routine. As soon as the recess bell went off, we'd dart towards the cycle stand, whisk our bicycle out—me jumping on to the back seat—and off we'd go, peddle-peddle-peddle, all the way from school to home in exactly twenty minutes.

Gugu would be a delight to behold; an endearing little bundle with sparkling eyes lying in the sunlit veranda under a sky-blue net. He'd start smiling as soon as he caught sight of both of us ... Uff! We'd fuss over him for a few moments—quickly lift the net, plant kisses on both his

Didi, Gugu, and I.

cheeks, then just as swiftly, before Mama came out of the kitchen hearing our voices, surprised to suddenly find us home in the middle of a school day, we'd rush off again, peddling furiously in the great summer heat. We somehow always made it back in time just as the end-of-recess bell went off.

Nehar outing with Gugu and Gyaniji.

Though Gugu was generally a happy, well-behaved baby, he did manage to surprise us at times. On one of our Sunday nehar outings, when Gugu was still small, he jumped into the nehar along with us girls. Suddenly, we noticed that Gugu had disappeared from the edge of the canal where he'd been sitting just a few seconds ago, giggling as he watched us girls splashing about in the water. We all panicked. Didi instinctively plunged her hands into the water and pulled Gugu out by the collar. I still remember the relief on my parents' face when they saw our little brother emerging from the water, face down, his collar in Didi's hand, yellow mangoes floating away from the overturned bucket in the water.

∽

Another evening, as I was in my room ironing my school uniform, Mama came in carrying my baby brother, and sat him down on top of the dining table. 'Keep an eye on him, Deepi,' she said and hurriedly walked away. Little Gugu sat on the dining table playing with a steel rod in his hands. I noticed that it was a pedal crank arm of a bicycle. He seemed quite content playing with the rod, and beamed at me every now and then, so I went back to humming and pressing down the pleats of my green uniform, until all of a sudden, the steel rod came flying across the room and hit me bang on my head! *Thhaa!* I staggered back, stunned. *What the HELL!* Holding my head with both my hands I swung around to give the brat a piece of my mind. So angry was I at Gugu, I could strangle him. But when I looked at his face, I saw my little brother clapping soundlessly, gurgling with laughter!

Whenever I remind Rohit of the incident, he says, 'Are you sure Chhoti Didi, it really happened? Because I don't remember that!'

'Well *I* do. Because *I'm* the one that got hit on the head!'

∽

Mama doted on Gugu, while Piti was more reserved with him. Predictably, he had great expectations from his son, just as he did from his daughters. At this time, as a rule, we were required to sleep for two hours in the afternoon. At 4.30 p.m. Gugu would get up from his nap and come sit at the small gate, dressed in a romper. This soon became a vantage point for him to watch the mochi boys play with marbles. At age five, all my little brother wanted were his own set of marbles, a wish that was fulfilled by Telu Ram, a servant in our house at the time. Telu Ram was a bit of a buffoon, a cockeyed, scrawny Pahadi man, who had protruding ears, a drooping moustache, and deep crevices around his mouth. He was deeply affectionate towards my brother and would sometimes win marbles for him. Gugu would hide them from our parents in the dark staircase across their room.

Knowing of her son's fascination with the little iridescent glass bantae, Mama allowed Chetya and Mooseya, two mochi boys around the same age as Gugu, to come inside the house and play marbles with her son. She gave Gogi, Raj Aunty's son, a rupee, and sent him off to buy twenty marbles. The boys would then play in the soft mud patch in the vehra.

Summers were soon reserved for marbles. The rules for the marble game were simple. Kholi, a hole, would be dug in the soft ground, the maata. You throw eight marbles towards this hole. If three go into the kholi, the balance of marbles remaining would be five. Gugu would say, 'Neele vaale noon nishana lagao.' (Target the blue one!) If Gogi could hit the blue marble after touching it to his lips, 'shoo karke', then all the marbles would go to him. If not, all five go to Gugu.

Gogi was an absolute master at the game and had, in fact, kept three Dalda tins full of marbles collected over all his childhood years. He kept these with him until his death in 2006.

That summer, the marble games almost came to an abrupt end, just as soon as they'd begun. Gugu had lost three marbles and, out of sheer frustration, he uttered a Punjabi abuse that he'd recently picked up:

'*Maaaaaeeeen ...!*'

Mama heard that. She didn't see left or right and gave four–five tight slaps across Gugu's face. The mochi kids were barred entry into the house. Forever!

Next summer, playing marbles with the mochi boys was a thing of the past but Gugu and Gogi found a way out of the situation. This time Gogi took my little brother upstairs to his home. They made a hole in the ground in Gogi's bathroom for playing marbles during those hot, hot summer days. Chaee, the Sardar boy, was their partner in crime.

When Piti wished to see Gugu, he'd clap for his son to come down. One day, when he didn't come down for some time, my father went

upstairs to Gogi's house in search of him. And sure enough, he caught
Gugu and Gogi playing marbles in the bathroom. He was livid seeing
his son with bantae in his hand. He asked Mama, 'Why did you give
him two rupees for marbles? What life is he going to make for himself
playing these damn marbles?' There was a fight in the house that day.
Didi and I looked on. Mama finally cried.

∞

The season changed. Spring was in the air . . . kites soared in the clear blue
sky. Glassy strings criss-crossed overhead. Hall Bazaar was buzzing with
villagers streaming into the city for the big mela, wives and children in
tow. A man was carrying a baby in yellow on his left shoulder, and on the
right a jumbo size transistor, blaring. The radio sang on . . . songs of Basant
resounded everywhere . . .

> *Yeh duniya patang, nit badle yeh rang,*
> *koi jaane na udaane vaala kaun hai!*

I loved a sky filled with kites and I loved the song, the deeper meaning
of the words . . . the metaphor of kite for the transience of this world,
and, uncertainty of life and death, which is not in our hands . . . Happily
I skipped along the pavement, checking my reflection in glass windows,
when I saw the tall, statuesque figure of a Jat, clad in a white lungi-kurta
and an enormous white turban on his head, striding down the street, his
face framed by the red arch of Hall Gate. What magnificent statures some
of these Jats have! I slowed down my pace, admiring this Greek god-like
apparition gliding towards me in slow motion. Then as we crossed each
other, me gazing up at him almost in a trance, the man suddenly spewed
out paan peek, and there I was, standing in the middle of the bazaar,
streaks of red spittle dribbling down my face. '*Blooddy* . . . *JJJJ* . . . *JATTT!'*

Disgusted, I darted home in tears, and ducked my face under the
tap in the vehra, hissing, '*I will* . . . *I will* . . .!' Didi, watching me from the
kitchen burst out laughing! 'Someone *spat* on your face? There's your
reality check!'

Basant time meant kite-flying, and this season my little brother insisted
on flying a kite. He went up to Gogi's terrace. Four annas would get
him four to six kites. Two rupees, and he'd get one gitth dor (length of

string) at Dwarka's shop. Once Gogi taught him how to string a kite, kite-flying became my little brother's new obsession. He'd managed to find a mentor in Gogi, who seemed to be a connoisseur in the art of flying kites. Gogi was my age and Gugu was by now six years old. Both Gugu and Gogi would go to the uppermost terrace of Gogi's house, stand on the absolute edge of the rooftop and fly their kites. Seeing the two boys so dangerously close to the edge, Mama would panic.

'Gugu! ... Get *back*! Get *away* from that edge, you both! *Get away at once!*'

The dor would run short and Gugu's kite would get cut off by the mochis' kite who'd tie little stones on strings and throw them up to cut their kites.

'*AAAAAEEEEE ... BOOOOWWW!*'

Gugu would get very upset at this and end up putting the entire blame on Gogi. 'Gogi ne meri guddi bo karaa ditti.' (Gogi has made me lose my kite!) and he'd walk away in a huff.

Speaking of his kite-flying days in Amritsar, Gugu once narrated to me this little incident:

'One day, when a ten-rupee note dropped out of Mama's cupboard, I quietly took it to Dwarka's shop and bought kites. I hid them on top of the dark stairs in the veranda but felt very guilty about my actions. Later, the presswallah's son also stole money from his home, bought lots of kites and came and hid them with me. They were kept under our stairs without anyone knowing. I had sensed that the boy was doing something wrong as well and that kept me on edge for that whole season.

'There was an elderly Sardar at the end of the gully opposite Gyaan Halwai, I don't think you ever noticed him. He was extremely skilled in kite-flying and I was very impressed with him too. I remember the Sardar's kites had "Chartered Bank" written all over them. He used a very curious technique to win over his young opponents. He would just hold the dor and stay very still. When another kite came to cut him off, he'd tug at his string a wee bit, and the other kite would instantly snap off and swiftly go down, nodding in the breeze, to the excited shrieks of: "*KAATAAAAA ... BOOOWWW ... !*"

'It was the Sardar that I lost my kites to, the ones I'd bought from Mama's ten rupees. And, believe me, rather than feeling upset, I actually felt a great relief at losing those kites! Good riddance, I thought.'

∞

Once when we girls wanted to go and see a film and asked for our mother's permission. Mama said yes, but on one condition. Gugu would go with us. He was seven. We were amused, but since we had nothing to hide, we happily let him escort us.

We were all sitting in the theatre enjoying the film, giggling, laughing, crying—all emotions the film evoked. During the interval, we decided that since Gugu was our escort for the day, he should be the one to buy us ice cream. Gugu quietly got up from his seat and went out. The interval was over, the film restarted but Gugu did not show up, nor did the ice creams. Didi, now worried, got up to look for him and found him standing at the door in the dark, looking terribly upset. 'What happened, Gugu? Why are you so upset?' He lowered his eyes and in the most heart wrenching tone, said, 'I don't have enough money to buy ice cream for all you Didis!' Didi hugged him. For the rest of the evening, we all ended up fussing over our little brother.

Gugu and Didi

Gugu had taken his role as our escort rather seriously. Another time, another film, and at the end of the show, walking across Bhandari Bridge, we were animatedly discussing the story of the film. There were some boys following us that only Gugu had noticed. He sulked all the way back home. When Mama asked him how it went, Gugu instantly blurted, 'Mama, you know what! There were boys following them, and all the Didis ... Chhoti Didi, Badi Didi, Munni Didi, Nonu Didi, Pemu Didi—all of them were giggling away on the street! Shamelessly!' What was normal for us was somehow inappropriate behaviour in the eyes of our little brother.

∞

When he was around six, Gugu and I brought home a bird. We'd found her displayed in a cage off the pavement in Guru Bazaar one hot summer afternoon. We were captivated. She was a beautiful bird; red feathers speckled with yellow and black dots. We decided to call her Bandhani, after the chunnis that the mochi women wore.

Bandhani was placed in a cage, hung in the veranda of the house. We'd decided she was a *she*, a female bird, though we had no clue how to figure that out. We both grew very fond of her. We'd bring her food, take turns cleaning the cage, pull the cage inside when it started to drizzle or when there were signs of a dust storm. I'd put my fingers inside the cage and touch her soft feathers, petting her gently. After school we'd run up to the cage to spend quality time with Bandhani.

I don't remember what season it was, could be summer, when the family had gone out for days together. On our return, both Gugu and I ran to the veranda wanting to be the first ones to look at Bandhani. When we swung the cage in excitement, Bandhani did not move. She did not flutter her wings in response. To our horror, we found that Bandhani had been pawed at by the wretched cat. She now lay in the cage, completely still.

My little brother and I were heartbroken. We sat on the steps of the veranda for a very long time, the cage in my lap. Mama didn't say a word. She thought it best to let us be silent in mourning. As the sun went down and the shadow of the mosque stretched across the yellow wall, we dug up a part of good soft earth and buried our little birdie below the bougainvillea in the vehra. Then, we both wept.

∽

Gugu in Mama's arms, with Didi, Munni, and me.

I remember a cute little habit of Gugu that I still tease him about. During the Rakhi festival, there'd be a lot of fuss over the ceremony. After we sisters tied rakhis on our little brother, Mama would make Gugu hand over little envelopes filled with crisp five-rupee notes to both Didi and me. Our brother would walk around the whole morning, flashing the silver and gold tinsel flowers on his wrist, then by late afternoon, quietly come and hand the rakhis back to us, saying, 'Didi, here . . . take your rakhri. Now give me back my money!'

That's how adorable Gugu was, our little brother!

18

Piti Goes Abroad

In the year 1961 my father had the opportunity to go abroad for the first time. Didi was eleven, I was nine, and little Gugu was a year old. He was one of the ten people selected from India to go to the US for a Work Study Program. It happened at the behest of David Beynon, an official of the United Nations, who'd come to India at the invitation of the Lions Club. My father and Kapoor Singh Uncle, Secretary of the Lions Club, had both met Mr Beynon on the occasion of the UN Day Celebrations in Delhi. Because of his keen involvement in the Productivity Council, Piti was selected to participate in this program, and in the summer of 1961, he left for America. A photograph shows him with a garland of marigolds around his neck standing next to Mama.

∽

This was the year Lily Aunty came to live with us with her family and took over the Green Room. Our cousins, Pinky, Nidhi, Kaku, and Sanjay, were a couple of years younger to Didi and me and a year apart from each

Lily Aunty   *My cousins and I.*

other. Together, the six of us had, what I remember as, a riot of a time during the year my father was abroad.

Piti wrote to us regularly from America. Whenever the blue aerogrammes arrived, there'd be much excitement in the house. Both Didi and I received our much-awaited letters that we'd open with a lot of anticipation. We so wanted to know about Pitaji's new world out there. He sent us lovely picture postcards and wrote in detail about

Karya Jaanch: Kyoon Aur Kaise

the places he visited. The ones that had Mama's name on it, would read 'My darling Winnie ...' always, 'My darling Winnie' ... I loved the equation between my parents. It left me with a lot of tenderness, thinking about the bond between them. The earlier anxiety in their relationship seemed to have, with time, melted away. I felt good seeing Mama read the letters sitting on the wicker chair in the veranda in her sky-blue flannel dressing gown.

Soon after he returned from his tour to the US, Piti got down to writing a book called *Karya Jaanch: Kyoon Aur Kaise* and became the author of the first Asian-language

Piti with David Beynon and Kapoor Singh Uncle.   *Piti with Pandit Nehru.*

publication on a management technique called 'Work Study'. The book was
published by Vivek Publications, Amritsar. Tata Iron and Steel Company
bought 500 copies. He even received a letter of appreciation from Prime
Minister Pandit Jawaharlal Nehru, addressed to 'Dear Professor Naval'.
He always held that letter dear and even carried it with him to the US
when he emigrated. I'd always see the letter in a glass frame, hanging on
the wall of his study in Long Island.

Dear Professor Udaychandra Naval,

I have received your letter of July 5th with attached papers. I am
glad that you have written a book in Hindi on Work Study. I am
unable to find time to read this book but I have glanced through
it and it seems to me a very useful work, which ought to do good.
I hope many people will read it.

    For the last few years I have been much interested in the
subject of Work Study. We have been utilizing this method in
some of our Embassies as well as our Ministries in Delhi and
it has produced good results. I am sure that this approach is
profitable and, if generally adopted, will produce good results.

Yours sincerely,
Jawaharlal Nehru
Pahalgam (Kashmir)
July 10, 1962

∽

In 1962, when my father returned home after a year in America, he came bearing gifts for his family. Piti showed us the 8 mm films that he had shot of Syracuse, Washington, DC, and the countryside of upstate New York. There was footage of his trip to the Niagara Falls as well. All these places seemed so beautiful and magnificent—smooth wide roads lined with lovely houses on either side. It all looked so dreamy . . .

Family portrait at Dhruvji's studio, 1961.

The 8mm camera remained with us for many years and it recorded some interesting images of our growing years.

The first glimpses that I saw of myself on a moving camera were in those blurry 8mm images that we shot, moving about the house, and then repeatedly played them back to the camera's scratchy soundtrack. I see Mama painting at her easel, me in two braids wearing a brown sweater and blue-grey pinafore. As I get up from the bench in the foreground and step to the back, my skinny legs move out of frame. The camera shifts and zooms in and out on Gugu laughing in the vehra, perched on his baby cycle, and many more . . .

Piti also brought back from America a reel-to-reel Grundig tape recorder that was massive. It was a bulky grey, square piece of German technology that became an instant fascination for both Didi and me. There was a lot of excitement over the clunky German beauty. The family would fuss around the voice recorder; it was a time of great joy. We'd record our voices in it and then repeatedly hear them back, watching with awe, the thin glazed brown magnetic tape go round and round in two clear plastic spools. I was quite tickled by the sound of my own voice. I would have liked to sing in it, recite poems, do so many things, but was shy in front of everyone else. Mama did once sing a Juthika Roy bhajan that my father recorded; she had a beautiful voice. As we all went about the house living our lives, Jeet would quietly go and press the *Record* button. Later when it got played back, we'd all get embarrassed and die laughing.

I don't recall whatever happened to that film camera or the tape recorder later, but what those spools captured were pretty precious. We must have left them behind when the family emigrated to the US ten years later. If only I could have saved them, had them with me today, the laughter of all of us together—Mama, Piti, Didi, me, and the gurgling chuckles of little Gugu and his baby sounds—a record of a time that was never to come back the same way ever again.

SECTION IV

WARS AND REBELLIONS

19

An Unreal War

Up in the north, further north than the north we lived in, a war was being fought in the Himalayan region, the China war of 1962. I was ten. In October that year, China invaded India. It was the voice of Lotika Ratnam, the English newsreader on All India Radio, New Delhi, and Devki Nandan Pandey, her co-newsreader, that announced:

'WAR HAS BEEN DECLARED!'

India was taken unawares by what was supposed to be a brotherly neighbour. Even as he extolled the mantra of camaraderie, Hindi-Cheeni Bhai Bhai, the Chinese Premier Zhou Enlai betrayed our leader Pandit Nehru who had till then done his best to foster cordial ties with our neighbour.

On 21 November 1962, the Chinese declared ceasefire as they withdrew from the disputed area, but only after swallowing Aksai Chin, a large part of India's territory, and breaking the spirit of our Prime Minister, Jawaharlal Nehru. We took a great beating at the hands of China in that war. After losing Gilgit-Baltistan and Azad Kashmir to Pakistan in 1947, this was the third major loss of territory for India.

Though this was a war that happened during our times, it did not directly affect our lives. The main theatre of war was the northernmost region of Ladakh which, for us, was quite far away. That didn't stop us from speculating about what was going on and suddenly expressing opinions on all things Chinese, much of which was sadly just short of xenophobic.

I began to think of the Chinese as hostile aliens—small, narrow-eyed, unfathomable of speech, unpredictable of movement, and so on. I'd imagine small Chinese people scuttling over each other to build the Great Wall of China, scampering over the border, and overpowering our brave Indian soldiers like malevolent hornets. Stoking my paranoid fantasizing was the fact that there was very little I knew about the Chinese. The only thing that was recognizably Chinese in my home environment was a drawing book that Mama had in the house that contained ink sketches of Chinese landscapes. Mama loved those images because they reminded her of her childhood in Burma. I, too, liked the dreamlike drawings—trees and cliffs and clouds lying low in the valleys. However, this didn't help me gain any real insight into either the Chinese or the war. My schoolmates didn't know very much either, mainly because we weren't taught much about cultures of the world. The only things we studied were British empire and the history of the Mughal empire and, to put it bluntly, we had no world view—our ignorance was boundless. All we knew at the time was the Chinese were the bad guys and therefore needed to be slammed.

Confusing my patriotic wrath was the fact that I did actually know a Chinese man, perhaps the only one in the city of Amritsar. We'd frequently visit his store across Bhandari Bridge, a small Chinese shoe shop. Apart from the Bata shoes that I wore to school, I had shoes made by this Chinese shoemaker on Cooper Road. He was the humblest person I'd ever known. Unlike the Punjabi men around me, he was a gentle soul. There was nothing else Chinese that I knew. Except perhaps for the china crockery stacked in the dining room cupboard.

And then, as abruptly as it had begun, the unreal war came to an end. Our lives went on as before. But what emerged out of the war for posterity and for all times to come was an unforgettable patriotic song:

Eh mere watan ke logo, zara aankh mein bhar lo paani
Jo shaheed huae hain unki, zara yaad karo qurbaani . . .

I would sit on the swing in the veranda and sing along every time the song played on the radio, and in those days that was most of the time. A few months after the war ended, when Lata Mangeshkar sang the song on 26 January 1963, during the Republic Day Parade in Delhi, it was said that Pandit Nehru cried.

∽

I recall the day Chacha Nehru came to our hometown. On Baisakhi day, 13 April 1963, the whole city was tense with anticipation as we waited for the Prime Minister's convoy to pass through town. It had been raining since morning, which was very unusual for that time of the year.

We were told that the convoy was going to enter through Hall Gate, pass through Hall Bazaar and then move towards Golden Temple, where Pandit Nehru would give a speech. There was much excitement amidst us children as we were for once going to be able to see, actually *see*, Chacha Nehru.

Kids in our lane ran around wearing freshly washed clothes. The little naked urchins put on clean banians and kachhis, the strings, for once, firmly knotted and tucked in. The entire length of Hall Bazaar, all the way up to the Town Hall and beyond, was lined with people, all windows dotted with faces. The men styled and smoothed their hair down even if they were going to get only a top angle view of Pandit Nehru. What if the Prime Minister of India were to look up and wave in their direction?

For us sisters this was cause for major excitement, but also much anxiety as our house was tucked away in the third lane off Hall Bazaar, at the back of the mosque, from where there was no way we were going to get even a glimpse of the passing convoy, even if we hung over the banister of Raj Aunty's house. But no way were we ready to miss out on this event. Mama thought of a way out. She arranged to take us to Dr Bhandari's house, the red-brick corner building in the last lane to the left just before the Hall Gate. It was a spot from which we were guaranteed to get the best view of the convoy as the open cars cruised in through the Hall Gate.

So, there we were, leaning over the parapet of Dr Bhandari's terrace, waiting for the great event to unfold. There were police everywhere. I had never seen the bazaar like this before. Policemen in uniforms flashed their batons to keep the crowds behind the roped footpaths. For hours we stood, despite the drizzle, watching from above the stream of black umbrellas sliding down Bhandari Bridge right up to Hall Gate and lining up on both sides of the street. People were falling over each other on terraces, waiting to get a glimpse of their leader. Every now and then the crowds broke into cheers whenever there was the slightest indication of anything happening, although, without exception, these were false alarms.

'Aa gaye! Aa gaye! Aa gaye!'

Finally, the convoy arrived. Dr Rajendra Prasad, the President of India, rode in the first open car. The crowds were ecstatic! Everyone cheered, shouted, waved their umbrellas in sheer ecstasy! Men whistled; women waved with their chunnis. Then, about fifteen minutes later, Pandit Nehru's jeep entered Hall Gate. A sudden hush fell on the crowd. A whisper ran through the streets. 'Pandit Nehru aa gaye! Pandit Nehru aa gaye!'

We held on to each other tense with anticipation. At the first sight of the Prime Minister of India, I remember we were all spellbound! There he was, our dear Chacha Nehru, standing in an open jeep, wearing a grey achkan and a Nehru cap, the famous red rose in his sherwani. He was glowing!

We held our breaths as the jeeps cruised by in super slow motion, the Prime Minister of India smiling and waving at the people of Amritsar. Slightly behind him stood his daughter Indira Gandhi, wearing a black chiffon sari, her hair cropped short. Her personality was striking. The moment stretched out. Then an ecstatic slogan broke the spell.

'Chacha Nehru . . . Zindabad!'

The crowds cheered. The children of Amritsar cheered the loudest.

'Chacha Nehru . . . Zindabad!'

The drizzle intensified. People flung their umbrellas away.

From our rooftops, on the streets, our faces flushed with rain and tears, we roared out our love and support for our greatest ever prime minister.

'Chacha Nehru . . . Zindabad! Chacha Nehru . . . Zindabad!'

In a public meeting held behind Durgiana Mandir, Pandit Jawaharlal Nehru stood at the dais and gave his speech, one that the Ambarsaris would quote for a long time to come . . . Huddled around the brown radio with the yellow knobs, we listened intently.

On 27 May 1964, when Chacha Nehru died, every child cried. It was a dark day for the children of India.

∞

Later that year, a stirring movie about the war with China, called *Haqeeqat*, was released. Directed by Chetan Anand, and starring Balraj Sahni, Dharmendra, and a new actress called Priya Rajvansh, it became our way of memorializing the China war of 1962. The song '*Hoke majboor mujhe usne bhulaaya hoga . . .*' played on the radio all the time. The landscape of Ladakh left an imprint on my mind. I'd never seen high-altitude cold desert mountains like that before. In school the Ladakhi word 'julay' became our favourite term of address. Instead of a 'Hello' or a 'Good Morning', we'd greet each other with a 'Julay!' This curious memory of a bunch of Punjabi kids using a Ladakhi greeting sort of set the seal on the way I remember a tragic year and an unreal war.

My movie-going experience was also gathering intensity around this age. I loved standing still for the national anthem just before the film began; I felt in a good way about my country. I perceived it as a new emotion.

20

Once Upon a Time in Ambershire

The year Chacha Nehru visited the city I moved up to Middle School. I was eleven years old. When we got to the fifth standard, our class was divided into four houses, each house represented by a different colour. There was St George, blue house; St Patrick, green; St Joseph, mauve house, and St Thomas was red. On the morning that we were to be told which house we'd be in we were all pretty excited, rather like the pupils of Hogwarts School in J. K. Rowling's Harry Potter novels waiting for the sorting hat to inform them which house they were headed to. When the names got called, I was assigned to St Patrick House, whose house colour was green. I remember being terribly disappointed. Green? The school uniform was already green, for heaven's sake! I'd have to live with the colour green for the rest of my school life! Green was such an unimaginative colour, I felt. There was no mystery about green. Such a common colour, it was everywhere. The fields were green, the trees were green, my frock was green, my sweater was green, my blazer was green ... I pleaded with Sister Rita to have me sent to another house, but she said no—firmly.

When the girls from all four houses stood in neat rows in the assembly hall, wearing the reds, the greens, the mauves, and the blue net veils across their shoulders, I would look longingly at the rows of reds, mauves, and blues. Blue was the colour I *actually* wanted. But that wasn't meant to be.

'You don't like green? Mama asked, looking at me quizzically, unable to fathom how anyone could dislike a colour so vehemently.

'All colours are beautiful, you silly girl! Every shade has its beauty!'

I raised my head from my copybook and tried to bring up irrefutable arguments with all the wisdom I could muster at age eleven:

'For green you forever have to look down—green of fields, green of trees—whereas for blue, you had to look up ... like the sky? It's blue!'

'And water ...?' Mama looked amused.

Nevertheless, when it came to the house colours, I wouldn't be loyal to my house, I decided, and continued to harbour a deep dislike for the colour green. This finally passed when I joined Sister Gabriel's painting class on the first floor overlooking lush green fields, and began to look upon the colour green with new eyes.

∞

The nuns of Sacred Heart Convent were strict as hell. If there was one thing they drilled into us it was a sense of discipline. They also carved into our psyches a deep sense of right and wrong. No matter what price had to be paid, we were taught to tell the truth.

In school we were not allowed to speak in any other language but English. If we did, we'd be fined right away. We couldn't, for the life of us, be caught speaking in Punjabi or Hindi. It had to be only English. The nuns would sneak up on us ever so slyly, and catch us red-handed. Each time we were caught speaking in our mother tongue, we had to pay eight annas. During recess, as we dug into our lunch boxes we'd be happily yapping away in Punjabi, discussing the latest films that we'd seen, till a Sister came along, and instantly, switching over to English our *Ambarsar* would turn to *Ambershire*. It was sort of a joke the girls enjoyed.

∞

Reading the *Schoolgirls Picture Library* series was an addiction with us girls during our Middle School years. We'd exchange *Schoolgirls* with each other, hiding them under the desk during class, whispering excitedly about the action happening in *The Adventurous Four* and, during recess, discussing in great detail, our obsession with *The Secret Three*. The nuns knew what we were up to, but they chose to ignore it. We never once got punished for reading *Schoolgirls*. I was particularly hooked on to the series as there were so many unpredictable things happening in their lives all the time! They always seemed to be charged about something, a mission they were set to accomplish, and that was so infectious. There were other girls in class who read the romantic *Mills & Boons*, but I somehow was never drawn to those love stories. It was the *Schoolgirls* comics that excited me and set me off on adventures in my head.

∞

One of the things I still possess from those years of my life is an autograph book. Mama sat me down one morning, opened up my newly bought autograph book that I'd picked up at Sharma Book Depot, and showed me how to make the 'Gateway of Friendship'. She'd done the same thing with her own autograph book when she was in class six in Wesley School. She folded the centre spread, two pink pages, turned them in, and pressed them down. Then she took the scissors from her sewing box and cut the top of the folded pages diagonally across. Inside the flaps she drew horizontal lines and outside she made vertical lines to make it look like a barnyard gate, and then made me write on top:

'Gateway of Friendship'.

Next day in class when I pulled out my autograph book and passed it around, there was much excitement. The girls all clustered around the Gateway of Friendship, eager to get through and write their little messages for me. They all wanted the same thing done in their autograph books as well and I ended up making similar Gateways of Friendship for each of the girls in my class. Pemu did half the job with scissors; her diagonal snip was perfect. My autograph book quickly filled up with comments from all my friends—sometimes funny, and mostly sweet nothings … reading them today, poor grammar, misspellings and all, fills me with nostalgia.

Daljit Sandhu wrote on a yellow leaf:

'When you are tired, sit on a rock
Take off your shoes and smell your socks!'

Dear Deepti,
'I slept and dreamt that life was a beauty,
I woke and found that life was a duty.'
Love and best wishes, Jaspreet

'When your heart is full of hope
And away is despair
If you feel sad and lovely

Remember my naughtiness dear!'
Prem Lata (Pemu)

∽

To my dearest Deepti,
'Policemen, policemen, be on your duty!
For here comes Deepti, the Indian beauty!'
Your loving friend
Madhu Sadana

∽

Jyoti Kakar's handwriting is the neatest on the page.
'I met you as a stranger,
I shall leave you as a friend,
May we meet in heaven,
Where friendship never ends.'
Forget me not—
Your loving sister Jyoti

∽

There's also a page that is written by Didi.
'When the baby Deepti was bathing in her tub,
Her mother forgot to put the plug,
Oh my goodness. Bless my Soul,
Down goes Deepti in the HOLE!'
From your pal Smiti

Trust my sister to write something like that! And I celebrated that comment by drawing a tub next to it. Moron me!

∽

We middle school girls lived in awe of our seniors. Whether it was Prathibha or Beevan, Neelam Mansingh or Ratan Bhandari, Kittu, or Kamaljeet Sandhu, Kiran Pashauriya or Tina Kumar—we held them in high esteem.

The one girl who stood out amongst them all was Kiran Pashauriya (later Kiran Bedi). She was three years senior to me and was friends with Didi. My classmates worshipped her. There was something special about her. I used to find a quality in her that I hadn't seen in any other girl in school. She was always definite about everything. She knew her mind. When she spoke, she would speak with precision and to the point. She was extremely motivated. I was in awe of her and knowing that I was Smiti's younger sister, she was extra sweet to me. I remember on one occasion, at the end of the school day, I rushed over to my sister waving a piece of paper in my hand. 'Didi, I wrote a poem today! Look!' When I saw Kiran standing there with her, I quickly tried to shuffle the paper back into my schoolbag. Kiran saw that.

'What's that you have written? Let's see!'

'No, no . . . it's nothing . . . just something . . . I wrote in class.'

'Let's see your poem. Please let me read it,' and she took the paper from my hand. It was a poem about clouds and rain and I was terribly embarrassed when Kiran started to read it aloud.

'Baadal aaye, baadal aaye . . .'(The clouds have come . . .) it said, and then the second line said, 'Paani bhaaga bhaaga aaye' (Water comes running), or some such rubbish. I thought both Didi and Kiran would burst out laughing, but Kiran looked at me earnestly.

'This is good!' she said. 'You have written exactly what you have felt, so this is great! Have you written more poems?'

'No, this is my first . . .' I said, knowing very well that she was being awfully kind to me. I mean whoever would write a poem with a line as silly as Paani bhaaga bhaaga aaye? I wanted to kick myself but Kiran Pashauriya was not one to discourage anyone.

'Please keep writing,' she said, 'you must write more poems! And with each poem you write, you will be writing better, I promise you that!'

Another senior who stood out during those years was Neelam Mansingh, a very pretty girl with a striking face. I remember a time when there was a huge mystery attached to her name: the mystery of the letters. We heard that Neelam received letters from across the school wall from an unknown person. The mysterious letters came from across the back wall of our school, near the banana trees, where there were remnants of a graveyard. The entire school was consumed by the story.

Every morning we'd hear a fresh bout of rumours elucidating the scenario of *Neelam Mansingh and the Mysterious Letters*. The schoolgirls had a fertile imagination, no question about that.

'M e e e e e t me in the G R A V E Y A A A A A A R D … at t h r e e e e in the N I I I I T E …'

They came up with all kinds of concocted rubbish, like Neelam had been seen at night standing under the banana trees talking to shadows. Once the nuns got embroiled in the situation, we began to see the amusing side of things. 'If it was a ghost writing the letters,' we'd lightly mock, 'it would be completely acceptable to our strict nuns, but God forbid if it was a boy! *Oh Boy!*'

Neelam and the Letters was a mystery that till the end of school remained a mystery. No amount of growing up on *Schoolgirls*, *The Secret Three*, or *The Adventurous Four* could help us solve that one!

∞

An absolutely bizarre incident happened during those days—less 'incident' and more 'accident'. One rainy morning a girl from my class was standing at the cyclewallah's shed outside Hall Gate, getting air pumped into her bicycle. A Punjab Roadways bus, parked just behind her, slipped on the wet ground and slowly started rolling towards her, as she stood with her back towards the Gate. The cyclewallah was busy pumping air into the tyres. No one noticed the bus gliding towards the schoolgirl. Then, the dreaded thing happened—the girl was gently pushed to the ground. She fell on her face and fainted, as the bus started to roll over her.

People gasped as they stood witnessing the horrific sight. Everyone thought she'd be crushed to death. But to their utter surprise, the girl slowly shifted, regaining consciousness, then seeming a bit confused, she rose from the slushy ground, slapped the mud off her uniform, paid the cyclewallah who stood stupefied, and merrily peddled away towards Bhandari Bridge. Before she reached school that morning, the news had spread like wildfire.

'Run over by a *bus*? My God! She could have been squashed to death! How close was she to the tyres? … It was sheer luck!' The discussions went on and on in the minutest of details—how unsuspecting schoolgirls get run over by Punjab Roadways buses—the inexplicable incident being recalled, reimagined, re-enacted over and over in class—not only for that monsoon season but for all times to come in the history of Sacred Heart Convent of Amritsar.

∽

I have another bicycling accident that I would like to narrate, this time featuring me. I was probably around eleven years old and sure enough should have been riding my own bicycle instead of sitting behind my sister and letting her continue with the drudgery of carting me all the way to Majitha Road and back. One afternoon returning from school she tells me to keep sitting and not get off at the incline of Bhandari Bridge. I dutifully follow instruction. Didi has not got off the bike, is still peddling uphill when suddenly the bike wobbles all over the place—a sudden swing to the left, then sharply to the right, and then I realize that my foot is caught inside the back wheel of the cycle.

Ow! . . . ow! . . . ow! . . . OW! . . . and the bicycle gets stuck and I fall. Didi steps down, horrified at what has happened. We are both looking at my foot. My skin has been scraped off as though with sandpaper, revealing from underneath a fresh fuchsia layer, bright and shimmery. Sure, I'm in pain, but more than that I'm surprised at how pink the flesh is under my brown skin. My pain is visible on my sister's face. She is so sorry for what has happened and keeps apologizing. But I hardly feel she is responsible; I should have gotten off the bike at the incline in the first place.

Nervously and slowly we both move to the extreme corner of the bridge and start walking towards home. I'm unable to put my peeled foot flat on the ground so I walk on my heel, tilting it up to keep it from bleeding. It seems like a long shamble through the length of the bazaar till we finally reach home. Seeing me, Mama freaks out and quickly rushes me to the one-stop-shop for all medical debacles—Dr Atam Prakash's clinic—where for once, instead of the purple tincture, my grated pink foot is Burnoled and bandaged in good time.

∽

Once, in school, an exam got interrupted by a dust storm. I had just settled down to answer the paper, when I noticed the sky had started to change colour. From a clear blue it turned to a deep yellow, then to an orange. The girls shifted in their chairs with excitement.

A strong wind wailed.

Sister Rita stepped out on to the veranda and looked across the green fields. Holding her rosary in her hand she walked back into the class and nervously whispered:

'Looks like there's going to be a storm!'

The wind whipped the glass doors of the corridors. White paper sheets fluttered on desks. Then the sky turned an orange-red. At ten o'clock in the morning the nuns had to switch on the lights in the classrooms. Everyone looked around, excited.

Before we knew it, the sky was a deep crimson and then the lights went out and it was pitch dark all around. The nuns ran up and down the corridors between the classrooms carrying candles. The girls lost no time. What a heaven-sent opportunity to cheat! Everyone began whispering loudly to each other asking for help to answer questions. Notes were passed around. Even as the nuns ran around holding candles in glass jars they were shouting above the howling din:

'NO CHEATING GIRLS! PLEASE! NO CHEATING!'

Poor old Khoga! She was literally in tears, pacing up and down the corridor shouting, '*How* can you do this, girls, how can you?' The girls loved her dearly. Normally they wouldn't hurt her for anything, but this one black, wind-struck morning they chose to ignore that sentiment. They simply put their emotions aside and did openly what they always wanted to do—cheat! Shamelessly cheat! All hell broke loose. Sister Rita's voice had now begun to crack.

'THIS STORM WON'T LAST FOREVER, GIRLS! GOD WILL PUNISH YOU! HE WILL DEFINITELY PUNISH YOU FOR THIS!'

Holding on for her life to the glass lamp, limping on her sprained foot, she hobbled up and down the dark corridor pleading for high conduct, for strength of character, for fear of God, for the voice of conscience ... her voice crackling to a high pitch, as she tried to bring order to a class running riot!

'STOP IT GIRLS! STOP IT!'

The nun in white was a dark silhouette against a burnt-red skyline. Paying no heed to her entreaties, most of the thirty-one girls in the class got out of their seats and stumbled around in the dark, shamelessly tallying answers and scribbling on palms, until suddenly the lights came back on, blinding, white. The girls darted to their seats and began to attack their answer sheets with a vengeance, writing down ferociously their freshly acquired knowledge on the blank sheets of paper on their desks.

I have memory of our dear Khoga standing in front of the class, in tears, hurt, and trembling with humiliation.

'SHAME ON YOU GIRLS! SHAME ON YOU! This is a DISGRACE! Wait till Sister Jacinta hears of this! You will have to *hang* your heads in SHAME!'

Retribution didn't take long to arrive. The storm did end. The sky did clear up and the girls did stand in the classroom, their heads hanging in shame. There was only one voice, the voice of Sister Jacinta—sharp and menacing. She declared that the entire test paper stood cancelled and Class VII would need to take the test all over again.

Served us right. You know the strange thing about this incident is that I have no memory of *me* cheating! None! I'm blank. Did I cheat? To be honest, I don't remember. All I remember is being an enthralled spectator to the entire episode, standing there by my desk, taking into account every little detail of how the sand storm had tossed into thin air our strict convent upbringing. I remember the dust storm, Sister Rita's anguish, the chaos in the classroom, but as to my own part in the play, my mind is a blank. This is not unusual. Whenever I feel sheepish about something, I end up suffering from memory loss.

∽

I have one final startlingly clear memory of this phase of my childhood. When I was twelve, Didi and some other girls were going to Darbar Sahib to buy costume jewellery for a school dance they were participating in, and I insisted on accompanying them.

As the girls disappeared into the narrow gullies around the Golden Temple chattering about bangles, parandis, trinkets, and such-like things required for the next day's performance, I was asked to wait for them by the side of the road.

I stood still for a while on the spot looking at life around me.

To my left I noticed a white gate-like structure, with a board that said ... 'Museum'. A museum? In the middle of these gullies? It got me curious. I moved a little towards it, then, stopped. It would be getting dark soon. Didi and the others have asked me to stay put right here at this corner, so I'd better be here.

All around were tiny shops with drains flowing under the wooden thresholds, displaying gota work—the dazzling silver, papery borders stitched on the edges of shawls and veils. Red dupattas hung from turquoise painted wooden doors, and heaps and heaps of reds, yellows, and pinks bordered with gold.

'Little sister!' I heard a shopkeeper addressing me from across the lane. 'What are you looking for? Dupattas? I have the best georgette in town ... better than Lahori georgette.'

'No, I don't need ... thank you ... I'm not buying.'

'But did I ask you to buy? O-ho ... tell me, did I even *once* ask you to buy anything? But sisterji, since you are here, just please look at least ... it doesn't cost to look. You don't pay anything ... no money for looking! Hain?'

I stood across the lane, looking. Then, as the shopkeeper turned, I moved away.

'O, sisterji ...'

More to escape him than anything else, I entered the so-called 'museum'. The place was dingy and unkempt. Inside there were paintings of Sikh Gurus painted in blaring blues and yellows. My gaze settled on one of the paintings—a striking image of a beheaded man. It was a representation of a Sikh Guru, a headless warrior, charging into battle, brandishing a sword in his right hand, and in the left, he held his own severed head. I stared, disbelieving what I saw, then quickly left the museum. Standing at the corner of the narrow lane, watching the handcarts and rickshaws manoeuvring their way through, I little realized that what I'd just seen would be one of the strongest images implanted on my mind for all time to come. When Didi and the other girls returned, I started walking along with them without a word, and never mentioned this strange warrior to anyone.

No one ever spoke about Sikh history in the house. But Mama loved listening to the shabad emanating from the Golden Temple. At times, while passing by the inner lanes of Darbar Sahib she would ask the rickshawallah to stop for just a while so she could hear the Gurbani. 'How beautiful that sounds!' she'd exclaim. At other times she would take Didi and me inside the Golden Temple where we'd sit by the holy water listening to the Sikh priests chanting from the Guru Granth Sahib. Mama would sit in silence for a long time and then quietly walk away. Even though that image of the headless warrior piqued my curiosity, my understanding of the city's history and involvement in Sikh traditions remained limited for much of my childhood.

21

Introvert Drama Queen

Puberty was a difficult and confused time for me. As my hormones went into overdrive I was plunged into all sorts of dilemmas, some of which resulted in actions that I might otherwise not have taken. I'd been a rather friendly, happy, and largely content child up until this point in my life but my nature began to change when I turned thirteen.

At thirteen I started feeling alienated from my environment, as if I belonged elsewhere. I grew quieter, smiled seldom, and became something of a recluse. I'd created my own little inner world where I dreamt of living in the mountains, being free like a shepherd, wandering in the meadows...Now when I think about it, the older I grew, the more withdrawn I became. Nonu claims she had to bend backwards cracking jokes, 'trying to *make Deepi smile!*'

I was beginning to be a loner and I liked being that...in my own little world. No one knew a thing about what was inside of me. Poetry became a means for me to strengthen my tenuous connection with the world. Whenever I liked a line, a verse, I'd carefully jot it down in my grey diary.

'Heard melodies are sweet, but those unheard . . . are sweeter'.
—John Keats

Daydreaming in class and writing poems was as crucial for me as passing maths, english, physics, and history tests was for other girls. Nonu tells me, 'You were not interested in what the teacher was saying. You were forever looking outside the window, counting birds.' It wasn't so bad though, let me tell you, she exaggerates. I did do my share of studying and was fairly okay as a student. But being average unnerved me; I had to excel in *something*.

'All that we see or seem, is but a dream within a dream.'
—Edgar Allen Poe

Seasons came and went by. I wasn't much enamoured of either maths or science. I did find geography interesting and quite liked history. But mugging up lines was not my forte—that was Didi's domain. I would quickly learn a chapter, and then, just as quickly, forget it.

The only thing I could remember by heart were the verses of poems that I kept filling my diary with—

Hope, like the gleaming taper's light,
Adorns and cheers our way;
And still, as darker grows the night,
Emits a brighter ray.
—Oliver Goldsmith

And of course I knew all the film songs by heart.

At this time, I'd be happiest left to myself. I loved the prospect of making dialogue within, or with the mirror. Bizarrely, my only friend during this anxious, unsettled time was a hat stand in which a mirror was embedded. I'd spend long moments gazing at it, would talk to my reflection every so often and regularly shared all my secrets with it. As this phase of my life peaked, I became a complete introvert and lived in my own world.

Such were my teenage years, years of yearning for an extraordinary life ... as Pitaji would say, 'A Life of Consequence' ... and surely my life was charted to be different. I would do *something* to make a difference. I'd touch other lives, touch hearts ... that dream would surely come true. But how would that ever happen in a place like this? I worried. The more I was left to myself the more convoluted my mind became. I felt I was different, I didn't belong, I lived here, as the saying goes, but life was elsewhere ...

∞

I'm afraid I cannot complete this memoir unless I write about this time, in the thirteenth year of my life, when I did the the most irresponsible thing I had yet done—I ran away from home. At first, I thought I'd skip this chapter, pretend like it never happened, but as I continue to write, it coaxes me to tell the whole truth, about my act of rebellion. But if I was a rebel, I was surely a rebel without a cause.

Besides the act of leaving home, I had no concrete plan in mind, no real idea of what I was hoping to achieve, nothing beyond an ostensible desire to see the mountains of Kashmir. This was because I'd seen a series of movies shot in Kashmir in the period before I set off on my great escape.

In November of 1964, I saw *Kashmir Ki Kali*. Then came *Aarzoo, Janwar, Waqt, Mere Sanam, Himalay Ki God Mein*, and finally, *Jab Jab Phool Khile*. All these films were set in Kashmir and Kashmir was on my mind. I felt there was no place on earth that could be more beautiful, more heavenly than Kashmir. I dreamt of sitting in a shikara in the Dal Lake, walking through a spread of orange chinar leaves, gazing at the snow peaks of Pahalgam. I became obsessed with the idea of Kashmir. All I wanted was to go away to the beautiful valley of Kashmir, and I did. Well, almost ...

Let me take you along with me on a train journey, one I embarked upon to reach Kashmir, and show you how I spent that cold January night—my night on a railway platform ...

∞

The wheels of the train start to move. I see my reflection in the glass window; a thirteen-year-old girl wearing a muffler around her head, a

white salwar, light green kameez, bottle-green sweater, and a dark green
blazer. Over her school uniform she's wearing a light overcoat, a greyish
brown. Her face shows mixed feelings; excited for sure, but also something
more ... something undefined.

I look in the other direction. A man sits across constantly looking
at me. I feel uncomfortable and turn my head back to look out of the
window. It is pitch dark outside. There are other people in the compartment.
A woman and child, both wrapped in a blanket, sleep on a berth, four
men, office-going middle-class types, play cards and joke with each other
in a dignified manner. A Sardarji sits on the berth above, dozing off. The
man staring at me has a pot belly.

The train halts at a secluded place: BATALA.

'Chai garam ... Chai garam ...'

There's a hospital-like building lit in dim yellow light. A stray dog
barks. Two men and the woman and child get off the train here. There's
a dark silence outside. Somebody switches on the radio. Old songs start
to play, songs that struggle to emerge from the static that clogs the radio
waves. Someone coughs. A man gets out of the toilet and snuggles back
into his blanket on the upper berth. The four men playing cards are
now talking politics.

I tilt my head to look out of the window. A green flag is waving.
The train, for an instant, starts moving in the opposite direction. One of
the four men jokingly remarks, 'Lao ji, gaddi Pathankot jaan di bajaye,
Lhaur nu tur pai hai!' (The train is moving towards Lahore!)

I turn my head to look at the remaining people in the compartment.
I fiddle with my bag and take out my diary. After looking out of the
window I begin to write ... notes on what I'm feeling right now. Soon,
I'm dozing off on my seat, clutching my diary and bag. There are now
only two or three men in the compartment. The train stops again, nowhere
really, as there's no sign of habitation in the darkness. I'm terribly sleepy.
I nod off, wake up, and find even fewer people in the compartment—the
man who has been staring at me has moved across to another window
seat, and half reclined, the old Sardarji on the berth above me is still
dozing. The whistle goes off and the train starts. It moves out slowly
and picks up speed again. A flood of light moves towards me. I open
the glass window again as the train comes to a halt at a platform of a

large station. The brakes hiss and screech when it slows down to a stop.
I look out and see a big signboard in black and yellow: PATHANKOT.

The suspicious character who'd been staring at me, has got off even
before the train pulls into the platform. He jumps out while the train is
still in slow motion, crosses the tracks, and disappears into the dark. The
old Sardarji sleepily gathers his potlis and bisterband, and begins to get
down. The ticket collector at the gate is checking the tickets of the two
or three passengers who have disembarked from the nearly empty train.
As I'm still looking out, an old woman steps down and is escorted by
a young man waiting for her and they also leave. The ticket collector
goes into his office.

I finally pick up my bag and step off the train onto a deserted
platform. There's hesitation, fear, but I decide to put on a bold front. I
look around confidently, and then, as if I know the place in and out, I
start to walk towards the main gate. To the left of the gate, through a
tall grille, I can see the main entrance area of the railway station which
is lit up. Against a wall, there are women and children sleeping on the
floor, working-class people. A beggar too is sprawled across the floor. In
the extreme left-hand corner of the entrance area a group of coolies
are sitting around a bonfire. On the front wall, right in the centre, a big
clock strikes eleven.

I take in this scene for a few minutes and then confidently walk
across this big entrance area, and out of the station. It has been drizzling
but as I emerge from the station the thin rain stops. There is a fenced in
roundabout outside the station. I begin to walk around it when I notice
a shadow following me. I walk around the roundabout; the shadow does
the same. I get tense. Then I hear a voice.

'Kithhe jaana hai?' Where are you going?

I don't look back. The man in a worker's purple uniform overtakes
me and blocks my way.

'Where are you going?' he repeats himself.

'Jammu.'

'Jammu? Do you have a ticket?'

'Yes!' I speak with nonchalance.

'Where are you coming from?'

'Where do I get a bus for Jammu?'

'Bus? There is no bus going at this time.'

'Isn't there a bus from here to Jammu?'

'Are you alone?'

Silence ...

'Where have you come from?'

'Where's the bus station?'

The man looks me up and down.

'Where's your ticket?'

I look at him as if insulted, and defiantly start to grope in my blazer pocket, revealing for the first time a school uniform. I stop. Without showing him the ticket, I look at him and say, 'How is it your concern?'

'You want to go to Jammu? Well, the roads are blocked. There's been a landslide ... There's no bus leaving for Jammu tonight!'

'So? When will it go?'

'At 5.30 in the morning.'

'Okay, fine!' I end the conversation abruptly and side-stepping him resume walking. He calls to me again.

'Oye girl! Where do you think you are going?'

I stop. He catches up with me.

'Why?' I ask.

'Chalo! Come to the waiting room!'

I look on blankly.

'You have a ticket, right? So, come! Come and sit in the Ladies Waiting Room!'

I do not know what to say. He looks at me suspiciously and points towards the left at the few buses standing in the rain.

'There's the bus stop!' I begin to get nervous.

'Is there a train that goes to Jammu?'

'Chalo! Go inside! We'll find out!'

He indicates for me to move first. I look at his face as I turn and reluctantly start to walk back to the railway station. Back on the main platform he directs me to a huge wooden door with a fly screen. Over the door a sign says: LADIES WAITING ROOM - III CLASS.

It's raining continuously now. The door to the waiting room is half open. Voices can be heard inside, voices of women. The worker knocks at the semi-open door. I see an elderly woman, standing with her back towards us, bent over a register on a table. This man calls out to her.

'Mai ... come here for a minute ...!'

The woman ignores us. The worker knocks again, and briskly the elderly woman turns and steps out. She is a thin, slightly greying woman, with a warm, but strong face. She is dressed in a white salwar kameez with long sleeves and has a shawl covering her head. The worker looks at me, and tells the woman called Mai that I have arrived on the train from Delhi, and am on my way to Jammu and so will need to stay in the waiting room for the night. Mai looks at me quizzically.

'Ticket hai?'

I nod, as the worker answers for me.

'Haan, hai ...' and takes Mai aside, just a few steps away, where I can hear them murmur together in low tones. The worker is saying to Mai: 'Mainu taan ohi gal lagdi hai ...' I feel it is the same situation.

After hearing this phrase, I, who was so far putting on a cool front, become suddenly alert and uneasy. They continue to whisper in even lower tones—I cannot any longer hear what they are saying. They turn around and walk back towards me. Mai asks me to show her my ticket.

'Where did you get on the train?'

'In Delhi!'

'Where are you heading?'

'Jammu!'

'Are you alone?'

'Yes.'

'Where's your luggage?'

'Don't have any.'

'Take out your ticket!'

I grope for the ticket in the pocket of my overcoat and hand it over to the old woman. The woman looks at the ticket, then stepping closer to the light, she scrutinizes it, and looks at the worker who has an expectant look in his eyes. The ticket has been issued in Amritsar, and not Delhi, but the woman discloses nothing to him. She asks me to step inside the ladies waiting room.

I go in hesitantly, but I'm still showing great confidence. Mai moves towards the worker and tells him something. The worker becomes very animated. After talking for a while Mai gives him what appears to be instructions and he leaves. I wait in the waiting room.

On the right side of the room there's a window that is shut quite firmly. Beside the window, against the wall, is a massive old wooden bench. To the front of this room is another huge wooden door which probably leads to the bathroom. On the left side is a bare table made of dark wood—longish; beside it, a bench made of the same wood. There isn't very much else in the room.

There are a few other occupants of the waiting room They seem to be village women and children who have probably arrived on the same train as I or the one before it and are still in the process of settling down. They have a little luggage: a bisterband or two; one of them spreads a sleeping bag on the floor and a child is put to sleep on it. Another of the women sits on a tin chest and rocks another child to sleep, one that has been crying. There's a woman in her early fifties, clad in a linen salwar kameez with a sweater and socks. She is heavily built. The women are making small talk as they wait.

I sit down on the edge of the bench on the left side beside the table. On the table is a thick register, which everyone staying in the waiting room has to fill in. Mai, who has been outside the room talking to the worker who brought me here, comes back in and starts to turn the pages of the register. She says to me:

'Yeh lo . . . sign karo . . . your name here, here, your home address . . . and here, the place you are going, write everything in this!'

I, who have been sitting prim and proper with my bag tightly clutched on my knees just looking at all these people in the room, now look at the register and do not move.

Mai is saying to the woman who has put the bedding on the floor.

'Why don't you place this dhurrie against the wall, the child is asleep here, he will be getting in the way!' With this she starts helping the woman move the dhurrie. This takes a few minutes. I sit totally tense and still, making no effort to move. Mai goes to the door to deal with two men who have called out to her. She talks to them for a while, a few hurried sentences, and then comes back to me. She looks down at the register, which is lying blank, points at it again and says, 'Chalo! Log in your name and address here . . . chalo!'

I move up to the table and stand beside it looking at the register.

Mai passes a pen to me, which is tied to the register with a string. I hold the pen and Mai says, 'Baitho!'

'Write! ... name?'

I'm still for a moment and then I write down Deepti.

'Poora naam ki hai ... write your full name!'

I write—Deepti ... Naval.

After a while, she asks me to go outside. I find a police inspector waiting for me. The inspector starts to question me. When I start being defiant, he slaps me across the face. I burst into sobs, silently. I'm brought inside the waiting room again by the old woman, who, in front of other ladies sitting there, starts talking about how the police have been informed, and how my family is looking for me. She starts to narrate an earlier incident about a brigadier's maid, who had run away from Srinagar and was raped here in Pathankot by thirteen men. I sit quietly on the edge of the bench listening to all this. Mai goes away after some time. Some more time passes, and a train comes in. The village women and their children leave on that train.

Two very polished young women now enter the waiting room. One is in a sari and has her hair up in a joora and sits down and starts knitting. The other is in a churidar, short hair, and is reading a fashion magazine. It gives me some comfort to see them. They mostly chat in English. The two seem to be waiting for the older lady's husband to come and pick them up. He is a Major in the army who is to join them here. He is driving down in his jeep. Apparently, he is driving here from Srinagar where the weather is really bad, and all roads are blocked. The older lady tries to speak with me. I'm unwilling to make conversation at this point. The younger one just looks on. After some time, both the ladies doze off.

A train pulls in to the platform. It is still raining outside. I sneak out of the waiting room and walk on to the platform. Here I see an old Pahadi man with a lantern, using a gunny bag as a covering to keep from getting wet. I walk up to him and sit beside him, watching the raindrops fall on the glistening tracks. We chat for a bit. He had dreamed about being a 'fauji' he says, but was disqualified due to his eyesight. I tell him about my school, the nuns, and my family. The old Pahadiya describes his life in Chamba.

'Can you see the mountains from here?' I ask the old guy.

'Oh you can, but only when the sky is clear . . . it is raining these days and cloudy!'

'But can you *see* . . . the mountains?' I ask again.

'Yes . . . I see them all the time . . . in my mind . . . my heart . . .'

'So do I . . .' I look at the old Pahadiya.

'What did you say?' he asks, looking distracted.

'I said, someday I will go to the mountains . . .'

I hear approaching footsteps and run back inside the waiting room.

The old Mai comes in again. After registering two new names, she leaves. Now, I decide to lie down on the bench. Somebody knocks and the two other women who are waiting with me get up when they hear a voice. The Major is at the door of the waiting room. The ladies start packing. He tells them he will go collect the luggage from the locker. The younger sister leaves the room to help him but forgets her keys. The older sister asks me to take the keys to her. I go after her to hand over the keys only to find a man and a woman locked in a passionate embrace behind a pillar. For a moment I think it's the Major, and . . . and . . . I am taken aback, I'm not sure. In my confusion I withdraw. With the keys in my hand, I walk back to the waiting room where the wife sees me looking shaken. She asks me what happened. I compose myself and say, 'I couldn't find them.'

Mai returns. The inspector comes in with her and so does the stationmaster. She tells me I'll be taken back in the morning by train to Amritsar, so I should get some sleep. I am unable to fathom what I'm feeling at the moment. She tells me not to open the door to anyone. Everyone leaves and I am left alone. I lie down on a mattress feeling very disturbed. Despite this, I close my eyes and quickly fall asleep as I am very exhausted.

After a while there is a knock on the door. It's the worker in the purple uniform. He tells me it is 5 o'clock in the morning and that my train is ready to leave. He tells me that Mai has asked him to help me board the train. Half asleep, I get up, grapple for my overcoat and bag, and follow the worker out on to the platform. It seems to be a long walk. I follow him to the end of the roofed section of the platform and stop. From here, I can see a train in the distance. The worker says that's my train. We walk up to it. There are no lights in the train and no passengers either. My mind starts to race.

'Come,' he says.

I keep standing looking at him, unable to understand why I'm required to board an empty, dark train.

'It's so dark ...' I utter.

'I'll switch on the light,' he mutters and steps inside the train, then comes out again.

'Come in,' he says.

Seeing the fear on my face his tone softens.

'Are you afraid?' Then I see fear on his own face. 'There's no need to be afraid of me ... I'm the one who saved you ...'

Just at that moment, better sense prevails. I realize that the big clock on the platform was showing three-thirty when we walked past and not five. Suddenly, I turn around and hurriedly start to walk back, running almost, towards the main platform. The worker follows me for a bit, but then decides to give up the pursuit. Rushing all the way back to the waiting room, I slump in a corner, drenched and breathless, and start to weep.

'Mama ...'

Outside on the platform, I can faintly hear the Pahadi man singing a song—

'Pal pal bahi jaana, bahi jaana, o jindua ... pal pal ...'

His voice feels reassuring and I fall asleep. Sometime later, Mai returns with her three-year-old grandson in tow. She puts him to sleep on the mattress and wakes me up. I sit up with a terrible start. My eyes are still wet. Mai gets alarmed. She asks me if anything is the matter. I stutter, trying to tell her that the man she'd sent to put me on the train tried to get me inside an empty dark compartment. Hearing this, Mai flares up.

'Hadn't I told to you not to open the door to anyone but me?' She continues to reprimand me as I listen, my eyes downcast.

Finally, Mai puts me to bed next to the baby boy, her little grandson, and says not to move till she wakes me up herself.

Morning sounds begin to filter in. Mai comes and wakes me up. The light changes. The door opens in silhouette. There are train sounds again on the railway station. The platform seems to be abuzz. A whistle goes off. As I get ready to leave, three people are waiting outside for me, including the police inspector. I am introduced to the two men who are designated to escort me back home. The old woman explains to them what is to be done. As I walk out of the Ladies Waiting Room, I see two rows of people lined up on the platform gawking at the *runaway girl*. I am terribly embarrassed and feel very ashamed.

The train is ready to leave. Mai has instructions for me till the end. I go inside and take my seat. The two men come and sit across from me. The train begins to pull out. I look back and wave to the people left standing on the platform. As the train chugs past the PATHANKOT signboard, way back near the railing, I see the worker in his purple uniform, standing apart from the others. The train picks up speed and leaves Pathankot behind. Outside my window I see faintly on the skyline, a sketchy impression of the hills ...

Mid-journey, at Batala, I am surprised to see my father along with Gyaniji and Dalip Singh Uncle, the DSP of Amritsar, come to fetch me. I'm nervous and joyous at the same time. From Batala, we get into Uncle's car and drive to Amritsar.

At home the scene is extremely sad. Mama is in her grey flannel gown lying in bed completely devastated. I can see that her eyes are swollen from crying all night. I go and lie down beside her. We both have had a bad night. My mother clings to me and cries her heart out ...

'Jaan vich jaan aayi hai!' So relieved, I can finally breathe ...

As I lie next to my mother, I see the neighbours standing on the veranda. Then I hear voices. Through the door to the hall, I can see Piti sitting at his desk, speaking to the people around. He holds up in his hands a couple of books—*The Adventurous Four* and *The Silent Three*. I can almost hear him telling his audience that it's the influence of comic books such as these that have led to his young daughter running away from home.

Later, Pitaji sits me down in the hall kamra and I narrate to him all that has happened the night before. After hearing my entire story, my father finally says:

'Deepi, you have, in one night, destroyed the reputation that took me ages to build.'

We both fall silent after that. Then, seeming unsure of himself, he asks me, 'Beta, why did you run away?'

'I ... I wanted to see the mountains ...' I reply without looking at him.

Piti is quiet for some time, then says, 'We should be thankful to Mai; she has been a godsend!'

Two days later, I'm told that Mai and the Pathankot police inspector have been invited home. Not only do my parents feel the need to express their gratitude to these people because of whom I have returned home safe and sound, but they also need to show our neighbours that the story that has been put out about my escapade is genuine.

My parents never mention a word about the incident after that day. Gyaniji offers to become my godfather and assures me that I can confide in him whatever I cannot confide in my parents.

Mama's words ring in my ears even today, when she clung to me that winter morning, and whispered . . .

'*Thand pai gai ae . . .*'

There are no words in the English language that can explain that feeling.

I went back to school as if nothing had ever happened. No one in my class knew about my night out on a railway platform. Even Pemu didn't have a clue. Nandini had no idea either. And soon everything was put away from my mind and was happily forgotten.

✑

I'm afraid I have to break the flow of events here, as I have run into a mental block. It's no writer's block. It's a landslide! Why on earth did I run away from home? Did my parents deserve this? The enormity of the situation dawns upon me only now—for the first time ever, and I'm questioning myself. How could I have done this to Mama and Piti? Was I justified in taking such a step? Whoever runs away from home to go and see the mountains? Just because my parents had never once brought up this incident in all my life, it had never really sunk in me for all these years. Having a wonderful mother and father like mine, it was blasphemous, what I had done in the thirteenth year of my life.

As I write this, I wonder if films were at the back of my mind and this was my grand gesture, at that impressionable age, of trying to fulfil what I believed was my destiny. If my running away from home had anything to do with the fact that Hindi films were forever being shot in Kashmir and I hoped to run into a film unit and get 'discovered' by the world of cinema—I would *hate* to admit that.

22

The Pak War of 1965

Less than a year after my act of so-called rebellion, a larger war arrived on our doorstep. Pakistan, the perennial thorn in our side, began a series of skirmishes starting in April 1965. This came to a head when they attempted to infiltrate thousands of troops into Kashmir, finally provoking India into a massive reprisal in August.

This war was much more real for us than the war with China that had taken place in distant Ladakh when I was younger. This time around I was thirteen and the war was, literally, next door.

It was the middle of September. Metallic news crackled in from All India Radio.

'PAKISTAN ATTACKS INDIA AT THE BORDER OF
KHEM KARAN!'

We jumped up with excitement! A real war? At the Amritsar border? Finally, *something* was happening in our lives! Something important! We were going to become part of history!

Hostilities in the Jammu sector had been mounting for some months now. As the pressure mounted, India realized that the offensive in the Jammu sector had to be offset by opening up another front on the Amritsar border. This was just after the rainy season when the Ravi River was in full spate, so the fighting took place in very difficult conditions. Even though the fighting was on the border of Khem Karan and Asal Uttar, forty miles away, there was plenty of action for us to follow in the city. There were garrisons of the Punjab Regiment and the Gurkha Regiment stationed at Amritsar. Truckloads of jawans drove through Chatiwind Gate. Once in Hall Bazaar we saw, with mounting excitement, units of Sherman and Centurion tanks roaring past. The entire mohalla turned out to watch the never-before-seen machines drone past. The city limits had stretched; makeshift hospitals had been set up to treat the casualties of war who had started streaming in.

The village of Loharka, only five miles away from Amritsar, had been bombed. When things were at their peak we could hear shelling all night long. Being a border town, just thirty-one miles away from Lahore, Amritsar was vulnerable and had to prepare for war. Overnight, trenches were dug all along the gullies, one being excavated just outside our gate. Around six every evening sirens would go off and people would run and hide in the trenches, an exercise later repeated several times a day in order to get us civilians used to the idea of war ... 'Just in case Pakistan decided to drop a bomb on Amritsar!' The practice of running and hiding in the trenches became a game for us kids. The whole exercise seemed immensely amusing and funny to us, and we could just not take it seriously. Every morning and evening, when the mock sirens went off, we'd drop everything and hurtle towards the gully, stumbling over each other, giggling our way in and out of trenches, *enjoying* the war!

Munni and Binder next door were sent away to their village in Doaba. We exchanged gifts. I painted a scene of our neighbourhood on a wooden plaque and solemnly gave it to Munni as a parting gift, telling her that in case one of us died, then there would be something for the other to remember her by. Soon, there was an announcement on the radio to say that Amritsar might have to be evacuated. Mama had heard that the people of Amritsar were leaving their homes and going away and the possibility that we may have to flee as well completely devastated her. But we were happy not to miss out on the action!

At Gandhi Ground, an anti-aircraft gun was set up in order to combat the onslaught of the Pakistani planes. The enemy planes could not be seen in the dark until occasionally one of them was hit, going up in the night sky like a firecracker. Every evening people would gather around to watch the fireworks! There'd be a major uproar and cheering amidst the crowds.

The real hero of the war for us kids was Raju Topchi, an anti-aircraft gunner, who was a great nishaan-e-baaz. Stationed at the Cantonment, just outside the walled city, Raju Topchi, one of the Indian Army's best anti-aircraft gunners, would shoot down the Pak jets as they came whirring through the skies creating a wave of excitement among the young, and panic among the city's old. With Raju Topchi's gun forever aimed at the sky, the Pakistani jets ran into heavy flak. They could never get past this soldier's nishaana. He is said to have shot down nearly thirty Pakistani Sabre jets.

Each time a Pakistani jet shot across the sky leaving contrails of smoke behind, we girls, instead of running downstairs for shelter, would run up to the terrace in order to watch the tamasha. We were in awe of the spectacle of war. We were sure that since our house was next to the mosque, we were safe; the Pakistanis would *never* bomb a maseet.

'Aeh gya! O gya!' the little urchins would shout, running through the gullies of Hall Bazaar. 'Go down, you!' Deoli would be heard shouting. 'When one bomb explodes na, then you'll come to know!' But for these kids there was no cowering under covers. They wanted to look the war in the face, their eyes squinting in the sun!

One morning, around 10 a.m., a plane came flying so low it nearly hit the minaret of Khairuddin's mosque. People ducked. Right behind it was another one, chasing it. In all the hullabaloo I wonder if we could even tell which plane was Indian and which Pakistani. Petrified, people began to run helter-skelter through the gullies. The noise was horrendous! Suddenly, the windowpanes of our house shattered and fell to the floor with a jingle. It was a sharp, stunning image. It happened in a split of a moment! But right after that everyone straightened up and composed themselves, saying, 'Ho gya! Ho gya! Ho gya!'

∽

The radio played a most significant role during the war of 1965. Wherever you tuned in, you would hear patriotic songs, songs that would charge your emotions, boost your spirit, inspire the nationalist in you. It was mainly because of these songs that I felt more Indian than I'd ever felt before! I can still hear snatches of those songs when I recall that time:

Eh watan, eh watan, hamko teri kasam . . . teri raahon mein jaan tak luta jayenge . . .

And:

Kar chale hum fida jaan-o-tan saathiyo . . . ab tumhaare havaale watan saathiyo . . .

Every morning at 8.30, we would sit in a semicircle around the
brown radio with the yellow teeth, and listen to our Prime Minister,
Lal Bahadur Shastri, addressing the people of his country, keeping their
morale up. His was the lone calm voice in the midst of the cacophony
of war and it did us a power of good—it gave us hope and brought
reassurance that the insanity of war would soon come to an end.

In an attempt to spread misinformation about the Indo–Pak war,
Radio Lahore would broadcast highly provocative and false propaganda
about India. The motive was to demoralize the local Ambarsaris. However,
most of the time, Radio Lahore's broadcasts were so patently false that
they provided comic relief to the Indian listeners, who would get the
correct feedback soon enough from the AIR. Indians called Radio Lahore,
'RADIO JHUTHISTAAN'.

Early one morning Radio Lahore had alarming news for us.

'PAKISTAN PAINDABAD!'

I shuffled in bed.

'THIS IS RADIO LAHORE! WE HAVE JUST RECEIVED NEWS
THAT THE PROMINENT FRONTIER TOWN OF AMRITSAR
HAS BEEN CAPTURED BY THE PAKISTAN MILITARY!'

I woke up startled and looked around. Everyone but Piti was fast
asleep. My father was listening intently to the radio. The announcer on
Radio Lahore continued:

'PAKISTAN KI FAUJ MUSALSAL AAGE BADHTE HUAE
AMRITSAR SHEHAR PAHUNCH GAI HAI—HAMARI FAUJ NE
HAAL GATE KI GHADI BHI UTAAR LI HAI!'

Pakistan's army is continuously marching forward and has reached
the city of Amritsar. Our army has ripped the clock off the Hall Gate
and brought it back as proof of victory!

Then, after a pause: 'PAKISTAN CELEBRATES THE CAPTURE
OF AMRITSAR!'

I peered out of the window. Even though we mocked Radio Lahore,
upon hearing this startling revelation, I wondered if I would see the
Pakistan army marching through the lanes of Katra Sher Singh, but no,
no sign so far. All was quiet in the gully. Had I heard right? Piti, who
was fiddling with the knob on the radio, managed to tune into Jalandhar
radio station.

'RUBBISH!' retorted the Jalandhar announcer, promptly retaliating with his own version of events. 'INDIAN ARMY CAPTURES LAHORE! THE CITY OF LAHORE HAS FALLEN TO THE INDIAN ARMY! THERE ARE INDIAN TROOPS EVERYWHERE!'

I ran up to the terrace and leaned across the parapet, almost falling over the edge, wanting to see signs of victory in the bazaar. The power of my imagination those days had hit an all-time high. The capture of Lahore! I visualized images of Indian soldiers marching through the streets of Lahore city. The Indian Army storming the Shahi Masjid! I imagined our troops walking down the famous Anarkali Bazaar. Indian soldiers taking hostage the prostitutes of Hira Mandi! Wow! Breathlessly, I waited for further news, my imagination running wilder.

'The wanton women of Hira Mandi captured and brought back to Amritsar!' Wouldn't that be something? We'd finally have the nautch girls of Pakistan, dancing to *our* tunes! Just like in the movies!

'The art of the mujra returns to Amritsar!'

But there was no sign of anything, anywhere. All was quiet. But the day's excitement hadn't ended. As people began to wake up, the fake news that had been circulating had the effect of charging them up. Men and women thronged the terraces of houses, at first whispering and then shouting across to each other.

'LAHORE JITT LEYA! WE'VE WON LAHORE!'

Mochistan came alive! Little children scrambled out of their mud huts and ran barefoot towards Hall Gate, their kachhis falling, shouting victory slogans.

'LHAUR JITT LEYA! LHAUR JITT LEYA!!!'

Little jingoists, brandishing corncobs! Blustering patriots, clamouring for war!

Melville de Mellow, a renowned Indian Radio Broadcaster at the All India Radio, was specially stationed at Amritsar to counter the Pakistani propaganda.

It was one of the more bizarre manifestations of the war, an epic tragedy playing out as a comedy. In reality, though, there was little to cheer or celebrate about this carnival of hate. Each country stoked its loathing for the other. Each flagged its fantasized victory over the other.

On the ground, in the city, the atmosphere was charged. Housewives volunteered their services for the war effort: working in hospitals, setting up stalls, collecting money, and distributing food packets. Young college girls went around collecting donations, a bangle here, a chain there; piling up magazines to take to the jawans convalescing in hospital beds. A major stall was set up near Hussainpura by the Women's Conference and another one by the Red Cross, collecting blood donations. Mama would go and distribute pamphlets and food to faujis in passing tanks and trucks, little Rohit trundling along with her in the rickshaw. She would take Didi and me along with her to donate blankets at the 'Donation for the Army' counters set up all along the Grand Trunk Road. She was not alone. The women of Punjab were out in force fighting the war their own way!

'Yeh waqt sone ka nahin, yeh waqt khone ka nahin, uttho watan ki ore se, jaago watan ki ore se, awaaz do . . . awaaz do, ham ek hain . . . ham ek hain!'

The words of the songs instilled into their mundane lives, a new meaning!

The college girls of Amritsar also pressed into service. They would go to the military hospital in the Cantonment where the wounded were brought in, sit by their bedsides, and write letters for them. Writing letters for the jawans was for the girls a very special privilege.

Elsewhere in the city, people were contributing in whatever way they could. Mastana Loudspeaker in Katra Sher Singh had taken it upon himself to boost the morale of the people during those seventeen days that the war lasted. Tucked away in his little shop in the gully, Mastana would keep the turntable of his record player spinning round and round and round. His would be the last shop to close down, and the last sound resonating through the gullies during the dark, blacked-out nights would be a song:

Tu hi meri aarzoo! . . . Tu hi meri qabroo! . . . Tu hi meri jaan . . .
Ae mere pyaare watan . . . eh mere bichhde chaman . . . tujhpe dil qurbaan . . .

All of Katra Sher Singh resounded with the unforgettable lyrics of Prem Dhawan, bringing a lump to our throats.

'Eh watan, eh watan, hamko teri kasam, teri raahon mein jaan tak luta jayenge!' were words that would choke you with emotion.

∞

One night we inadvertently got into trouble. To avoid enemy bombers, the city had enforced strict blackouts. As the war escalated, we would spend entire afternoons sticking black drawing paper on all the glass windows of the house, quite an undertaking as the Chandraavali house had an endless number of windows. Gogi and Pappu, the boys upstairs, were forever running to Rama Stationery to buy scrap-fills of Amrit Glue.

My father had the habit of reading every night before going to sleep and he would switch on the bedside lamp. But my mother would quickly switch it off, saying, 'Darling! Please! There's a blackout all over the city!' My father would toss and turn in bed, then, unable to take it any more, he'd switch the lamp back on again. Again, Mama would lunge over and switch the light off. Piti would try and be clever by throwing a newspaper over the lampshade to get the light to fall only on the book, but the paper would slip, and once again, there'd be light! Flashing brightly on the dome of the mosque ... on, off ... on, off ... on, off! This went on for two nights till my parents got into serious trouble for not following the blackout instructions.

On the second night of the blackout, there was a knock on the front door late at night. Then another. Then a major thumping on the big phaatak downstairs. Piti hurriedly went down. As he opened the gate, he saw a knot of heads, peering at him.

The crowd whispered, 'Bauji, we just saw flashes of light across the maseet! We suspect that someone is sending signals to the enemy from your terrace! Looks like the enemy is within! ... if you might allow us to search the house ... for your own safety!'

'No, no, no ... no need!' My father stuttered, quickly brushing aside the suggestion, and reassured the knot of heads ready with dandas, to go back to their homes. 'I'm here, I'll watch out!' he said reassuringly.

But the matter didn't end there. By the third morning, the night's flash-fiasco showed signs of ballooning out of control. The self-appointed vigil keepers of our gully had decided that the flashes across the mosque were signals being beamed to Pakistani jets to come and bomb the city.

That evening, before the blackout happened, it was evident that something major was about to take place. The spy story had infiltrated into every nook and cranny of the gullies and spread across the entire mohalla. People were now no more bothered with sirens and blackouts.

They had another agenda at hand—to catch the spy!

All of Mochistan was up in arms against this Pakistani spy. They'd all seen that light flash on and off...on and off...across the white dome of the mosque, giving out signals through the night. Action had to be taken immediately!

'How can we let this happen in our OWN mohalla? One of US? A TRAITOR?'

That evening when my father returned from college on his bicycle, he saw a crowd blocking off the gully, right outside the gate. 'Bauji, we'll *get* him tonight!' the cobbler clan said as one, waving their arms in a fury against the invisible traitor, the wretched deshdrohi!

'We've seen it with our own eyes, Naval Saab! Light being flashed on the mosque! On, off! On, off! There's a spy around here who climbs on to your terrace in the night, sending signals to Pakistan! Not once, not twice, but repeatedly—for two nights! We can't let this happen! Not in our neighbourhood! You don't worry Professor Saab, we'll get him! No Mai da Laal will sleep tonight! Tonight, we'll catch the miserable wretch!'

'And, and ...' Tota Ram's father's voice was a notch above the rest— 'And beat him to PULP!'

Watching from the terrace, Didi and I giggled nervously as Piti pulled his hat low over his face, and sheepishly, without making eye contact with anyone, dismounted and wheeled his bicycle into the house. He then shut the phaatak on loud slogans:

'DESHDROHI! ...TRAITOR! ...! We'll get you tonight, you wretched WORM! If we don't SQUELCH you under our feet na, you just see!'

Needless to say, my father's reading at night came to an end for the duration of the war.

Between Mochistan and Pakistan, life was in a complete quandary, and we loved every moment of it!

∞

On 23 September 1965, the eighteenth day of the war, a ceasefire was declared between the two countries. There was great relief. Everywhere in the city people rejoiced. But to our horror, that same night Pakistani Sabre jets unexpectedly pounded Chheharta, the industrial hub of Amritsar, killing nearly 100 civilians.

The news of Chheharta's devastation spread like wildfire.

'CHHEHARTA BOMBED! ALL THE PEOPLE IN THE AREA DEAD! EIGHT TO NINE HUNDRED HOUSES RAZED TO THE GROUND! THE FAMOUS PRATAP BAZAAR GOES UP IN SMOKE! CHHEHARTA IS FINISHED! FINISHED!'

The night Chheharta was bombed the walls and windows of our house shook badly yet once again. That whole night we heard nothing but shelling, as if there was no other sound on earth. No one slept. It seemed as if Amritsar would be blown up after all, the city of the Golden Temple turning to smoke! And for once, we were scared.

The night came in suffused with an unnerving calm. There was no trace of breeze on the barsati. Mastana's loudspeaker was the last familiar sound that resonated through the night—and we were grateful when we heard, in between the thump of the artillery shells, the deep, intense voice of Manna Dey singing the memorable *Kabuliwala* song:

*Tere daaman se jo aayen . . . un havaaon ko salaam . . . Choom loon
main us zubaan ko, jis pe aaye tera naam . . . Sabse pyaari subah teri,
sabse rangeen teri shaam . . . tujhpe dil qurbaan . . . Maa ka dil banke
kabhi . . . seene se lag jaata hai tu . . . Aur kabhi nanhi si beti . . . ban ke
yaad aata hai tu . . . eh mere pyaare watan . . .*

The next day, once it was clear that the ceasefire would not be broken, Piti rented an Ambassador and drove us to Khem Karan, the border on the Indian side, to impress upon us the tragedy of war. We'd got news that our older cousin, Gertie Auntie's son, whom we'd never met before, had been posted in the sector at Khem Karan and had arranged for our visit. My mother's anxiety mounted. She was excited as well as nervous at the prospect of meeting her long-lost nephew. Piti sat in front, next to the driver, while Mama huddled in the back with Didi and me, Gugu, my little five-year-old brother, tucked between the two of us in his soft pink blanket.

The thirty-five mile drive up to the border was an eye opener. As we left the outskirts of the city and approached the open fields, the atmosphere started to change. There was a palpable sense of gloom.

Tanks were spotted along the road, trundling towards the border. We drove past Asal Uttar, by now known as Patton Nagar, as a huge number

Kamal Bhaiya with his fellow officers at Khem Karan.

of Pakistani Patton tanks had been ambushed here by the Indian Army.
By the time we reached Khem Karan, the sun was going down. The
sight I saw there has remained embedded in my mind—it was my first
real look at war!

It was evening, the sun was going down, but there was still some
light in the sky, reddish, eerie . . . all was still, no breeze, no sound . . . and
in the muggy silence of a devastated landscape, I saw the severed head
of a buffalo, blown apart by a shell, impaled on an electric pole, a black
crow sitting beside it on the smoked-out wire.

The place smelled of metal as Khem Karan had become a graveyard
of tanks (I learnt later that this war had seen the world's biggest tank
battles since Second World War). The fields were badly scorched. Shattered
tanks were strewn all around the area. A few dead bodies lay sprawled
in the dust. Crows sat quietly on electric wires without cawing. It was
a very disturbing sight. I was scared and huddled close to Didi in the
back seat, but still took in everything. I wanted to imprint every little
detail of war in my mind.

As I absorbed the enormity of the tragedy that had taken place, I
felt deeply ashamed that while the Indian Army had given their lives

Kamal Bhaiya visits Chandraavali.

fighting for their country, we kids had been giggling as we ran in and
out of the trenches, *enjoying* the war.

We were shown the inside of an enemy Patton tank. The hatch of
the abandoned tank next to it was open, a dead soldier slumped out of it.
'They are in the process of removing the dead bodies', we were told. A little
further away, under a cluster of trees, a soldier was being buried. Buried?

'He is Pakistani . . . we are to give them their due burial', we were told.

Finally, we were ushered into a bunker to meet our cousin. A young
man, twentyish, stood smiling in front of us. 'Captain Kamal Sharma,'
he introduced himself. Mama dissolved into tears upon seeing him and
hugged him with all her heart. It was an intense emotional moment,
one that I would draw from several years later in my life as an actress.

Somewhere deep within me, something had stirred . . . a sort of sea
change. At age thirteen, I suddenly felt grown up.

An image still comes back to me sometimes—

Against a smoky red war sky . . . stuck on an electric pole . . . the head
of a buffalo . . . blown . . .

Later, during my Hunter College days, my friend Meenu Munavvar and I would sit together recalling the war—she on the Pakistan side and I on the Indian side of the border, just about thirty-two miles away from each other, but sharing similar memories of the 1965 war—the same emotions, same fears, the same excitement. Both of us remembered the same metallic sounds emanating from Lahore and Jalandhar radio stations, both falsely proclaiming:

'PAKISTAN CAPTURES AMRITSAR!' and 'LAHORE JITT LEYA!

Sitting on the corner of Sixty-eighth Street and Lexington Avenue in Manhattan, we'd be looking out at the world, reflecting...Why war? Why?...Why can't human beings just live and let live, when life was so beautiful?

23

The Elbow Crusade

It was the year 1966; eighth class girls were in full form. Since we were already in war mode, it wasn't difficult going from one battle to another. The winter after the war with Pakistan was won, we decided to declare another kind of war! A war against the disgusting practice of 'eve-teasing'—the precise and evocative Indian coinage for a widespread form of sexual harassment aimed at women and girls of all ages—that was rampant in the city and surrounding areas.

It seemed that in every other man on the street there was a hidden grabber. Every now and again, one of the girls would land up in class narrating some traumatic incident that had happened on her way to school. It was all too familiar to every one of us. You would see a guy move strategically towards you, from all the way across the street, looking elsewhere, of course, just to rub his shoulder against yours, to accidentally brush his body against yours, to somehow touch you. You could see it in the eyes of these men!

They were all around us—tall Jats from villages, built like icons, and despite their Greek-god-like appearance, putrid when it came to their behaviour with women and girls; lean and scrawny fellows on bicycles, their eyes focused at the *right spots*; harmless looking men on the bus; and even boys walking innocently along the road—they were everywhere and they were the enemy.

Most times the enemy had no face. Just a hand in an overcrowded bus that would suddenly grab you! Or pinch your bottom! Or give you an unwelcome back rub! Or squeeze your tit! Brazen and undeterred, these predators moved from bus to bus, crowd to crowd, in search of pinchable bottoms, grabbable tits. Pathetic creatures, they were not fit to be called men, these creepy-crawlies! They were just worms! Worms! It was sick!

And every so often it would get too much for us to take. Consider what happened to one of the girls in my school. Mona was from a neighbourhood called Batala—tall, Amazonian, true Peshawari blood! When we had all switched over to wearing salwar kameez, Mona continued to be in her frocks. One day, she came to the school crying. We were most concerned. What on earth could have happened!

Mona used to ride her bicycle to school. Apparently, a guy would follow her on a bicycle, shouting obscenities and making lewd remarks. Mona had so far managed to ignore him. But this morning obviously something drastic had happened.

Two men on a motorbike had driven past her, shouting—'Eh, patt dekhe! Patt!' (What thighs man! What thighs!) and she broke down again. Soon after, Mona had to switch over to wearing a salwar kameez. After all, we were living in Punjab!

My experience was worse. One morning I was on a bus that was unusually packed with people. It was Baisakhi time and hordes of villagers had come to the city for the mela. I was sitting pretty at a window seat, but as the school approached, I decided to get up and walk to the front of the bus. It was difficult to move through the crowd—men, women, children just stood swaying, jammed against each other. Unable to manoeuvre my way through the crowd, I stood holding on to the railing above. Suddenly two hands shot out from behind and grabbed my breasts. I gasped! My grip on the railing gave way! I swayed with the shock! Quickly the hands disappeared. I was so petrified I did not dare to look back. I started to tremble. A sense of revulsion came over me; all I wanted to do was get off the bus and puke. Somehow, I squeezed my way through the jam of people up to the front exit. At the next stop, a stop short of my school, I got off the bus and broke into tears. I walked the rest of the way to school crying.

When I got to class, I did not talk about this to any of the girls. But deep inside me, anger had started to build up, anger directed towards myself! Why hadn't I turned around and slapped the guy! Why had I not shouted and got everyone's attention? People would surely have lynched the creep! Why had I got scared and quietly moved away? Why the hell was I crying? I should have retaliated! Should have turned around and hit the guy! Mama would have!

But I did not have the guts. I was only fourteen.

This was the story of every young girl growing up in a city like Amritsar. I started to feel that this was not the place for any decent girl to grow up in. It was around this time when we girls felt that enough was enough. We had to *do something* about it. We decided that the only way to deal with it was to fight back—ferociously. We deliberated at length on this issue and decided: NO MORE! No more getting pinched in buses and being rubbed against in the crowd! No more being frightened and embarrassed at being pawed. Coming to school in tears was *not* the answer! Now *we* would be the ones to attack! We decided to go to war! Against eve-teasing!

It was towards the end of the fourteenth year, during the fall of 1966, that it was actually launched, and it lasted for a whole year—we called it 'The Elbow Crusade'.

The girls club elbowed their way through that time. Strategies were worked out. An unofficial slogan was coined. 'Touch me not!' was too tame. 'You DARE touch me!' was the new war slogan.

We now observed all hands with great suspicion. Hands holding bus railings, hands resting on thighs, hands carrying bags or books, especially unseen hands in coat pockets, were all potential weapons to be guarded against.

The enemy was well-versed in the art of the skulk. A hand could appear in the middle of nowhere—from within a crowd or on a lonely street. The biggest challenge was to defend yourself in a chest-to-chest, jostling bus ride, with one hand carrying books and the other holding on to the railing above. The enemy in the shape of hands had to be combated with instant, reflexive actions, accompanied by a barrage of gaalis to no one in particular and to one and all in the bus.

Mostly the enemy would appear from behind. When such creepy-crawlies attacked, one would have to swirl around and hit! A sharp jab of the elbow right into the ribcage! So, the enemy would lose his balance as he lurched back in sudden awe of the victim. Yes, slap! If need be. Do not shrink into the crowd. Face the situation squarely. Retaliate! Do something! But don't just take it! Launch a verbal attack, in which case the people around would suddenly be galvanized into action against indecent behaviour—in such cases you yourself wouldn't have to do much. Let the crowd take over. You would just have to step back and watch the fun as the enemy got flogged right there on the spot!

The attacks did not let up right away. Neither did the defence. Sharp! Focused! In the mornings before classes began, the teen infantry would huddle together in the school corridors, reporting on incidents of the day before. After school the modus operandi that had been decided upon would be put into practice. Then, at night, we'd all talk to each other on the phone to review the day's incidents. Overnight, strategies would be changed, amended, reworked. New counter-offences would be thrashed out, to be launched the next morning. When we were younger, and learning about the predatory male gaze and other forms of daily sexual oppression, we were taught to ignore taunts and stares by keeping our eyes lowered and walking swiftly away. This would no longer be the way in which we'd deal with such behaviour—our eyes would *not* be lowered, but wide open and alert, watching on all sides. We had learnt three new words from the dictionary—circumspect, adroit, alert!

From playing defence, we became counter attackers. At times these attacks would be lethally comic, and, splitting with laughter, the winners would narrate their tales of conquest and courage. The enemy was often stunned by the defence, and had to take to his heels or duck and dodge his way through the crowd lest he got beaten to a pulp!

The biggest counterattack we mounted against our oppressors took place in May the following year when the cornfields were nice and ripe. It was called the 'Chappal and Jutti Offensive'—a well-planned action, worked out with precision. The offender would be lured to a secluded corner behind the school and then beaten up. Even the dialogues were rehearsed. 'You bastard! Don't you have a mother and sister at home?'

We counted on Mona to entice the creep on the bicycle to his doom! She would lure the skirt-chaser towards the back of the school into a secluded corner flanked by cornfields. The plan went as follows—when the scumbag peddled past her uttering obscenities, instead of abusing him, she would give him a faint smile, and tilt her head away from his gaze. Bas! That was all it would take; the moron would assume the girl was saying 'Yes!' And that is exactly how it played out.

While Mona was doing her bit, we all went and hid in the cornfield. Mona rode into the field behind the wall of the school, the area we had designated our battleground. The jerk happily followed her, peddling his way right into the trap we had laid for him. At a distance Mona dismounted from her bike, slanting it against a brick wall. Then she moved behind the wall to where he could no longer see her. The guy threw his bike on the ground in his excitement and hurried after the girl, looking all around him nervously. He now stood in front of Mona, breathless, panting!

We were ready, on our marks! We had decided to count up to ten before we made our move. Let the creep move towards the girl and we will...The creep moved barely one inch, and before he could lay his hands on the girl, we attacked! Suddenly, a brigade of schoolgirls came screaming out of the field swinging their shoes by the laces, and before he knew what hit him, we had clobbered the fellow to the ground and continued to thrash him.

'Maaf kar deo! Maaf kar deo!' squirmed the enemy—'Sorry, sorry, sorry, sisterji! Please...maaf karo! I will never...Never, do it again!'

The worm screamed for help, but we were relentless. We wanted to pound him to a pulp! I saw Nonu pull out a ruler from her bag and repeatedly poke the man writhing on the ground with it. That day I found an innovative way of using my freshly sharpened drawing pencils. Kiran whacked him in the face. Finally, the enemy was screaming for mercy, all of us having at once been converted from 'prey' to 'sisters!'

Victory! Victory! Worms of the world—squirm!

By the time we emerged from the field, we had the look of warriors being hailed for winning a battle. When Sister Jacinta saw us in the assembly later that morning with our socks full of slush, her eyes narrowed. She looked us up and then all the way down, squinted at our dirty shoes and socks again, but surprisingly did not utter a word. Nothing, it seemed, could mar our moment of victory!

24

Coming of Age

Growing up on our street was quite something and, in a way, it prepared us for life. When we switched over from wearing frocks to salwar kameez, Mama became stricter. Didi had already switched over to wearing the chunni, while I was still showing my skinny legs.

I remember a very interesting conversation once between my mother and my sister. There was this boy at the Sardar tailor's shop who'd keep staring at us each time we passed by the gully on our bicycles.

'Mama, that boy in the tailor's shop, you know, he is very kharaab! He keeps staring at us every time we pass by.'

'Does he? Then keep your eyes on the ground and walk on!' Mama's reply was short.

A few days later Didi again complained.

Didi in salwar kameez, with me in a frock.

'Mama, that fellow *na*, that creep—he is still staring at us!'

'Yes, still staring at us ...' I confirmed, standing right beside my sister.

'How do you know? You must have looked at him!' Mama glared at us this time.

'To check if he is still staring!' Didi logically answered.

'No need to check!' Mama brusquely said. 'Put your head down and walk straight through the gully! No need to look at anyone, is that clear?'

'Yes, Mama!' said Didi.

'Yes, Mama!' I parroted, looking at my sister to make sure we both understood that.

∽

Not all the boys and men around were creeps, in case you are beginning to wonder. It was around this time that we started getting interested in boys. There were nice boys at St Francis School whom we met when we went there once in a blue moon, for some competition or to take part in a debate or a festival. During festivals, music was played on request. Requests were written out on pieces of paper and given to the DJ sitting under a tent—so and so boy wishes to play a song for so and so girl. The girl whose name got announced followed by a song, would feel embarrassed, and blushed. There was romance in the air, but that's where it remained, in the air.

∽

Around this time, I also started maintaining a diary that I kept safely hidden in my wardrobe. I had all kinds of *feelings* written in it and couldn't afford to let anyone read it. Each time some little thing happened, I'd come and pour it all out in my diary, sharing with it my deepest thoughts and emotions. In order to guard it strictly I would slide it all the way to the back of the shelf, under the neatly arranged stack of clothes. Many years later, when it was time for me to leave Amritsar, I put a matchstick to my diary and watched it go up in flames—a greatly dramatic moment in my young life.

∽

It was at this time that I had my first crush. Our eyes had met once or twice, and I thought he was awfully cute. Seemed like a charming, shy sort. At times I'd see him ride down the lane on his motorbike and I'd stand in the hall kamra convinced that he was passing by my house only to get a glimpse of me. Other times I'd imagine him speaking to me—that was the extent of my imagination those days—him speaking to me, him asking my name, and telling me his name. I'd spend considerable time imagining what his name would be. In my mind I conjured up all kinds of names, somehow starting with a V, and then settled for a 'Vikrant'. And when he spoke to me, he'd obviously speak perfect English. Polished, well-spoken, shy, intense—that's what he'd be.

Half a season passed but nothing happened. We never confronted each other on the road. He never stopped for me, nor did he ever get off his motorbike to speak to me; I never found out what his name was.

Then, one day, returning from my morning walk with my father, I saw him standing at a window at the corner of our street and Hall Bazaar. Yes, that was surely him, at the first-floor window, with a stick between his teeth, doing datun.

Datun? How *desi*! In that instant the entire romantic edifice about him that I'd built up in my head came crashing down. How could I romanticize being with a boy who did not even use a proper toothbrush? The thought horrified me.

Though he continued for a few more days to exist on the periphery of my heart, my mind was occupied with so many other things that were more exciting at the time, and it did not take me much to forget all about the boy with the datun, or Vikrant, or whoever he was, my first crush.

∽

Along with my first crush, there was another first in my life at this time— my first period. I'd been aware for some time that I was the object of some curiosity among my friends and one day I discovered why. I was ironing my uniform when Didi and Munni cornered me.

'Have you got it yet?'

'What?'

'Your period.'

'What the hell is that? I pretended not to know what they were talking about.

'Menstrual cycle, stupid! Every girl gets it. Don't you know? Don't tell me you haven't got it yet.'

'No, not yet.'

'Are you sure you haven't? Honestly?'

'Nope!'

'You are what, fourteen already? When are you going to start menstruating?

'Arrey!' What is this menses mania, I thought.

Then one day Mama decided to educate me about the monthly periods, and soon after, Didi took it upon herself to expand my knowledge on the subject.

'What? Once a month? Every month? For life?'

'Yes, for life ... till you are old and haggard!'

The whole thing sounded quite awful to me.

'No, no, I don't want to get all this!'

'Yeah, sure! You're *Miss Special*! You'll go through life without having to deal with it!'

Finally, when I did get my period that season, everyone promptly lost interest in the subject, and life went on much as before.

∽

Attaining puberty was naturally followed by dreaming about love and romance, another rite of passage for a young girl, ready to blossom into womanhood. But while we girls did entertain the idea of having a boyfriend, it remained limited to a fancy. We discussed boys, and we'd be curious to talk to them, and, for a while, we went no further than idle curiosity. Slowly but surely, we came up with an ingenious way to talk to boys without any of the actual trouble of meeting them. We'd dial random numbers on the black dial phone and wait for a young voice to pick up the receiver on the other end. We had no clue whom we were speaking to, but if we liked a voice, if it was deep, resonant, with a good English accent, we'd shyly start chatting him up, three or four of us huddled around the phone, giggling. The receiver would be passed on from one girl to the other in hushed whispers. The yellow phone directory was there for us to pick numbers from.

This was how we'd end our schooldays, by dialling 'wrong' numbers. If the guy on the other side turned out to be a nerd, we'd simply say, 'Wrong number!' and hang up. We made up fake identities, fake names, fake accents, gave any rubbish information about ourselves, never revealing our true identities.

The boys at the fancy store down at Queen's Road were an easy target. We knew the bunch there were not bad looking, and the numbers were quick to find. So, we started chatting them up. Once we told them we'd meet them at a certain spot, dressed in such and such colours but we had no intention of actually meeting them. We went there wearing the exact opposite colours just to check if they had showed up!

Finally, one guy beat us at our game. He figured we were making an *ullu* out of him. Nonu was on the phone. Didi, Munni, and I stood around in the corner of the hall.

'So, what do you do, I mean, for a living?' She asked him.

After a pause, the guy replied: 'Meri bra ki factory hai, main bras banata hoon.'

Nonu turned pale. She covered the receiver with her hand and turned towards us.

'He has a bra factory, he says, he makes bras!'

'Haaawww . . . How cheap!' We were scandalized.

'Bloody rascal! How *dare* he!' Disgusted, we rang off. That was the end of our wrong number caper. Not once after that day did we dial another wrong number. We figured it wasn't worth talking to boys. Boys were cheap—they had only one thing on their minds!

We went back to books, and the more dream-like world of Hindi film songs.

∞

Aah, old Hindi film songs . . . we heard them all the time, if not on our radio, then from the house next door or the radio down the street. As a girl, I was hooked on to the radio, forever tuned in to Vividh Bharati or Radio Ceylon, my favourite being *Binaca Geet Mala* by Ameen Sayani, *the* voice from my girlhood years! Lying under the open sky with the transistor on my tummy, it was old film songs I'd doze off to night after night. I also loved Lahore Radio as I was enraptured by the mellifluous sound of the Urdu language and it was around this time that I developed an enduring love of Urdu poetry. But old film songs transported me to another world. It was songs from good old black and white movies that gave me all kinds of notions about life and about romance and I continued to dream my dreams...Whether anything else worked in life or not, romance was crucial to existence. If one could not fall in love like in the movies, what was the point?

What with sleeping on the terrace, gazing at the stars...the clouds drifting...the faqir singing his lone song...the pigeons taking flight, their wings set on the wind...and old songs playing on the radio...how could one have not been impacted by all these romantic images?

∞

Times had changed. I was now a young girl, no more *little*. The hat stand that kept a close watch over my stepping into puberty, stood in the

pillared veranda, more towards Mama's room against the wall facing the vehra. It was once too high for me to reach and would take me years before I would get the first glimpse of myself in the mirror.

During my baby years, it would see a glimpse of my confused little head, when Piti had me in his arms, shaving with his right hand and holding me with the left. When Mama occasionally glided in from somewhere, my face would be swept away from its mercurial surface. Then I was on my own two feet, trotting forward mostly, taking tiny steps against my will, as if someone was poking little fingers in my back. Then there's the time I'm dressed in a frock, holding Didi's hand, ready to go for a day out with Mama and Piti.

When I was small, I tried several times to stand on my toes and get a glimpse of my face, but it was far from reach. My foot slipped several times as I tried to lift myself up on that rod. Initially, a fringe and two eyebrows appeared in the mirror, no more. But this much was okay for now, at least I could see my French cut was intact. I shuffled some hair in the front brushing them down with my fingers over my eyes, still not visible at that height.

As I grew a little older, I'd be able to look into the mirror by standing on the rod. I'd prop up on the hat stand and stare for long moments, admiring myself, asking, 'Mirror-mirror on the hat stand, am I a pretty girl?'

That mirror was perceptive for sure. It studied me while I studied myself, my feet perched up on the horizontal bar to reach my reflection in its freckled face. I considered the angle at which I looked best. I turned my face in all directions in order to ascertain that I looked good from every angle. I thought I had beautiful brown eyes. Not that anyone had particularly told me about that, it was just this inner feeling.

Whenever Mama called for me and I ran barefoot across the courtyard to her room, I'd never forget to step up at the hat stand just for a split second, for a quick 'all okay?' look at the person in the mirror. Mama had noticed this ritual several times but pretended she hadn't. She didn't want to make me feel self-conscious. I suspect my mother saw a whole lot of herself in her younger daughter.

Around eleven, I remember, each time the doorbell rang, I'd hoist myself up on the wooden rod and with a tilt of my head, shoot an angular glance in the mirror, to make sure I looked presentable before answering the door. I'd always make it a point to tip my head a bit at that particular Sadhana angle where she looked her best, making sure that the same effect was achieved in my mirror as well. But the girl in the mirror always seemed startled by her undefined looks. Of course, I never forgot to smile. How come no one had noticed my smile? Couldn't it ... I mean ... it could change the world, right? ... Sadhana's did!

I didn't just stand and stare into the mirror—I'd talk to the person inside it always. The hat stand stood there, with the patience of saints, taking into account each flickering indication of bloom on my face, the first flush of youth, recording each moment of doubt, anxiety, disappointment, and joy. Come to think of it, if the hat stand could speak, it would blurt out many secrets that I kept to myself and regularly shared only with the mirror.

When, at sixteen, I wore a sari for the very first time for Brian Uncle's wedding, a lime-beige cotton, and stood in front of the hat stand, pinning my pallu to my shoulder, I smiled into the mirror, and I swear, for once, it smiled back.

Years later when the house in Amritsar got demolished, I let go of everything else, but just the hat stand I retained ... and it stands today, framed by snow peaks, in my little art studio in Himachal.

25

The Other Side of Madness

Didi had just passed out of school winning the title of 'Miss Charming' and we all had now acquired the new rank of 'seniors'.

Didi and Munni.

My years in high school, up to the tenth standard, certainly had some highlights, big and small that I'd like to describe. One of the things I delighted in was getting my own bicycle. After years of riding pillion on my sister's cycle this gave me a palpable sense of freedom and independence. I loved riding a bicycle. In the first months after I got my bike, we were still wearing frocks and had to be extra careful not to let the breeze lift the hems higher than was considered 'decent'. Later, when we'd shift to salwar kameezes, it would be the dupattas that would have to be kept in check. They'd go flying all over the place, those two metres of soft chiffon forever threatening to get caught in the wheels of the cycle.

The best part of the bicycle ride was the slope down the Bhandari Bridge. What joy that was! Especially on days of sweltering heat, this part was the best. Both feet on the pedal, but no peddling, just letting yourself go. The wind in your face, and you went winging downhill, your chunnis flying, the breeze tingling the pores of your body, exchanging glances, grinning at each other—the sheer joy of being girls! No other bicycle ride in the world ever matched the one down Bhandari Bridge.

Didi, Munni, and I in our teens.

Winters would be a challenge. Riding the bikes to school in the biting chill was something else. In the early morning hours, your ears felt like frost, like they weren't there at all. The wind would turn our faces so cold our noses would become sniffling red blobs and our eyes would start to water. But we were young and bursting with vitality and high spirits and we deemed these minor inconveniences. In fact, I quite liked the winters and preferred the cold weather to the dry heat of Punjab. The morning fog, the feel of the blazer, the knitted socks, the laced-up shoes, there was something about winter that perked me up.

The only fascination I had for the summer heat was the onset of the monsoon. Whenever the sky rumbled and the sun went behind the clouds, we'd pull out our bikes and go off cycling on the long empty road towards the Raja Sansi airport. My favourite time of the year though, was the fall season. Cycling back from school I'd at times take the scenic route home and follow the tree line along Thandi Khui peddling by the old eucalyptus trees swaying in the breeze. How tall these trees were, and how old...Autumn in Company Bagh was a splendour to behold. I'd stop a while and watch the dry leaves falling...they'd fall in clusters with sudden gusts of wind and then scatter around in a mosaic of rusts, browns, and yellows. Fall was a season I'd wish would stay the whole year round. To watch yellow leaves falling from trees was a moment your heart locked in.

∞

Once we grew out of wearing frocks, our outfits came under the tight scrutiny of Sister Jacinta's stern eye. We could not wear churidars and tight, hip-hugging kameezes like Asha Parekh and Sadhana in the movies of our days. Our kameez had to be a certain length. Sister Jacinta would actually take an inch tape and measure the slits on the side. If the gaps were less than the required length, she'd simply take the scissors hanging on her rosary, and cut them open. She walked around with those scissors in her hand, forever looking out for girls in tight fitting kameezes.

∞

With Sister Jacinta, eighth standard.

The ninth standard girls were forever up to mischief. We simply couldn't be contained no matter how strict the nuns were.

One day, we all let out the air from a bicycle stacked in the bicycle shed. When the school bell rang, Miss Sudesh, our Hindi teacher, came out and walked over to the shed. Seeing us, she smiled, and then to our horror, she pulled out the very bike whose tyres we'd deflated. She saw what had been done and then looked at us. We all looked elsewhere. Instead of losing her temper, she quietly wheeled her cycle out of the school gate and had it repaired at the wayside 'Tire-Painture' wallah. I felt quite bad for Miss Sudesh, as I rather liked her. Though I was never the one to initiate any of this mischief, my friends had my full support—I never let them down.

A few days after the incident, just outside Mother Superior's office, Miss Sudesh walked over to her bicycle and found the back tyre had gone flat. Nonu and I were standing near the gate, innocently chatting. She looked towards us with a knowing look. We straightened up. But swear to God, this one time we hadn't done it and though we weren't guilty of this particular infraction, when Miss Sudesh passed by us with her flat tyre, we both looked sheepish and apologetic for no reason. Not that she held it against us. In my second autograph book from the year 1968, there is only one page written in Hindi and that is in Miss Sudesh's handwriting:

Sach-charitra, namrata, Mata Pita ki seva hi jeevan hai.
Purushaarth, tatha Ishwar par vishwaas,
Jeevan mein Unnati pradaan karte hain.
(Good character, humility, hard work,
trust in God, and service to ones parents
enhance one's life and make it worthwhile)

With Love,
Sudesh
S K Sayal, House No. 238
Opp. Gol Bagh, Asr.

Miss Sudesh came into our lives when we were in the seventh standard. I took to her almost instantly and became quite fond of her. There was something very amiable about Miss Sudesh, something very

reserved, yet easy, about her demeanour. She'd come to school riding on
her bicycle. Tall and well built, she was always dressed in a salwar kameez,
hair in a single braid, and wore a bindi. She was quite fond of me, I
could see and I'd quite look forward to my Hindi class. She would say,
'Honhaar birwa ke chikne-chikne paat' (If there are qualities, they'll be
visible in you as a child).

Skit for Miss Sudesh.

Miss Sudesh opened up the world of modern Hindi literature for me. We
had the opportunity to study an anthology of Hindi short stories that
included greats like Munshi Prem Chand and Mahadevi Verma. But more
than prose, whether fiction or essays, it was poetry that actually drew me
to Miss Sudesh's class. I got to study all the major modern Hindi poets like
Ramdhari Singh Dinkar, Nirala, Harivansh Rai Bachchan, Sumitranandan
Pant, and Mahadevi Verma. Hindi poetry changed something within me.
Inspired by the poetry of Nirala in Miss Sudesh's class, a group of us
girls called ourselves the 'Nirala Group'. We had the audacity to think
that we were special and unique and were the *Niralas* of the world. We
were four of us in the group: Prem Goenka, Kiran Duggal, Nandini
Puri, and me.

Besides the modern poets we also studied classical masters like Kabir,
whose work impacted my thought process in a way that nothing else

The Nirala Group

had. There was something deeply philosophical and universal about Kabir. He would take me back to the faqir in my gully whom I'd encounter during the winters of my early childhood. I now recognized, that what he sang in the wee hours of the morning was a lot like Sant Kabir:

Othhe beej lae taranaan vaali kiyaari,
Jithhe papaan vaale khet beej laye . . .

&

For the entirety of our school life, we only ever had one male teacher, Mr Soni, who replaced Mrs Mahindru, the Maths teacher, once she retired. He was a tall, lanky man, with legs much longer than the desk he sat at in front of the class—it could hardly accommodate his entire being. This resulted in him perpetually sitting with an arch in his back, which, coupled with his old age, led us to call him the Hunchback of Notre Dame. Whenever in class he would notice Nonu up to something, he'd say to me, her benchmate:

'Can you push that girl out of the class?'

'No, sir . . . I . . .' I'd stutter.

'Then you also go out!'

He was an odd fellow for sure, but in due course Mr Soni did help me get over my mathematical anxiety.

∽

Besides Miss Sudesh and Mr Soni, the other teacher I have never been able to forget is Miss Hussain, our History teacher. Strangely, I remember everything about her except her face—I have no memory of what she looked like. I have only an *impression* of her personality. There was something about her, something unexplainable, but I didn't know what exactly it was that made her different from the rest. She seemed a bit strange at times. Gradually we came to learn of her life story.

'She's off her rocker!' said one of the hostellers in class.

'Really? No wonder she's strange!' the girls whispered. I was curious, rather concerned, I'd say.

It was said that Miss Hussain had vowed to consecrate her life to the service of God. She went through rigorous training in the convent in order to become a nun. She had been accepted as a postulant, even lived several months in the order taking classes. And now, finally, she was going to be consecrated in a formal ceremony. But the night before she was to take her final vows, she ran away from the convent.

It was also rumoured that since that day Miss Hussain lost her mind because she believed she had betrayed Jesus Christ. It didn't occur to any of us geniuses that if she was 'crazy' she wouldn't have been allowed to take classes for us. But then the imagination of teenage schoolgirls isn't exactly rational!

Our speculation about Miss Hussain led us to briefly delve into the intricacies of what it took to become a nun. Pemu promptly pulled out her dictionary and looked up the word 'nun'. She read aloud—

'A member of a religious community of women, typically one living under vows of poverty, chastity, and obedience.'

'Poverty, chastity, and obedience,' said Nonu. 'That's too much!'

Kiran didn't think so. 'It's a way of life you're choosing, it's not a joke . . . Go on, what else does it say?'

'Once a woman decides to become a Catholic nun, she applies to join a specific order by undergoing an aspirancy.'

'Aspirancy?' interrupted Nonu. 'What's that?'

'... which,' Pemu continued, 'is a period of two to four weeks in which she lives with the other nuns of her order.'

'Then?' I was most attentive.

'If ... if the nuns of her order determine she is a good fit, she will be accepted into a postulancy. After several months of living in the order and taking classes, a prospective nun then enters a novitiate.'

'Yes, that's right!' said Rani, the only Christian girl in our class. 'At this time, she will be assigned a new name.'

'Wait ... there's more.' Pemu insisted on reading on. 'After two years as a novice, the nun then takes her first vows.'

'Oh man! This is endless!' Nonu was losing it.

'And then ... then after three more years, takes her final vows.'

'Oh ... Boy!' We were exhausted simply listening to this five-year saga of the preparation that went into becoming a nun.

'No wonder,' said Pemu, 'she ran away from the convent!'

'I would too!' Nonu agreed finally.

∞

Our fascination with nuns in general led us to invent all sorts of things about them, including wicked tales about unsavoury goings-on between the Sisters of Sacred Heart Convent and the Fathers of St Francis School. Sister Jacinta would be paired with some Brother, as would others. We'd question their vows of poverty, chastity, and obedience.

To our feigned horror and delight, it was Sister Jacinta, we heard years later, who had run away with a man and got married. The strictest nun in our school ... married ... so our wild speculations weren't completely imaginary!

∞

While in these pages we girls sound a bit distracted, we were actually all made of tougher stuff and sought to follow our dreams! Didi would become a biochemist and work at the Memorial Sloan Kettering Institute in New York. Among the seniors, Kiran Pashauriya would become Kiran Bedi, the super cop, first woman police officer of India. Recipient of the Padma Shri, Neelam Mansingh would go on to carve a niche for herself in the world of theatre. Kamaljeet Sandhu would become famous as an athlete, representing India on the international stage. As for my classmates, Prem Lata Goenka would join the Khalsa College University for boys, becoming the first girl there to get her Master's in English Literature. Madhu Sadana would go on to become a doctor, following in her father's footsteps. Kiran Duggal would choose to be an educationist, and I'd pursue fine arts and writing, and one day achieve my dream of becoming an actress.

∞

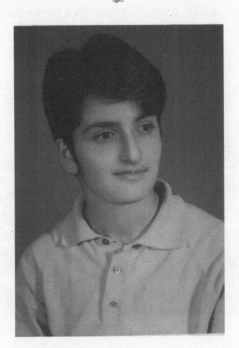

Neeta Devichand

Down in the valley near Simla skies
I fell in love with two brown eyes . . .

These were the first two lines of a poem she'd written that she read out to us in class and that's how I would like to remember her.

Neeta Devichand joined our school in the summer of 1966. We had finished with the eighth and were moving up to the ninth standard. It was a year in which life revealed itself to me in totally unexpected ways.

Sister Jacinta walked into the classroom one day with a boy, or so we assumed.

'This is a new student and she will be in your class as of today.' She? We all looked at each other. But she looked exactly like a boy. She came from Simla and was quite unlike any other girl I'd so far known. She had a boy's haircut and even spoke like a boy.

'Main jaounga … Main karoonga … Main aata hoon … main jaata hoon!'

We girls were maha amused at her way of speaking and giggled a lot initially in her presence as we found her behaviour rather cute. When she was asked to pick a seat, she came towards the back and sat down next to Nonu and me.

Me, Kiran (standing), Nonu, and Pemu.

Neeta was born in February 1951 and was an Aquarian like me. She had studied in Simla and eventually made her way to the Sacred Heart Convent where she lived in the hostel for two years. Neeta was an enigma in many ways, and everyone was fascinated by her. We became friends and she was the fifth member to join our group—Pemu, Nonu, Kiran, Neeta, and I sat together in class; outside the class, we hung out together, all five of us, the *Nirala* bunch.

She seemed enormously talented and showed great potential as a student. She was surely above average, and seemed to be much sharper than most girls I knew, and far more confident; I found her confidence somewhat intimidating. She wrote poetry and took part in declamation contests, winning every single debate. Neetu also acted in plays, even directed some of them on stage. I was amazed to see the abandon with which she performed, the manner in which she could, in a split second, transform herself into something completely different. That certainly needed talent.

Neeta would make the whole classroom come alive with her presence. Everyone in our class, the girls and the teachers, were awed by her.

But there were things about her that no one could understand. She would run away from school. We didn't know where she went, but it seemed she really had a history of disappearing. She had even run away from home a few times. She was missing once for two days—her family looked everywhere, and after two days she came out of the attic.

Neeta would tell us all about her adventures in Simla.

'One night,' she said, 'it was wintertime. The whole valley was covered with snow. I was in my room upstairs, studying. I had this strong urge to get out of the house and go somewhere. I just needed to go out in the open. Once everyone in the house fell asleep, I quietly opened the window and crawled out.'

'At night? All by yourself? Where did you go?'

We all were now huddled around Neeta, her adventures being no less exciting than those we read about in our *Schoolgirls* comics.

'Through the sleet I walked up and down those steep winding roads, and once the chill got to me, I went and sat inside a cinema hall on the Mall Road and watched a movie.'

'A movie? So late?'

'Yes, I watched the last show, then returned home and crawled back into my room through the same window. No one had any inkling that I'd been missing. I loved sneaking out of the house to go and see movies!'

'Did you ever get caught?'

'No! Not once!' she said.

Neeta spoke very fondly of her father, who doted on her and called her his 'Prince of Wales'. But she said that she had a stepmother who treated her really badly. We felt awful listening to Neeta's stories. Poor girl, how miserable her life had been! We couldn't help but empathize with her and vowed to stand by her at all costs.

Each morning as we entered school, we'd get to hear of something new—what Neeta had done the previous night.

'She sleepwalks, you know!' the hostel girls would report.

'Really? We didn't know she had that habit!'

'I swear she does! She got up from her bed last night and went and crawled into another girl's bed. That girl flew out from her quilt, shrieking, thought it was a ghost. When the warden switched on the lights, she found Neeta standing barefoot on the cold floor looking completely lost.'

Girls in the hostel said that during drama rehearsal one evening Neeta fell down in the corridor and her body throbbed on the floor. The nuns went berserk running around with shoes in their hands trying to make her smell leather. Sister Rita tried shoving a bunch of keys in between her teeth to bring her back.

Neeta's actions soon became the talk of the conservative convent. Sitting next to me in class one day, Neeta opened the desk, placed her hand on the edge, smiled, and smashed the lid down on her hand. My head jolted back in shock. I looked around to see if anyone else had seen her do that. When she drew her hand out from the desk, it was gashed. Before I could stutter the word 'H a e l l l p!' she tapped my arm. She also picked a stone one day and hit herself on her forehead, then entered the classroom bleeding. Another day, she dug her teeth deep

The school choir

into her writst, then cried, 'I'm in pain ... I'm in pain!' That day I realized something about Neeta. She was hopelessly addicted to creating drama around herself. She could go to any length to seek attention, that it had become difficult to tell what was real and what was make-believe—both for others around, as well as for herself.

Come winter, and the school would get galvanized into preparing for the annual concert, something we all looked forward to. There'd be elaborate preparations for the event months beforehand, and great expectations as well. There would be plays, skits, songs, dances and the girls were encouraged to take part in everything. I was good at singing so it was mandatory for me to be in the chorus. Though inside me, I

In costume before a dance performance.

always knew I could act, I was too shy to go up on stage and perform in front of everyone. But I loved singing and dancing, and would happily stand in line with the other girls singing away in the glittering lights against the backdrop of our painted forest stage.

Shakespeare's *A Midsummer Night's Dream* was being performed on stage
this December. Some of us girls were given the task of ushering in the
parents and families into the hall and making sure they found their allotted

seats. Ratan Bhandari, a senior, made her formidable appearance on stage
wearing purple breeches and a silver crown, her hair falling around her
shoulders. Didi stood on stage wearing a long robe, and curiously enough,
she had a moustache.

The play was well on its way when I desperately needed to go to
the loo. But how was I to go out there all by myself in the pitch-dark
playground? Kiran Duggal offered to accompany me. As we carefully
opened and closed the door of the hall, we found Neeta standing outside,
anxious, fidgety, smoking. She had been hugely involved in the production
of the play and was a bit on edge. She offered to escort me up to the
loo and back. Kiran decided to wait at the entrance, while Neeta and I
walked across to the loo. The night was crisp and my hands were cold.
Once I was done, we hurriedly walked back towards the auditorium down
a darkened passage. Suddenly Neeta grabbed me and put her mouth to
my lips. I froze. A shudder ran through my body. This was insane! I tried
to free myself but Neeta's hold on me was firm. For a moment I wasn't

sure what was going on, and then I remember feeling extremely revolted. In that brief dark moment, all kinds of thoughts rushed through my head. How forceful a tongue could feel, how wet and sinful the act of kissing!

I jerked myself away and broke the moment, breathless. When I emerged from that dark passageway, Kiran was still waiting at the entrance. One look at my face and she asked me:

'Did she kiss you?'

I looked at her incredulously.

'....Yes...' I stuttered. 'How do...you...?'

'Your face is white!'

Kiran grabbed my arm and took me inside. Wait a minute; did she know things about Neeta *I* didn't know? Before I could ask, the dialogue from *A Midsummer Night's Dream* washed over us as we walked inside the hall. On stage, a girl in ringlets was delivering Helena's famous monologue:

'Love looks not with the eyes, but with the mind,
And therefore is winged Cupid painted blind.
Nor hath Love's mind of any judgment taste;

Wings, and no eyes, figure unheedy haste.
And therefore is Love said to be a child,
Because in choice he is so oft beguiled.
As waggish boys in game themselves forswear,
So the boy Love is perjured everywhere.'

As I sat down, what I'd just experienced hit me. I could not believe what had just happened. That was my first kiss . . . and I got kissed by a *girl* . . . gross! I looked at Kiran hopelessly.

For days I sulked. The experience weighed on me in a variety of ways. My first kiss had *not* been with the boy of my dreams. It was nothing like I'd imagined. No looking dreamily into his eyes, no feeling butterflies in my stomach, no first look, first touch, first anything . . . What an awful turn of events. My imagination began to spiral out of control. Now, when I meet the boy of my dreams what would I tell him? That I was not a virgin? I decided I'd be partly honest. I'd tell him I'd been kissed before, but I wouldn't say by a girl. That would sound bizarre. Those were the ideas we grew up with. You'd get intimate with only one man, the man of your dreams, the man you were going to spend the rest of your life with. Any other sort of intimacy was out of bounds. Till you met *him*, you'd wait. At least that's what the films propounded.

After the episode during the concert, I withdrew from Neeta completely. That I had started to avoid her must have been obvious to the rest of the girls in the group, but I remained tight-lipped about it. I wanted to wipe it out of my mind. Like it never happened. Other than that, I went about my routine normally. It was a huge relief when I noticed that Neeta's attention had moved on to another girl, a tall, pretty looking, light-eyed girl in class.

One afternoon, when the bell rang at the end of recess and the playground quickly emptied out, I found Neeta sitting on the veranda steps by the merry-go-round. She said she wanted to speak to me. I felt instantly ill at ease, but not for long. Neeta spoke at length. I do not recall exactly what she said but I'd like to imagine that she said her behaviour that night had been inappropriate, and that she regretted it. I do remember her telling me how she felt drawn towards this other girl and how she needed her to feel the same way towards Neeta. Finally, she said something I had been subconsciously waiting to hear.

'I care about you, Deepti, I don't want to lose you as a friend'.

I'd been listening all this while. Now it was my turn to speak.

'Me too.' I said quietly, still struggling to gauge my own emotions.

'Can't we continue to be friends?' Neeta implored.

We both sat there without saying another word for a while looking at the banana trees in the back of the playground. Then I turned towards Neeta and smiled.

'Friends?' she gushed awkwardly.

'Friends.' I repeated, rather less emotionally.

When I came away to class that afternoon, I was back to being my old self again and all was well with the world.

Neeta stayed in school for two years, but she never gave her exams, never completed her studies. She left in between. She studied all the way, preparing for exams alongside the rest of us, but she did not appear for her final papers.

I remember the day of the examination, she did not want to study. She ran away from the hostel, got into a rickshaw and came all the way to Pemu's house. She knew we were all going to be there. When she arrived at the Garden Bungalow, she was bleeding. One look at her, and we freaked out! Her face was cut across, slashed diagonally from the forehead to the chin. We rushed her to the V. J. Hospital. Back in school she lied to the sisters saying it had been an accident, that her face had been slashed by a wire protruding from the rickshaw she got into. In reality she had cut her face with a blade.

Next thing we knew, she was in a psychiatric ward. Monday morning when we arrived in school and heard the news, we were terribly upset. Everyone was talking about the dramatic turn of events.

'Neetu has been sent to a mental hospital . . .'

The nuns tried to downplay the matter, even hush it up, but it was the only thing everyone wanted to talk about. Only Sister Rita was her usual compassionate self:

'Don't worry girls, she'll be all right. Right now, she needs care!'

As the days passed, we got more and more restless wanting to get some news of Neeta. We could no longer just sit and wait. We had to do something. We *had* to go see her. But how would that happen? A dark gloom took over me at school and at home. I couldn't concentrate. I knew she did things to get attention, but she was no raving lunatic that she should be put away in a mental institution! She was *one of us,* for God's sake, how could we just let her be in there and not do anything about it?

I remember that day with such clarity, the day we visited Neeta in the mental hospital: Pemu, Kiran, and me. As we walked in through the big yellow gate of the hospital, a man passed by on a bicycle wearing a chadar, carrying a dead goat on his back. I noticed there were kikar trees planted all around the vast premises. We were asked to wait in a large empty room, supposedly the waiting room. I have clear memory of the muddy brown and yellow dhurrie on the floor, and pictures of Gandhi and Nehru hung from the walls. The grilled windows of the waiting room threw sharp streaks of sunlight across the floor.

'Government Mental Hospital Amritsar was established in the year 1948 when non-Muslim patients admitted in the mental hospital of Lahore were transferred to Amritsar and were . . .' Pemu was trying to read what was written on the display board when an attendant walked in with a file in hand. We stood nervously around as he started reading aloud from it.

'Neeta Devichand was taken into the custody of Punjab Mental Asylum by the gazette medical officer, Mr Baldev Kishore, who had assessed her an "alleged lunatic" on grounds of: she refuses to eat, is obstinate, lies a lot, does not work, is suicidal . . . hates her mother, sings all the time' etc. etc. She was admitted by her father, Mr Rajinder Lal.' Another page had something called: Statement of Particulars. 'Neeta had her first attack at age fifteen and she'd been admitted before at the PGI Chandigarh.' When asked whether the patient was subject to epilepsy, it said, 'Yes, Temporal seizures.' Whether suicidal? 'Yes.' The document was signed by Baldev Kishore, the Medical Superintendent of the Punjab Mental Hospital, Amritsar.

The attendant then asked us:

'Who are you? . . . Relation?'

'She is in school with us. We are her classmates.'

He disappeared inside the hospital. A little while later, the curtain separating the waiting room from the rest of the building was pulled back and Neetu stood in the doorway. She looked at us and smiled. She seemed so . . . so normal. Why in the world was she in *here*?

'What happened Neetu? Are you okay?' I asked a very obvious question, my mind unable to construct anything more appropriate.

'Main bilkul achcha hoon! . . . Nothing wrong with me!'

'What on earth happened?' I wanted details.

'Just because I cut my face in that blessed rickshaw the other day, they've brought me here. You know me better . . . I'm just acting.'

A glint appeared in Neetu's eyes. She smiled at us standing in an ankle length robe. Pemu and I glanced at each other. We wanted to say something, but before that, Neetu said in her usual mischievous manner:

'It's a lot of fun. I can emulate a mirgi ka daura. It's very exciting! Everyone here gets psyched out, you should see! Want to see me do it? Watch!'

Before we were able to utter anything Neeta was on the floor thrashing her limbs, her arms flailing in the air. Violent spasmodic contractions of the muscles, her face distorted, her expression changing several times over. We panicked. Neeta worked herself up to the point of frenzy, frothing at the mouth. Flecks of saliva flew from the corners of her mouth, dribbling down her chin.

No, no, this can't be an act. A hand grabbed me on the inside. Her rigid body jerked on the floor as I watched in horror, our perfectly lovely friend come to *this*! What in God's name had gone so wrong that she had ended up in such a state? Her eyes rolled up, her head stiff and tilted, as if unseen hands were wringing her neck. We stood there horrified. Hell, this was no *acting*, this was for REAL! We yelled for help. In a flash the attendants were there, holding her; three of them dragged her out of the room, her body shimmying on the floor. Any hope in my mind of Neeta's recovery was completely annihilated that afternoon. But just then, something happened. Before disappearing behind the red curtain, Neetu turned her head, winked at us, and grinned!

That grin of hers was the last I was going to see of Neeta Devichand. We could not utter a word to each other. All three of us stood there shaken, then quietly walked out. All I could whisper was one word:

'Brilliant.' That was a brilliant performance!

But was that a performance? . . . I would never know.

Was it possible that the line between real and make-believe had become completely blurred? It will always remain a question whether her brilliance was in making others believe her in what she did, or making herself believe that that was reality ... which reality did *she herself* live in?

Deeply distraught, we waited outside trying to flag down a rickshaw. My mind was tormented with questions that seemed to have no answers. And, although we didn't know it at the time, we were to never see our friend again.

About six months later, when I'd gone to the Krishna pharmacy to pick up something, Vibhu, Munni's older brother, said to me, 'O, teri saheli hai na? That friend of yours in the paagal khana ... she has written poems all over the place.'

I couldn't speak at first. I just stared at Vibhu. I knew this was bound to be. How could Neetu be somewhere, anywhere, and not leave her imprint? But I feigned casualness.

'You saw her? You saw the writing?'

'I've been going there for a project,' he said. 'Go and see for yourself! Her poetry is written all over the walls of the asylum!'

I wanted to go, but I didn't. Not then. I would, but ... I would.

A little later, on Neeta's birthday I went back to the asylum, and this time alone. But I was told she'd already been discharged and that her father had taken her away earlier that week. I felt happy and sad at the same time. I walked around the wards. Her handwriting was all over the walls. I lingered there a long while, touching the whitewash, reading her poems, getting to know ... her soul.

It was a season that was to shape things later in my life as a student in America and as an actress in the Bombay film industry. It would not be an unnatural choice for me to take up Abnormal Psychology as one of my major subjects at the City University of New York. It was something I had to deal with, I felt it was my calling. It was important for me to understand the other, deeper, darker side of the human mind, and also probe the areas where genius dwells.

It was only when I was at Hunter College in Manhattan, reading the poetry of Sappho, an archaic Greek poet who was born in 630 BCE and came from the island of Lesbos, that I realized where the word *lesbian* came from, a word I hadn't ever heard before, not during all those years at school in Amritsar. Sappho was a lyrical poet who wrote love poems for other women. I connected everything back to Neeta. If only we had known about lesbianism earlier, how it was simply another sexual orientation, perhaps we would have handled things better.

In the mid-90s, I was out with my film crew doing a recce for a TV series called *The Path Less Travelled,* and decided to explore the Kinnaur valley, as I'd never seen that region before. Simla was the first stop out of Delhi on our way to the mountains. I met up with old friends Manisha Banaerjee and Jessi Gill and we were all sitting in the dining hall at Davicos when a man walked in whom Jessi introduced to us as, 'Kappi, my lawyer.'

I asked around if anyone knew a store in Simla called Devichand's.

'Are you looking for the old Devichand showroom?' asked Kappi.

'Yes ... I'm looking for my school friend, Neeta Devichand.'

'Neeta, their elder daughter, who left for Austria?'

'Austria? ... perhaps ... we haven't been in touch for years!'

'She is no more ... Neeta died in Austria years ago. She died under tragic circumstances ... suicide, they say.'

I broke down! My friends were shocked to see me howling. They couldn't figure out what had suddenly gone so wrong.

I was told that though the Devichand's store no longer existed, the house was still there. Neeta's mother lived there. Oh yes, her stepmother, I recalled. Kappi wrote down on a piece of paper a phone number for me to call.

'Mrs Devichand?'

'Yes ...?'

'Aunty, I'm Neeta's friend ... my name is Deepti ... Deepti Naval.'

The voice at the other end sounded excited.

'The actress ... Deepti Naval?'

'Yes, Aunty ... Neeta and I ... we were together at Sacred Heart Convent in Amritsar.'

'My God! I've seen so many of your movies! I love your acting!'

It was a steep road off the Mall where Neeta's mother had asked me to meet her. I stood there feeling extremely vulnerable, literally on the edge. I saw a lady, not so elderly, walking up the path towards where I stood. She was petite and pleasant-looking. When she came up closer, and smiled, I thought, oh my God, she looks exactly like Neeta! She is no stepmother!

'Aunty, I ... I'm very sorry to hear ...'

'Deepti Naval ... of course!' She beamed. 'I didn't know Neetu and you were friends ...' And then a cloud of reflection appeared in her eyes.

We both were quiet for a long moment as we stood there sharing a pain we knew could not ever find words ...

Neeta's mother was a mother like all mothers, had always carried twice the burden, and yet tried to do the best for her daughter as was advised by all the doctors possible. That day she spoke to me from the heart.

Neetu suffered from a kind of schizophrenia—she had two personalities—one full of life and fun, the other where she lost herself somewhere and became another, so difficult to watch and bear. Hers was a cry for help, but medical aid for mental health in India at that time was non-existent, and drastic measures were taken to treat people like her.

As I said goodbye to Mrs Devichand and moved away from the ridge, I began to reflect upon Neetu's life and circumstance. She died near Munich, in a town called Unterschleissheim on 5 April 1985. Her father had been completely heartbroken when he'd left her at the mental asylum in Amritsar, and could not deal with the fact that his 'Prince of Wales' was so seriously ill and they could not find a cure. And for her, what torture she went through—just to survive as being different from everyone else. She was brilliant and that cost her dearly.

Her family recalls: 'We do not know a single person who knew her closely and did not love her, because God had made her just so special, and we are blessed to have been a part of her. May she finally rest in peace as she is now set free from the shackles and chains that bound her spirit and soul.'

I will always remember Neetu as a most caring and lovable soul, her love for life and people, her *zindadilli* are forever etched in our hearts. She bonded with everyone at a personal level, changed every single person she met, impacted every life she touched. She enriched and added a dimension to each of our lives as she taught us love and laughter. And like someone very close to her said: 'She is like the wind, let her go ...'

26

Goddess in Green Fields

Although the tragedy of Neeta loomed large in my final years in school, there were still exams to be prepared for, and hopefully passed. But I remained distracted for much of that year despite the fact that the final exams were drawing closer. Nonu and I were by now getting pretty restless in school and also, in a pensive sort of way, adventurous. Though we were two opposites and had contrasting personalities—I was far more subdued a person, and Nandini Puri was a riot—but we liked doing the same things. We'd look for any excuse to step out of school and wander off. During recess, the ninth and tenth class girls were allowed to step out of the school. We'd go sit on the little bridge over the naala for some time and then return to class as the bell went off.

∽

At times we'd wander off after school, hop on to a passing bullock cart, take a ride on the gadda for a few furlongs, then get off the cart and hop on to the Punjab Roadways bus, honking for villagers going to:

'*Ambarsar . . . Ambarsar!*'

I recall one particular gadda ride so well. It was the month of October, the last period of that day, a few minutes were left before the bell would go off. Both Nonu and I sat in class, looking glum. We looked at each other—surely there were more exciting things to be done outside this classroom! Nonu slid out first with the excuse of going to the loo, then, I excused myself under some pretext.

At the gate we both stood smiling about nothing in particular. The air was nippy and the sun was a white ball lower in the fields. We saw a bullock cart coming lazily along the deserted Buffalo Road. As it approached us, we placed one foot on either side, and climbed on to the haystack. The old Sardarji riding the gadda simply smiled, he knew we were going nowhere!

Lying back on the stack of hay, taking in the early winter air, gazing at the blue, white-streaked sky, the lazy jingle of the bells in our ears— this was the good life! For once we didn't want to hop off quickly. Swaying on the promise of life, we teetered towards Pind Majitha, softly murmuring things that were close to our heart, at times reflecting over little personal details.

It was quite a distance that we'd come along, I realized, as I sat up looking all around. School was left way behind, a distant dot on the horizon almost invisible now. We were in the middle of nowhere—it was just the autumn fields and us, and the old Sardarji, who hadn't turned around even once to ask where we were heading.

Finally, the gaddewallah doubled back to a bus stop and stood waiting beside us by the roadside, to make sure we got a safe ride back towards our school. As we stepped on the Punjab Roadways bus headed for the city, I glanced through the back window to catch the Gadda's lazy wobble into the foggy blaze of the brick-gold sun.

∽

Couple of times I strolled into the fields behind our school all by myself. I loved the thrill of being out there, one-on-one with nature, without anyone knowing about it. On one particular day, I ventured a bit further and discovered a little ruin of a temple. Inside was a broken image of a goddess. She held a trishul in one hand. Her head was adorned with a tinsel crown and a few glittery rags hung from her dark body. Her eyes sparkled with black kohl and there was a huge red teeka, oil-painted, in the centre of her forehead. Part of the trishul was broken; the crown was tilted, hung low aslant her forehead. The silver frill of her veil brushed her dark stone face in the soft breeze. Her eyes were captivating, gleaming in the afternoon sun. Who was the artist I wondered, who had so beautifully captured with bare hands, the spirit of the goddess! I stood gazing at her for a long time. Then, carefully crouching, I sat down beside the idol, lost in thought, until the school bell startled me back to reality.

I was strangely drawn to the little ruin, as though I was looking for a past connection ... it was a déjà vu moment for me ... like I'd *been here* before and that it meant something to me. There was mystery to it, a little secret I'd keep to myself.

'Where were you?" asked Nonu one day. 'I was waiting for you the whole hour.'

'Oh, just ... walking around ...'

'Aren't you scared being out there by yourself?' asked Pemu. I looked at her as if not understanding what she meant. No, it hadn't occurred to me to be scared. Being out in the open? In broad daylight? In the lap of nature? No, it's only the dark that gets me.

Next day after school I took Kiran along with me and we both sat there next to the nameless goddess. A bullock cart jogtrotted along the Majitha Road, its bells tinkling in the distance. A cool breeze wafted through the barley fields. That evening we saw the sun turn our magnificent school building into myriad shades of ochre.

These excursions continued, until our actions were brought to Sister Jacinta's notice.

'Jumping across the wall into the fields!' she walked into class, looking at all of us suspiciously.

'Which one of you is it?'

The girls looked at each other, confused.

'No, Sister, I don't know anything about ....'

'Who's been running across the fields during recess?' I'm told a girl in uniform was seen out there ...'

'Not me, Sister!'

'No, not me either.'

'Me? No.'

'I don't know anything, Sister.'

'No ...'

'Not me!'

All the girls denied the charges. Obviously, none of them knew about the goddess in the green fields, she was all mine. I stood quietly in the back looking most innocent.

'ONE more time if I hear of such outrageous behaviour, girls ... I don't know whom you are protecting, but the consequences will be severe!'

Sister Jacinta looked at each one of us with her famous sinister-squint. I stood there with my chin-down-look-up baffled expression on my face. She, of course, didn't suspect *me* of being up to any such thing. As she turned to go, Nonu looked at me, a goofy grin pasted across her face. Sister Jacinta stopped, turned back from the door, glared at Nandini Puri, then eased her scrutiny, and uttered just one word:

'Out!'

∽

Exams were such a pain I felt, a complete unnecessary evil in life. Why did we ever have to give exams in the first place? Wasn't being interested in knowledge enough? If there was one human being adroit at learning by rote, it was my sister. She'd be pacing up and down the room, reading aloud, mugging up pages of Physics and Chemistry. I was sure she could recite them backwards too. I, on the other hand, always found it difficult to retain what I read. My memory of things was more impressionistic.

Didi and her friends took a tablet called Methedrine to stay up all night studying for their exams. Catatonic, Dexedrine, Methedrine, when consumed, could keep you awake all night long. You didn't require endless cups of coffee to stay up; one little pill did it all. I was curious. I too wanted to try out this wonder pill, but Didi didn't allow me at first.

Then came a day when Mama sat up with me all night long trying to get me to learn chapters from my history book. I felt horribly sleepy but Mama kept me up till I got all the passages right. Next morning as

I sat on the desk ready to write my paper, my mind went blank.

That's when Didi decided it was time for me to try the wonder pill—and it worked. I found a new life with this tiny little tablet. Now I'd be up, awake and alert all night, studying right up till the wee hours of the morning. Only when Lata Mangeshkar's voice went up from the loudspeaker at Sitla Mandir, singing '*Jaago Mohan Pyaare*', a wake-up call for one and all at 4 a.m., did we finally close our books, and put our heads to the pillow.

We were in the tenth standard, with the matriculation exams looming in our near future. We were preparing for pre-exam tests and were all hooked on to this stuff—Pemu, Nonu, Kiran, me—all. Several times during those Methedrine nights we'd call up each other on the phone, and repeat all we had covered so far, sometimes even going over the chapters together, word by word. Nonu did not have a phone at home, so it was mostly Pemu, Kiran, and I forever ringing each other in the middle of the night. It would be Kiran's duty to call up the fellow sitting at the telephone exchange at Katra Sher Singh and ask him to connect all three of us on a conference call.

Then, Lata Mangeshkar's melodious voice, with the first note— '*Jaa . . . aaa . . . aaa . . . aaa . . . aaa . . . aaa . . . a a a . . . Go . . . ooo . . .*'—would remind us to grab the little bit of sleep we could manage, before rushing off to school for the first paper at 8 a.m.

I remember the very first time I used Methedrine; it was the night before the Physiology paper. I straightaway went into *happy* mode.

The night was heightened. In my head I could hear sounds, enhanced sounds of the train whistling past Bhandari Bridge and the chowkidar's baton on the street as he bellowed, 'Jaagte . . . Raho . . . ' I could even hear the pigeons on the dome, sleeping.

We were studying in our parents' room, both Didi and I. They had already gone up to the terrace and were probably asleep by now. Didi sat reading from her Physics book, but me, instead of revising for my exams, I'm dancing all night in front of the mirror. I was wide awake, much like an owl, alert and excessively hyper. The little pill sure was doing the job it promised. Exam or no exam, I couldn't keep still.

My mind buzzed with songs. I couldn't stop myself from getting up on my toes and cavorting to songs in my head. Tonight, not even the four-o'clock '*Jaago Mohan Pyaare*' was going to put me to sleep; the little pill was so potent. I was now an Asha Parekh, dancing to '*Raat ka sama, jhoome chandrama . . .*' and now a Helen, my toes spinning to '*Mera naam chin chin choo*'. But mostly I was Asha Parekh, prancing on my feet, to '*Tum jaise bigare baabu se main akhiyaan churaoon . . . thin-gin thin-gin naachoon,*' and I whisked away the book in Didi's hands. A cold stare stopped me in my tracks, but not for long. The next beat, I was back to '*Aur duniya ko nachaaoun . . . !*'

This was me at fifteen, a full-fleshed teenager, but so foolish until so late in life.

∽

Next morning in the examination hall, all the other girls were busy scribbling away their answers on the sheets provided. I was the only one not writing. Instead, I was drawing, making a diagram, in answer to questions about the pulmonary circulatory system. I drew in minute detail, somehow remembering everything, the vast network of arteries, veins, and lymphatics that function to exchange blood and other tissue fluids between the heart, the lungs, and back. I indicated the names of each blood vessel and every artery, colouring them in red and blue. Last night's Methedrine had heightened my senses and was now working overtime.

Sister Rita came and stood by me, watching me use a different colour pencil for each organ, and each artery. She was impressed, I could tell. Where else had she seen a student make such a perfect drawing? Theory didn't matter. It was the practical that counted in life. Glances from other girls only went to show that my decision to draw instead of writing wasn't such a sacrilegious act. Pemu turned her head every now and then wondering what on earth I was up to. 'Start writing, for God's sake! What are you doing doodling?' At the end the period, when the class submitted their papers, and the girls got to see my drawing—I took my diagram and set it on top of the heap of sheets on Sister Rita's desk. When my classmates exclaimed, 'Wow! . . . how beautiful!', I was sure I'd be walking away with a hundred on hundred for this one.

Three days later the result of the Physiology paper was in Sister Rita's hands. She called out each girl and read out the marks she'd obtained. I waited in anticipation. My name hadn't been announced yet. Finally,

Sister Rita held up the drawing I had done, the last sheet in her hand, flashing it in front of the class.

'Now this, this drawing...what can I say girls...it is beautiful!'

I rose from my desk, acknowledging my talent. Surely, I had set an example in school.

'But not a word...not a *single* word has the girl written.' Sister Rita continued. 'There was a questionnaire given, but Deepti Naval has not answered, not even *one* word.'

I could see what was coming.

'She has simply made a drawing...just a very nice drawing, that's all.'

'But, Sister, she has made such an elaborate drawing...' said Pemu, the studious one amongst us, defending me. Sister Rita held her ground.

'Yes, surely, but there's no answer written. How can I possibly give her any marks even if I want to, when she hasn't answered the question paper? So, I'm afraid, I'm going to have to...'

'*No*...Sister!?'

The class rallied behind me. 'How can you do this? Please give her full marks. She has drawn everything and marked each and every organ and artery, it's all there...she knows it all, *na*, you can see! Please, Sister, please pass her...'

I stood at my desk; my eyes lowered to the ground. Sister Rita stepped down, looked at me ruefully, wobbled up and down the aisle a few times shaking her head, then went back and sat at her table.

'Sorry Deepti—you...fail.'

∞

My final year in school passed in a blur of late nights, sometimes fuelled by Methedrine, as all of us studied frantically for our exams. In August 1968, the Punjab University matriculation results were out. I went through the list put up outside the board office. I was roll number 54257, and I had...I had...had PASSED! I had passed the six subjects I was studying, obtaining 493 marks in the Second Division—and I was fine with that. A little later, though, holding the report card in my hand I was startled to realize how average I was. Average was an adjective that had for me a sense of fear in it. Fear of being ordinary, of being mediocre, of being someone whose existence didn't matter in the world. And that was an unsettling thought. Coming from a family of academics, I had just about managed to *pass*? No, I couldn't let this result define me, I would have to live a life less ordinary. It was now that I became even more determined to live the life of an artiste. Come what may, I would achieve something in the world of art—painting, dance, acting—whatever it maybe. But one day I would surely be somebody.

SECTION V

DREAMING OF AMERICA

27

A Time of Change

My exams done and dusted, I joined the Government College for Women in Amritsar and became a collegiate. Although I was, to all intents and purposes, a college student, I was actually in the equivalent of the eleventh standard in school and the course I was doing was called 'Prep'—a year before BA first year. While some of the girls like Madhu Sadana, Nita Mehra, and Neeran chose to stay back in school another year and complete their Senior Cambridge, we matriculates were relieved to get out of school and join college.

New friends entered my life, girls from different schools, different places. Preeti from Tarn Taran, Neera Puri from the Alexandra School, Santosh (Toshi) from BBK, Promilla Luthra from Ram Ashram School, all became close friends.

I chose to study Psychology, a subject after my heart. I wanted to have an insight into the inner recesses of the mind, and understand what all really goes on in there, the aberrations of the human brain. I was also happy to continue studying English and exchange notes with Pemu over our nightly phone calls. Didi had moved from Hindu College to the Government College as well. While she enrolled for Biology and Chemistry, I took up Singing and Dancing as serious subjects. That I was going to be an artiste was clearer to me now than ever before.

∽

This memory belongs to my first day of college; a memory that still tugs at my heart. Piti gave me a hundred-rupee note to pay my fees at the office in college. I put the note between the pages of my book and went off on my bicycle. On the college campus with its wide passages, huge grounds, students from different schools, new teachers ... I walked around with my school friends discussing the subjects we'd be studying, the classes we'd be taking together, and exploring various permutations, combinations, the start of a new life.

When the day came to an end and I returned home all excited, Piti was sitting out in the veranda on his wicker chair checking some papers. I was telling Mama all about the new campus and the girls I'd met there and the new teachers, when my father asked me, 'Did you pay your fees?' That's when I remembered. I looked back and forth in my book but did not see the note.

'No ... Piti ... I think the note ... fell out from my book ... I don't have it.'

My father did not utter a word. I only saw a lump going down his throat as he gave me a dismal look and then turned back to his papers.

That memory has never left me. It disturbed me for days, the fact that Piti hadn't said a word. That hundred-rupee note must have meant a lot to him, his hard-earned money, and I'd been so careless about it. Not only that, I hadn't even uttered the word sorry.

I still recall the lump in my father's throat when I told him the note was lost.

∽

College brought us new freedom. The little things that would excite us in school were now a way of life. We didn't have to sneak out or hide doing things that we loved. One of these things was walking out in the rain. Beyond the little bridge at Kennedy Avenue where Nonu lived, there was a woman on the roadside selling corncobs. We'd walk up to her and sit on the rickety bench under the blue plastic shed, watching her stoke the fire with her right hand and with the left she'd be rotating the chhallis till they were nice and well-done. Whenever it got cloudy and there'd be signs of a slight drizzle, we'd pull out our bicycles and peddle away on Court Road getting wet in the rain. These little pleasures meant so much. That was the good life.

∽

It was sort of understood in my family that I would take to the arts. Pitaji wanted me to pursue painting since I had already been groomed by my mother and was quite good at drawing and sketching. As for me, I actually nurtured a desire to join the J. J. School of Art in Bombay at some point in the near future. But, for now, the only professional training available to me was at the Thakur Singh Art Gallery.

It was in the year 1969, while I was studying for Prep, that I joined the Thakur Singh Art Gallery, a heritage place created by S. G. Thakur Singh, a painter of high repute, famous for his oils, pastels, and watercolours. The gallery was a beautiful building on Egerton Road, its facade having an arched exterior that gave way to pillared verandas on both sides. The central hall exhibited the works of Thakur Singhji—I loved the 'Golden Temple'. His style was realistic, gentle, and colours were soft. I remember standing before his famous *Taj* with the view of the Yamuna, his landscapes and portraits in soft pastels, and the famous female figure in the painting titled *Bath*, admiring that work. I was inspired. I started to work daily with oils during those evening classes. I would go every day for the art class, which had a few other students from other schools and colleges. I remember I didn't speak much to anyone really; I'd quietly stand at my easel and paint.

The popular images in the art of Punjab at that time—anguished female faces, women silently suffering, rooted in deep earth, unable to break free of their shackles—made me somewhat uneasy. I could not relate to their angst. Why should women remain shackled? Why could they not find their place in the sun? But those images were a mirror to the society. I may not have been enamoured with the style of painting of that time, but I was learning. It was Sardar Gurdit Singhji who taught me oil painting, I also studied with Mr E. K. Raj, a fine water colourist. I learnt colouring, mixing of colours, and the application of transparent layers of paint; Mama had pretty much made sure I knew how to sketch.

Promilla Luthra, soft-spoken, dark and attractive, was the only girl I befriended in the art class. We were to become friends for life.

∞

We were given an assignment at this time to make a portrait. You could make a self-portrait or you could paint a portrait of anyone you wished to make your subject. So, we all got down to work. One evening I came to class a little earlier than usual. None of the students had arrived as yet and I had the opportunity of looking at what the others were working on. So, I wandered around the studio until I stumbled upon a canvas with my own face on it. Someone was painting *my* portrait? Without even *asking* me? I was scandalized. I wasn't going to allow this. I must destroy it! But how? Should I reprimand him? Should I complain about him to the teacher? But who was he? I had no clue and I didn't care. So psyched was I by the lewd male gaze and the *eyes-down-walk-through* stifling culture of Punjab that I felt as though blasphemous act was being performed. I took up my brush, plunged it into my palette, and slathered black paint all over the portrait, wiping out all traces of me. Then I went out of the hall.

Later, when the other students entered, I followed and sat down at my easel. To my horror I realized that the Sardar boy, the gentlest person in class, was the one who'd been painting my portrait. *No*, not *him*! I didn't dare look him in the eye, but I felt mortified as he stood before his canvas in a state of shock! That very moment I regretted my act and felt terribly small. That whole evening I couldn't draw one line.

At the end of class I found myself walking with my bicycle along the footpath towards Pemu's house, but instead of taking the usual right turn, I wandered off towards the Thandi Khui peddling along the old eucalyptus trees, my mind filled with conflicting thoughts.

∞

Back at the Garden Bungalow, Pemu and I sit and analyse life.

'Art is supposed to free you, isn't it? ... not chain you down.'

'What happened?' she says.

'A guy was making my portrait ... and I splashed paint on it.'

'Are you serious?' Pemu puts her book away. She is listening ...

'I need to analyse my own thinking. I can't afford to let my mind be chained into "should be's" ... as a kid one was so free ... Since when has my thinking become this convoluted?'

I look at my friend for her reaction; I know she will understand.

'I'm an artist, Pemu, why am I trying to conform?'

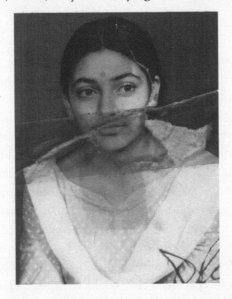

'You already know your mind, Deepi, where's the confusion?'

I take a long deep breath. We remain quiet for a while.

'What about you? Any thoughts about the next thing?' I ask.

'My master's, yes ... but the only course available is going to be at Khalsa College University, and that's all boys!'

'And? ... what does your father say?'

'He's very quiet ... If I get it, I'll be the first girl admitted there.'

'He was the one, remember, who held you up in front of Indira Gandhi's car when we were little, showing you off as a child of great promise?'

We both lie back on the grass and let ambiguities waft away.

She picks up her book from the grass:

'Read from some humbler poet,
Whose songs gushed from his heart . . .'

I continue:

'As showers from the clouds of summer,
Or tears from the eyelids start . . .'

I sigh. Pemu whispers, 'Longfellow.'

∽

At this time, as my interest in painting grew, I came across and immediately became attracted to the work of Amrita Sher-Gil. At home, I was sitting in the Green Room one day, leafing through the pages of the *Illustrated Weekly of India*, when I came across her paintings. I simply gazed at the images. There was something deeper about her work. Her lines were straighter, simpler, with a striking colour palette. There was a quiet intensity about her figures. Unlike the images I'd seen so far in the art coming out of Punjab, this Hungarian–Indian painter had something so modern about her work. Something more universal perhaps; I didn't quite know how to put it. I carefully cut out the pages from the magazine and placed them under the sheaf of papers in my cupboard. A few weeks later I had turned out a work of art to display before the family. I had made an exact, I presumed, copy of *Hill Women*. Both my parents were extremely happy and a little amused as well at the neatness of the work, especially my lines.

'Very good copy, I must say!' Piti said, with that slight jerky movement of his right shoulder, which happened when he wasn't sure about something. He clasped both his hands and bent over the still-wet oil work lying on the dining table.

Mama loved it. 'You painted this?' she asked.

'Yes.' I said proudly. 'It's a copy of Amrita Sher-Gil.'

'You can now try and paint something original,' said my father. 'Something that comes from your own head, perhaps?'

'Or heart?' said Mama. I was extremely encouraged by their response. If I could make such a good copy perhaps I had it in me to become a painter!

Years later, Pitaji told me about his meeting with Amrita Sher-Gil.

'You've *met* her?' I sat up. 'Yes, it was in Lahore', he said. He'd gone to someone's house with Professor Dickenson when he saw her, dressed in a dark georgette sari, her hair tied back in a single knot.

'Very Indian in attire,' he said.

'Did you actually meet her, Piti?'

'No, we didn't really meet. I just saw her kneeling on the floor across from a man selling chunky jewellery in the narrow balcony of that house.'

'And? What do you remember?' I was curious. Piti took a moment.

'The first thing, I remember was that she found the jewellery quite expensive ... and was coaxing the man to lessen the price so she could buy some of the pieces.'

'She was haggling?'

'Yes, she haggled over the price of a turquoise necklace that she had taken a fancy to.'

'Then? Did she buy it?'

'She raised a piece of uneven turquoise stone and held it against the light in the balcony, as a result, lighting up her own profile. She wore a deep coloured lipstick.' I was sure Piti just stood there looking at her, after all he was an art lover, and she was supposedly a thing of beauty.

'What did she look like?' I wanted details.

'She was ... not just beautiful, but something more, her face ... was certainly captivating. That she was half firangi was obvious from the way she knelt down, but I noticed that she bargained like any other Indian woman, except that her way of bargaining was a lot subtler.'

'Did she buy the necklace?' I wanted to know.

'I didn't stay that long, I quietly slipped away to another part of the house in order not to embarrass her, and left her to bargain in peace.'

∞

20 July 1969 was a landmark date. The newspapers flaunted an extraordinary headline: 'Man Lands on the Moon.' It was reported that Neil Armstrong, the American astronaut, commander of the Apollo 11 manned lunar mission, had walked on the moon.

Nearly 240,000 miles away from Earth, Armstrong spoke these words to more than a billion people listening at home: 'That's one small step for man, one giant leap for mankind.'

That night when I slept on the terrace, I looked at the moon with new eyes. Metaphors seemed to shift and drift away and new images started to appear in the night sky. As I lay awake, my thoughts were thousands and thousands of miles away. All I could think of was man's first slow, bouncy step on the surface of the moon. From there, they drifted to the time when Piti had gone to America in the year 1961. Upon his return I had engraved with a knitting needle on the whitewashed pillar of the veranda, my address—

Deepti Naval,
Chandraavali,
Katra Sher Singh,
Hall Bazaar,
Amritsar,
India,
World,
Universe,
Cosmos,
SPACE

It was Piti who had first noticed the inscription.

'Who has written this address?' he asked.

'It's Deepi's doing,' replied Mama.

'Achcha, achcha,' said my father with a faint smile on his face before becoming thoughtful.

Years later, in America, he told me that it was when he'd read my writing on the pillar, that he had made up his mind to leave Amritsar, emigrate to the US, and provide for his children a wider stage on which to enact their lives.

28

Flirting with the Future

College was the time I finally began thinking seriously about my vocation in life. I knew that my parents would never, ever, allow me to become an actress. Leave alone that, I would never have the *guts* to express such a desire to them, to even bring up 'films' or 'acting' as a career option. I was unaware of the existence of any sort of a formal institute, or drama school, that trained you to be an actor, like the Film and Television Institute in Pune or the National School of Drama in Delhi. I had no idea how I'd follow my dream, but I had blind faith it would happen one day.

As I attended college, dabbled in art and other ways of expressing myself, I was seized by the desire to travel and see all those places in the *Reader's Digest World Atlas* lying in Pitaji's bookshelf. Without telling anyone, I quietly answered an ad for air-hostesses for Air India. The call

for the interview came much earlier than I'd expected. The letter from
Air India required me to go to Delhi and meet the team at the head
office. I was nervous and excited but deep within I was sure I was going
to be selected. I took the letter to Mama and Piti and Didi and everyone
knew that this time I was serious about leaving home.

I was packed off to Santosh Aunty's house in Nizamuddin and Indu
Bhaiya escorted me to the Air India office for the interview. I don't have
any real memory of the interview but I'd like to believe that I made an
impression. I didn't hear anything back from Air India for a while, and
then Piti took the decision to emigrate to the US, and all of us grew
excited by the future that beckoned. In the middle of all the excitement
I received a letter from Air India saying I'd been selected, but by then,
of course, it was too late. My future lay elsewhere.

❦

For a very brief period I had also thought of modelling as an option. I
loved the Ponds Girl. I would see her in an ad, wearing a red sari, her
short hair falling around her shoulders. And then there was the Miss India
contest. I started putting two-and-two together. Leela Naidu had been
Miss India and then she became an actress. Nutan was crowned Miss India,
became a film star. Persis Khambatta was Miss India, 1965, then cast in the
film *Bambai Raat Ki Bahon Mein*. I had a soft corner for Yasmin Daji, Miss
India, 1966. Could that be my way out? But Femina Miss India meant
height and stature, and I didn't have the height. I was only five feet and
two and a half inches tall.

Sitting in the shade of the mango grove, Pemu and I chat. 'Will you
be able to wear a swimsuit and parade in front of everyone?' She looks
me straight in the face. It takes me a beat to say, 'So what?' and I look
away. 'Achcha?' she says teasingly. We roll back laughing, thinking of all
these crazy ideas.

❦

Didi had gone away to Chandigarh to do her masters in anthropology
at the Punjab University. Munni, after the untimely death of her dear
Phaiyaji, her father, had been married off and sent away to Delhi. I was at
home with my parents and my brother. What could I do that would take

me closer to the land of my dreams—Bombay?

'Art School,' I said sitting across Mama and Piti at the dining table. 'What art school?' my father asked casually. Mama looked up.

'J. J. School of Art. That's where I'd like to be...Bombay...I mean...I'd like to study at the Sir J. J. School of Art in Bombay.'

My parents looked at each other for a long moment. I watched their faces in anticipation. I could hear my own heartbeat as I waited for them to say something. But that moment between Mama and Piti became so long drawn out, I lowered my eyes and went back to nibbling at the food on my plate. For the rest of the meal, silence engulfed the dining table.

After dinner my parents went to their room and shut the door. Knowing my father, he would be discussing all the pros and cons, making notes, jotting down all possibilities, and the impossibilities...I was nervous. Had I done the most insensitive thing of my life by making that request? Had I asked for too much? Wasn't I aware of the financial constraints? I was surely unrealistic. While reading in my room, I glanced several times at the veranda, waiting for that door to open and for my mother to come out and tell me something positive, perhaps? No one came out. I quietly put my books away and changed into my pyjamas.

That night, as she would when I was a baby, Mama came to my bedside where I was sitting up writing something in my diary. I shifted over, making space for her. I had hope still written all over my face, as I looked at her once again, not giving up in my heart my dream of going to Bombay. Mama began to speak slowly.

'Deepi beta, we know how keen you are to study painting. We'd be really happy if you pursued your passion in art and found a life as an artist, but...'

I remember the look on my mother's face as she continued speaking: 'There isn't enough money, beta. Expenses are high at this point of time...and we discussed it, your father and I...we tried everything to somehow fit this in...but we figured...it...it won't be possible for us to bear the expense of sending you to the J. J. School of Art.'

I sat there numbed, seeing my hopes draining away, looking on this moment as a turning point in my life. Mama looked at me like she knew what I must be feeling. She'd had to give up a similar dream, similar passion...we both became quiet.

'There'll be other opportunities in life, beta, don't lose heart.'

All through our growing years, my parents never let us feel that there was any financial crunch. Whatever we needed somehow always got provided for. We never felt the lack of anything. If there was a dearth of money, we were not aware of it. I do recall that my parents rarely spent money on themselves, in fact, almost never. It was always Didi and I who needed little things that quickly got provided for. And our demands were quite simple. We didn't have many needs either. This was perhaps the first time after my request for a doll at the fair in Delhi that I was refused something I so desired. The pensive look on my mother's face touched something within me.

'It's all right, Mama ... don't worry ... I'll think of something else.' As Mama left my bedside, I slipped under the brown and yellow velvet quilt and burrowed into myself.

That night I slept with endings inside me.

∽

But I didn't sulk for long. Soon after, I took up dancing seriously and joined Guruji's dance class to learn Kathak. I had been a secret dancer all my life. As a young girl, I would practise my dancing in the gusalkhaana. I'd take the transistor radio into the bathing room, perch it on top of the shelf in the corner, and tune in to Radio Ceylon. I'd turn the tap on and let the water flow into the tub for the benefit of Shahni's buffaloes outside.

First dance costume made out of Mama's Banarasi sari.

That would also keep the sound of the music down. Then, standing there in my salwar kameez with my dupatta nicely tucked around my waist, I could dance to film songs for hours if it wasn't for Didi or Mama knocking on the door asking me to come out.

'I'm going to be a dancer!' I told friends, by now quite resigned to the idea that I'd never be allowed to become an actress. But classical dance was a respectable art form, wasn't it? And I loved dancing! Didi had already taken up Bharatnatyam and was performing in college. If I couldn't be an actress, I could certainly become a dancer, a Kathak dancer; that surely would be acceptable!

This is the time when Guruji entered the scene. Guruji, whose name was Sudarshan Kathak (Kathak was a takhallus, not his real surname) was a simple, slightly built, dark complexioned man, who belonged to the Rajasthan Gharana. Guruji taught me the intricacies of this dance form and I began to pick up all the subtleties of movement as well as the light-footedness, the quickness of step—the footwork in Kathak was a fascinating aspect of the dance form. But the one thing I could not pick up was the raising of the eyebrows, alternately. I could easily raise my right eyebrow, but the left one refused to move. I ended up distorting my face; it was quite

With Guruji and Preeti.

funny. I'd try to hold one eyebrow down with my hand and raise the left one but to no avail. I finally gave up on this nazaaqat and proclaimed to Guruji, 'We'll have to settle for only one eyebrow.'

Very quickly I started performing on the stage, representing my college at youth festivals, on the very grounds where many years ago Balraj Sahni had performed the play *Kanak Di Balli* and written his name in my autograph book. How I loved dancing! It was the new high in my life. There was no need to run away from home, I could fly! It was the

One of my Kathak performances.

world I'd always dreamt of, of being a performer one day. Instead of being an airhostess, wouldn't I rather be a dancer? Preeti, a pretty looking girl from Tarn Taran had also joined the dance class and we became friends. I was a year senior to her and was already performing as the lead girl on stage. We rehearsed during the day and after college hours we went to the Thakur Singh Art Gallery, where Guruji took evening classes. We were both chosen as partners in the dance troupe and we bonded over our mutual love of the arts. We diligently rehearsed for a dance drama called *Mathura Gaman* to be performed on stage in the Government College Performing Arts Festival. I was so committed; I completed an entire home science file for Preeti just so she had time to practise for the dance ballet. That was the kind of passion I had for dancing.

But there was a problem. Though we both had rehearsed for weeks, Preeti's father put his foot down when it came to her performing in public. I couldn't let that happen. We *had* to be part of the Youth Festival that year. So Preeti and I took a bus to Tarn Taran to go convince her family to let her perform on stage. We must have spent the whole day there in the village feasting on sumptuous makai di roti and sarson da

Performing Mathura Gaman.

saag but I was unable to persuade Preeti's father after all. There was no convincing him. He plain refused.

So, I had to dance without Preeti. I played Radha in our rendition of *Mathura Gaman* which was performed at the prize distribution function in college in 1970. I had cut up one of Mama's Banarasi saris and made it into a lehenga. I can't imagine how she even let me touch that; it was a beautiful magenta silk with bootis and a gold zari border. I have preserved that lehenga to this day. Before the performance I sat in front of the make-up mirror in the green room of our college theatre, white glaring bulbs in my face, horrified at the sight of my hair being combed in the wrong direction, ending up in a beehive. But once I began dancing to the classical song that was playing all was forgotten:

> Jaa . . . tohse naahi boloon kanhaiya . . . raah chalat pakde mori
> baiyaan . . . Jaa . . . tohse naahin boloon kanhaiya . . .

Mathura Gaman was a huge success and I had found new confidence. I don't recall being terribly nervous going on stage, but I must have been. I do remember at the end of the performance as the crowds cheered and clapped and roared with applause, I was suddenly overwhelmed by shyness. Instead of standing there and bowing to the applause, I ran away from the stage! I suffer this dichotomy to date—being confident and nervous at the very same time.

∽

Santhal dance

Rajasthani folk dance

Other performances I remember include one in which I performed a Santhali dance, wearing a white silk sari with a red border, worn a little high above the ankles like a half-sari, for the Old Students' Day in November that year. Next came a Rajasthani folk dance to the song, 'Mhaara Khetaan Oobi Baajri' performed by Jyoti, Harpreet, and me.

That same evening, I performed my first Kathak solo at the Youth Festival at Gandhi Ground on 6 December 1970.

The favourite of all the girls was the Punjabi Bhangra that we all danced—Preeti was my partner in this (allowed to perform only in college), dressed like a man with a pagdi on her head, and we danced together to the song '*Ni kudiye, Punjab diye, ni mutiyaare, Chanab diye . . .*'

I led the group on stage wearing an orange lungi and Bibiji's deep olive-gold collared kurti with zardozi work on the neck and sleeves.

Favourite of all the girls was the Punjabi Bhangra.

I didn't know why the other girls were dancing, but I knew why I was on stage in front of a live audience! I was determined to be an actress one day and dancing was an integral part of being a Hindi film heroine.

The irony of it all is that in my entire acting career I did not get a single dancing role! It's a dream that has remained unfulfilled and deeply saddens me, but I still hold my Kathak days very dear.

∞

I don't know at what point we discovered the Shivram Photo Studio, but the one recurrent stopover for us girls after every performance would be the studio at the corner on Cooper Road, next to the Chinese Shoemaker. We'd inevitably land up there with our fancy costumes, to now be properly photographed. Any little excuse and we'd be at the studio getting ourselves clicked in all kinds of poses, wearing different outfits. This was the time I was getting acquainted with the various angles of my face, through the lens of a camera, something that went beyond the mirror on the hat stand. I'd sit before the two huge floodlights, and let Shivram do his work, his head tucked behind the huge black box camera. A day later, I'd return to collect the freshly developed black and white images, and place them carefully in my photo album called the 'Shivram Photo Phase'. It's an interesting record of my teenage years.

One time, we girls decided to change into the Kashmiri outfit displayed in Shivram's show window and one by one posed in front of the camera. In one photo, I'm holding a kangri in my hands, there's a printed scarf over my head, and large silver danglers hang around my ears. In another, I'm carrying a basket full of plastic flowers on my back. Though there was nothing original about these photos—it was a typical North Indian studio thing, getting photographed in a Kashmiri dress—for me it was much more than that. It was my connect with the valley I continued to dream about.

Soon I had quite a collection. There are other photos that have me wearing a hipster sari with a short short pallu—a popular style those days. I'm quite fond of one picture where I'm wearing thick reading glasses pulled down to my nose, (à la *Angoor* style) and a funny looking cap, grinning away at an angle I know is my best. Another photo has Nonu and me standing side by side in our school uniform, bottle green sweaters with badges intact. In this photograph we seem like the most innocent looking schoolgirls you could ever lay your eyes upon! It is difficult for me to believe that we looked like *this*, while in our heads there was so much happening!

My last performance.

For all the joy dancing brought me, it too had to come to an end. I can never forget the last performance of mine, a Kathak solo, at the Thakur Singh Art Gallery auditorium. It was a ticketed show and there was much excitement about it. There were other girls performing various other dance items. Backstage, I was getting dressed in my white Kathak outfit with a turquoise vest, one I'd worn for the Youth Festival the previous year. All my friends were there, so was Mama, though she was extremely edgy as she wasn't comfortable with the security arrangements that had been made at the venue.

The atmosphere was charged. The other performances were going really well and I was impatiently waiting for my turn. Finally, I was on stage and dancing, when, suddenly, the lights went out. That was it! There was a huge uproar in the audience, and after that there was absolute chaos in the auditorium. I had to be rushed out through the back exit of the stage. Mama was in a state of panic. I don't remember how, but she hauled me out of that auditorium, brought me back home, then, standing in the hall kamra, she lambasted me. 'How could you be so foolish?' she raged. 'Why were young girls performing in public

without any form of security whatsoever?' She was livid with Guruji for taking such a risk, what if something serious had happened? That night as I stood silently before my mother in my Kathak outfit, Mama screamed:

'NO MORE DANCING! NO MORE OF THIS NONSENSE!'

I didn't say a word, but my heart sank ... None of the cultural and artistic dreams I'd had were panning out—my dream to become an actress, Sir J. J. School of Art—and now dance as well ... I remember I was left standing in the room for a long time, my mother's words echoing in my head. The silence around me was profound. It seemed to me that I was at last seeing a basic truth clearly. Could I possibly have a life without art? After a long cold moment, the answer was ... *No.*

29

Filmomania

A very blurry image comes to my mind, one of a picture postcard of the Marine Drive of Bombay. I don't know where I got that postcard, but looking at the sepia image, I imagined Rajendra Kumar's car cruising along the Queen's Necklace, or a Shashi Kapoor driving along the Chowpatty beach. I imagined all film stars zipping up and down the Marine Drive in their swanky convertibles. I had preserved that picture postcard with me for years, but when we emigrated to America it got left behind. So were my dreams of becoming an actress. At least for now. It would not be until after I finished college in New York that I would finally be able to tell my parents about my desire to join films.

∞

I grew up on commercial cinema. That was the only cinema I knew, and that was the cinema I loved. There were no art films those days. At least there was no such term those days. The one and only film that I could later identify as an art film, was Raj Kapoor's *Jagte Raho*, and even that had seven songs in it.

The eleven o'clock show at Adarsh Talkies kept us on our toes those days. This was one theatre that also ran all the old black and white classics from the fifties and the sixties. The morning show was a rage with the freshers in college. Every time the films on the roster changed, we'd come hurtling back to the theatre. We couldn't afford to miss any film. Even Regent Talkies, the infamous theatre at the end of our street ran a morning show. The boys of DAV College next door would call proxy attendance and crowd at that theatre. A shaky bell would trill from Regent Talkies at eleven, and half the college got emptied out.

We saw most of the movies by bunking classes. Didi was our saviour. Whenever we wanted to go see a movie and ran short of money, we'd run to Didi, and she always managed to dole out whatever extra we required. Did she get more pocket money than I did? It didn't really matter. As long as we could see all the movies we wanted to, the world was a good place to be in.

We watched film after film in the movie halls—all the girls—Nonu, Didi, Kiran, Santosh, Pemu, Munni, me—sitting in a row, whispering to each other, eating peanuts, drinking hot cups of tea, laughing and sobbing, while the boys sitting in the back rows shuffled in their seats and giggled at this mindless *rona-dhona*.

One time, Mama came along with us and I remember that so well. All of us were wearing ribbons in our hair. God only knows in which film we'd seen the ribbon look, but Mama got so annoyed, she snapped, 'Remove those ridiculous ribbons from your hair, or I'm not sitting with you girls!'

I found it curious that in the films of those days when things went wrong, they were never cleared up, no one ever talked things over, misunderstandings were just allowed to fester. But that kind of thing made sense when you understood the sort of trajectory the plot took. If things got cleared up in the first instance, how was the heroine going to sing that sad song wearing a black chiffon sari, like Asha Parekh in *Do Badan?* And that was the pivot of the story. The wrong impression had to be carried on for a whole one hour and fifteen minutes after the interval until you reached the climax when everything just sorted itself out on its own.

సా

One of the incidents I remember from my years as a teenager hanging out in the movie halls of Amritsar, had to do with the day we went to see a movie at Adarsh Talkies with a boy. He was a lean, fair, sharp-featured guy, not necessarily the kind that I found attractive but . . . at least we had a date—three girls and a guy. I didn't think much of it at the time but during the interval, Binder, Munni's brother saw us speaking to him. Before we got back home, the incident had catapulted into a nasty report followed by a major character assassination at the hands of our parents.

My father was livid. Sitting next to a *boy* in the movie theatre and watching a movie? A whole barrage of questions were thrown at us.

Since I was the younger one, I was spared somewhat and asked to go sit outside, while Didi was grilled. That evening she cried a lot.

How could he suddenly turn a tyrant? My father! Imagine! I was never going to forgive him for this. I also started to look at my mother accusingly. You too, Mama? After this incident I went into a shell. I wouldn't speak to my parents, unless absolutely necessary. I certainly could not confide in them. They became the *others* ... Growing up wasn't all that fun after all.

But the incident blew over soon enough, and we were back in the cinema halls enjoying the season's next releases. Of course, no boys after that were allowed to come and sit near us. All kinds of jerks would be sitting next to us but any decent guys worth talking to? Nope. Not allowed.

∞

Earlier I had spoken about the films I'd seen as a child. Here I would like to give you some idea of the movies and actors I watched during my teens, the formative years of my life; movies that consciously and subconsciously influenced and shaped my own career as an actress.

A major event during my girlhood days was the release of the movie *Dosti* in the November of 1964. This was the movie in which Indu Bhaiya played his first role—his decision to become an actor had caused a bit of an upheaval in the family, but things were eventually straightened out. There was considerable excitement in the family when the movie came to town; we girls were thrilled by the prospect of seeing Bhaiya on the screen. When he did appear, it was in a scene in a school where all the boys are teasing their disabled classmate. Indu Bhaiya's role entailed him running around the victim on one leg, teasing him, 'Langad-deen bajaaye been! ... Langad-deen bajaaye been!' Bhaiya's role started and ended there; a bit disappointing for us cousins who wanted to see much more of him on the screen. But we were sure that would happen in due course, he looked like Dev Anand after all!

∞

There were two films that went beyond the emotional connect, and became a cinematic experience. These were *Sangam* and *Guide*. With these two films, things had started to fall in a different perspective.

In the summer of 1964 when *Sangam* was released in Ashoka Talkies in the lane below the Railway Bridge, it rained pamphlets! Little white leaflets were scattered all over the city, from a helicopter, announcing the release of the film. I retain an image in my memory of people gasping as they tried to catch them. Such was the publicity campaign for *Sangam* that it got the entire city ticking with excitement. When we went to see the film, Didi sat next to Pitaji and I sat next to Mama. When she came back my sister told me she was embarrassed when Vyjayanthimala came on the screen wearing a swimsuit. I was very taken with Vyjayanthimala wearing white throughout the film, except for one song in which she wore the red swimsuit. There was something splendid about *Sangam*. It stood out as the film of the decade, and created waves in our little lives as well, and impacted me a great deal. After watching that movie, I believed I now understood the complexity of relationships at a deeper level.

Guide, the very next year, came like a fresh shower of rain at New Rialto. '*Kaanton se kheench ke yeh aanchal . . .*' was a celebration of life, and became the theme song of our girlhood days. Every girl wanted to be Rosy, breaking chains, starting anew, taking chances in life! I loved the way Waheeda Rehman danced. During lunchtime I'd stand around the banana trees near the back wall of the school and show the girls how Waheeda Rehman, dressed in red and black, dances the famous 'Snake Dance'. *Guide* was a film for all times. Dev Anand's monologue in the climax of the film was startling. 'Na sukh hai, na dukh hai, na deen hai na duniya. Na insaan, na bhagvaan. Sirf mai hoon, mai hoon, mai hoon . . . sirf mai, sirf mai!'

∽

'I'd be up there one day', I'd imagine, sitting in the theatre watching a movie. I'd be the face on the big screen, and all these people who are sitting in the audience, laughing and crying along with the stars on the screen, would be laughing and crying with *me*, connecting with *me*. They'd be impacted by what I'm going through. They'd feel what I was feeling, they'd dream what I was dreaming, my pain would be their pain, my joy would be their joy. They'd be bonding with *me*! That was the dream . . . to emotionally reach out to the audiences in a way that I'd matter to their lives. I wanted to be somebody who mattered.

None of my friends sitting with me in the theatre could ever imagine what was brewing in my head and in my heart. That I'd started to dream about becoming an actress would undoubtedly be a far cry from the kind of person they perceived me to be. They would have dropped dead hearing of it, or fainted for sure. On the outside my demeanour was of someone who needed to be protected, demure, soft-spoken, naive, and innocent. No one had a whiff of all the fiery, feisty ideas cooking in my head. Forget friends, even Didi had no clue, so seedha was I on the surface, so well I could underplay my true emotions.

∞

Before I go any further with the films of my teenage years, I must tell you about my Sadhana craze.

When I first saw Sadhana in *Hum Dono*, I was just nine and she seemed like a dream . . . so beautiful, such grace . . . and I wanted to be like her. Not like Mama, for the time being, not even like Meena Kumari, but like Sadhana. She was my new icon, the epitome of feminine beauty. The way she spoke, the way she sang, '*Sitaare jhilmila uthhe* . . .' touched my heart. There was no other heroine as beautiful as Sadhana and that was affirmed once *Asli Naqli* released. I became confident that Sadhana was worth switching loyalties for. Didi, me, Munni, Nonu, Pemu, Kiran—all of us girls went into raptures over Sadhana. She became our new fixation! *And* she was sensuous too. For us she was 'ultimate womanhood'.

'*Mere mehboob tujhe meri mohabbat ki qasam*' was the song that caught our imagination in a big way. It was a Muslim social, where Sadhana wore the most beautiful shararas in the film. After I saw her in *Mere Mehboob* in 1963, there was never any doubt in my mind that Sadhana was whom I wanted to be when I grew up.

The next year came a very different film called *Woh Kaun Thi*, in which Sadhana played a woman of mystery, a role very different from the ones she'd played so far. The movie took the city by storm, and I was blown away by Sadhana's presence on screen. She was magical. Literally! Girls in class discussed the plot of the film relentlessly—the stormy night, the car breaking down, the appearance of a hauntingly beautiful girl. There were two of her: the real Sadhana, and the one who claims to be the real Sadhana. I was a girl on the threshold of puberty, dying to become a teenager, and loved the mystery that Sadhana was in *Woh Kaun Thi*. I was completely hooked on to the songs of the film, and had quickly scribbled down and learnt by heart the words '*Adhoora hoon main afsaana, jo yaad aaoon chale aana*', and the classic '*Lag ja gale ke phir ye haseen raat ho na ho*'.

One day in school, as we were getting back to class after recess, we heard the shocking news that Sadhana had died. I was shattered. I ran away from the class. I ran all the way back to the far end of the playground and sat there on a swing, crying and singing: '*Naina barse rim jhim, rim jhim*'. I wanted to lament.

Nonu came looking for me.

'Deepi, come on, the bell has been ringing, come back to class!'

'No,' I said, without wiping my tears. 'Sadhana has died . . . I want to sit here and cry.'

At home that whole evening, I sat on the swing in the veranda.

'*Adhoora hoon main afsaana, jo yaad aaoon chale aana . . .*'

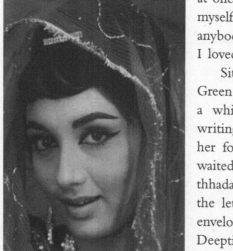

Next morning in school when it turned out to be a rumour, I felt at once elated and sheepish. I swore to myself: 'Never again will I sing songs at anybody's death, no matter how much I loved them.'

Sitting at my writing desk in the Green Room one day I pulled out a white sheet of paper and started writing a letter to Sadhana, requesting her for a fan photograph. For days I waited anxiously and ran out to the thhada every now and then to check the letterbox and see if there was an envelope from Bombay addressed to Deepti Naval. I cannot describe how elated I was when the envelope finally arrived. I quickly tore it open and pulled out from within, a beautiful black and white photograph of Sadhana, one from the film *Mere Mehboob*, where she has a tinsel veil over her head and is smiling, the fringe on her forehead intact. I still have that photograph. I noticed how her eyeliner was painted out longer than her upper eyelid to make her appear doe-eyed! Sadhana's photograph was the only fan photograph I ever asked for, and I still preserve it.

Next, we saw Sadhana sitting at a black piano in a glittering white chiffon sari, giving her slant glances to Rajendra Kumar and smiling her bewitching smile. When *Arzoo* released in the freezing cold January of 1965, my destination became clear to me. I will go to Bombay, join films, and become the next Sadhana. I was that crazy about her. I wanted to fall in love like she did in *Arzoo*, and when love didn't work out and I'd go into heartbreak mode, I wanted to sing a '*Bedardi baalma tujhko mera man yaad karta hai*' just like Sadhana did, walking around the pine needles and orange chinar leaves in Kashmir.

There's a picture of me with my classmates from the farewell party at the end of school where I'm in the same white outfit that Sadhana wears in the song. I managed to convince Mama to get me an identical outfit stitched for the event. I turned up in a tight fitting white churidar kameez, and on top I have the same flowy cape made out of white Leela lace. My hair is braided in a single plait, à la Sadhana style, and I actually managed to look like a startled version of Sadhana in *Arzoo*. Only the

Imitating the Sadhana look.

Sadhana Cut is missing; a thing that perhaps got left behind in childhood.

৵৹

I was now in the fourteenth year of my life and in the eighth standard when I got to see a huge number of films. Asha Parekh, Sadhana, Sharmila Tagore, and Mumtaz had taken over from the earlier galaxy of stars on the big screen. Among all the films I saw that year, there were two films that affected me deeply. *Anupama* was one of them.

The Sharmila Tagore–Dharmendra starrer *Anupama* released in the year 1966. And for a whole season I did not speak, at least I tried my best not to, because Sharmila Tagore did not utter a word in the entire movie. She only communicated through her eyes. Wasn't *that* incredible? Her furtive glances were so dramatic . . . I loved it!

Didi was amused; she kind of gauged what was going on in my silly head. She knew I'd seen the film and was *affected* by it, but she wasn't sure if this was for real. I'd spend hours sitting up on the terrace, in silent mode. Mama would call me, I'd hear her, sure I would, but I wouldn't answer. Instead, I'd quietly walk down the two floors, stealthily come and stand in the kitchen door doe-eyed and all that, waiting to be noticed. Didi would laugh, but my mother was annoyed. One day, I recall, I'm up on the barsati and Mama comes up fuming. She stands at the entrance door, glaring at me.

'*Good Heavens*! Did you *not* hear me calling you? Can't you for God's sake answer me? What on earth are you doing sitting up here when I'm looking for you all over the place?'

I look at my mother wide-eyed, as if I haven't seen this woman before.

'For heaven's sake! *Answer* me!'

I quietly get up without changing my expression, and without making eye contact with this beautiful woman called Mama, walk past her and start to descend the stairs ever so daintily. So serious was I about emulating in real life the Sharmila Tagore of *Anupama*, though my state of mind was more like Dharmendra's: '*Ya dil ki suno duniya vaalo, ya mujhko abhi chup rehne do . . .*'

Then I was back, on the swing, this time hissing under my breath, '*Kuch dil ne kaha . . . kuchh bhi nahin . . .*'

That euphoria remained all season. The whole summer I had not spoken. By autumn, as the leaves in Company Bagh turned to brown, we were jabbering away again tucked in our razais, discussing details of the mystery of *Teesri Manzil* and the romance blossoming between Shammi Kapoor and Asha Parekh, dancing at the Rock 'n' Roll Club, doing the Shake Dance to the loud and hypnotic '*Aaja aaja . . . main hoon pyaar tera!*', a challenge to the central nervous system: '*O aaja . . . a a aaja . . . a a a aaja . . . a a aaja . . . a a a aaja . . . a a aaja . . . a a a aaja . . . a a aaaaaaaa!*'

Incidentally, this was the number I gyrated to in my film *Chashme Buddoor*.

Of course, as the years rolled on, and I grew up to be a young woman, I would cause my mother much angst, but at this time, even through those non-communicative years, as I sat on the rolled-up mattress gazing at the clouds with Mama glaring at me from the barsati door, there was much beauty in life!

The other film that stands out in my memory chart is *Teesri Kasam*, the Raj Kapoor–Waheeda Rehman starrer that released in the same year. We all walked to Ashoka Cinema: Mama, Piti, Gyaniji, Didi, Gugu, and I. I remember on my return from the show, the whole family was chatting about the impact of the movie, but I walked up ahead, all by myself, wanting to be alone, thinking about the ending of the film. My heart kept saying, 'Why . . . why?' at Waheeda Rehman's decision to go back to her nautanki in the end. It pained me, the fatalistic ending. Shailendra's words haunted me for days.

'*Sajanva bairi ho gaye hamaar . . . chithiya ho to har koi banthhe, bhaag na baanthhe koye . . . karamva bairi ho gaye hamaar . . .*'.

The depth in Mukesh's voice had touched a cord, and was leading me to myself, a voice that made me contemplate the passage of time. These were songs that made me look at life from the far end, not what I was living now, but what it would be at the end of the journey . . . it was making me look back at things I hadn't yet lived. *Teesri Kasam* had quietened me down. It made me reflect, and I started an inward journey.

∽

The summer of 1967, when I was fifteen, all the cousins got together and went to Kullu for the holidays; I was down with typhoid. That whole summer I was quarantined, and sulked in what was once the Music Room. I was counting the days for my cousins to return, and once they did, they were all bubbling with excitement over the same bloody thing! *They'd seen a Shammi Kapoor film, and I hadn't!* I went into silent mode. Mama and Piti took it as a sign of this 'difficult teenage thing' and decided to let me have my time in the mountains. I was sent to Kullu valley to visit Shashi Bhua and that's when I saw a film shoot for the very first time, and had my second encounter with a real movie star, after my first meeting with Balraj Sahni as a young girl.

Bhuas, cousins, and Indu Bhaiya.

One day, we heard that Asha Parekh was in the valley, shooting for a film called *Kanyadaan*. We were told that a song was being picturized on her. So where was this happening? I was all excited to go see the shooting. We heard that the unit was shooting in such and such place, so we

Dressed as a Kullu belle.

In the Kullu valley.

quickly drove out there. But once we got there, we were told the crew was in another location at some distance. So, we rushed off there but once again, the unit had moved elsewhere in the valley. This went on for most of that morning. I was beginning to feel quite bad for both Uncle and Aunty, but they were great sports and we finally caught up with the film unit and Asha Parekh. She was dancing to the song, '*Mil gaye, mil gaye, aaj mere sanam*' in the lush green meadows of Katrain. We parked by the roadside and stepped down the slope to watch the shooting closely.

Here's what I see:
The lines of the song playing are—

Ae nazaaro zara kaam itna karo . . .
Tum meri maang mein aaj moti bharo . . .

The music stops. A dance coach jumps into frame and shows the dance step. Asha Parekh is sitting on a chair dressed in a red lehenga choli, checking her face in the mirror held by a young boy with a tray, looking drop-dead gorgeous. The coach steps back from the camera frame and Asha Parekh gets up and stands on her mark. The song starts again and she skips back into frame singing around a tree, holding it with her left hand, and with her right, the edge of her lehenga. It all looks so dreamy that I'm completely awestruck. After two rehearsals everyone gears up for the real shot. The song is played again. Asha Parekh jumps up on to her toes and runs into frame prancing around the tree, beaming.

On the second line, '*Tum meri maang mein aaj moti bharo*', she catches hold of a branch and shakes it. As she does that, beautiful white flowers start to fall all over her. That's awesome, I tell myself, but wait a minute, the tree didn't have as many flowers a while ago. Where are all these flowers coming from? That's when my eyes move up to the top of the tree, and to my astonishment and dismay, I realize there's a guy sitting up there holding a huge basket in hand, desperately throwing flowers down on cue. *Really?* Is *that* how it's done? It takes me a while to let that sink in. I look back at Shashi Aunty, disillusioned. She smiles her knowing smile. Never mind, I tell myself, it looks beautiful nevertheless. I'll settle for the guy with the basket!

Someone shouts for a break. People's body language changes. Suddenly everyone slumps. Their gait changes. Little fellows called spot boys spring to the scene with tiny glasses of tea, six at a time, carried in a wrought iron chhikka. The camera is now being placed on the opposite side. The large glaring silver boards on metal stands are being shifted as well. I see Achala Sachdev, the actress who'd been in Lahore with Mama, walking away with Asha Parekh. They disappear behind a huge rock in the far-off distance where there's no one around. I wait. Then I see them emerging again. I think quickly. I have, of course, carried my autograph book along, knowing fully well that film stars are forever shooting in the mountains. Our jeep is parked a good distance from where the shoot is happening. Both Uncle and Aunty have walked back and are waiting for me. This is the right time. I must get Asha Parekh's autograph before the shoot starts again. I run to the jeep. 'Are we done? Should we leave now?' asks Kapil Uncle who'd been waiting patiently for me to have my fill of a film shoot. 'Just two minutes, Uncle, I want to get Asha Parekh's autograph!' and I run back.

Now, here's the scene at hand. I'm standing beside Asha Parekh and Achala Sachdev with my autograph book in hand while the two are deeply engrossed in conversation. There seems to be no break in between sentences that would allow me to step in and say, 'Can I please have your autograph?' I'm standing there looking at them for a long, *long* time before finally there's a pause in their chatter. Asha Parekh, most graciously takes the book from my hand and signs her name as I gaze at her beautiful face in awe.

∞

Aamne Saamne, a 1967 release, was the film of our teens. Didi had a huge crush on Shashi Kapoor; his smile, she said, was to die for! I remember Sharmila Tagore in a red chiffon saree with a sleeveless blouse knotted in the back. The songs of *Aamne Saamne* were very popular. '*Kabhi raat din hum doore thhey, din raat ka ab saath hai*' and '*Nain mila kar chain churaana kiska hai yeh kaam*'. Didi's favourite was the other very popular song, '*Mere bechain dil ko chain toone diya, shukriya . . . shukriya . . .*'

Around that time came Manoj Kumar's *Upkar* with the song '*Mere desh ki dharti sona ugale, ugle heere moti . .*' and I quite fancied the idea of living in a village and working in the fields.

The year was 1968. I was in Matric class when we went to see *Sapnon*

Ka Saudagar escorted by Indu Bhaiya. We'd heard there was a new girl in the film called Hema Malini who was really good looking, danced like Vyjayanthimala, and was touted as the 'Dream Girl' of Hindi cinema.

∞

While we were busy watching all these new releases, I was strongly drawn to the enigma of the black and white movies from much before my time, the old classic reruns from the 50s and the 60s. So far, we'd only been listening to the songs on radio, songs that had become such an integral part of our lives. But now all those films were before us on the big screen.

In the rerun of *Baiju Bawra*, when I got to see Meena Kumari as a young girl, it only reaffirmed what I initially felt. I cried my eyes out when in the climax scene both Meena Kumari and Bharat Bhushan were drowning. 'They're dying, they're dying!' I sobbed. Kiran sitting next to me tried to console me. 'It's only a movie, Deepi, you *know* that.'

Watching *Jis Desh Mein Ganga Behti Hai* a second time in the morning show I also understood what Raj Kapoor was trying to say in the film! There was a strong message in most of his films. Nothing was just for entertainment, and I didn't care much for pure entertainment. I liked the idea that films left you with *something*—something that you carried back within you. They gave you an insight into life; they could touch your heart and mould your way of thinking.

I longed to see the other Nargis-Raj Kapoor films—*Aah*, *Awaara*, *Chori-Chori*, *Shree 420*—as there was a great love story there, but could not. I do have clear memory of *Aan*, starring Dilip Kumar and Nimmi, from the year 1952, the first colour film of that time, and discovered a striking presence on screen—Nadira. I waited for films like *Pyaasa* and *Kaagaz Ke Phool* to come to the morning show, but that somehow never happened. '*Jinhe naaz hai Hind par vo kahaan hain . . .*' and '*Jaane vo kaise log thhey jinke pyaar ko pyaar mila . . .*'—all those songs written by Sahir Ludhianvi remained scribbled in the pages of my song book and continued to be an enigma for me. Nutan and Balraj Sahni's *Seema* gave me a most compelling scene related to human dilemmas. This is when Nutan is sitting on the footpath, and someone, taking her for a beggar, drops a coin around her feet. Nutan's conflict, whether to pick up that coin or not—that scene went down in my heart as a great moment caught on camera, a piece of great acting.

I finally saw Helen dancing to '*Mera naam chin chin chu* . . .' the song that Mastana tweeter had been cooing away as it passed through our street, with the coming of *Howrah Bridge*. I'd been enthralled by Helen's dazzling presence on screen. I'd never seen anyone dance like that!

'Deepi, do you know, the dancer Helen is from Burma?' Mama said to me one day.

'Really . . .?' I was excited.

'Yes, Helen is Burmese.'

It was a reassuring thought that there was one person in Hindi movies who was from Burma, and yes, she did have a Burmese face. From that day, I felt closer to Helen.

∾

Coming back to the movies of our time . . .

When *Aradhana* came in the September of 1969, all hell broke loose! The female gender went bonkers over Rajesh Khanna, man for all seasons. We were not surprised when Sharmila Tagore in the film got pregnant and became an unwed mother. By now, we knew exactly how babies were made and how we all came into being. And getting pregnant with a Rajesh Khanna was perfectly understandable—he was *the* dream man of every girl. Nonu and I fell crazily in love with him. We loved the way he tilted his head and smiled, a mannerism that would become a craze with the public. I felt no other actor could have done '*Roop tera mastana* . . .' like Rajesh Khanna. Treading a fine line between forbidden love and desire, the crackling chemistry between the actors set alight a passion that blazed across the screen. *Aradhana* released at Adarsh Talkies, and we went to see the movie a second time during the same week to celebrate Didi's birthday. But that wasn't the end of it. Nonu and I, we saw that film thirteen times. The fact that Rajesh Khanna belonged to the interiors of the walled city of Amritsar and was born in Gully Tiwarian inside Lohgarh Gate thrilled the Ambarsaris no end.

The other Rajesh Khanna film that I adored was *Safar*. With it I found a deep internal connect. I also discovered that it was the tragic that drew me more. I wasn't so kicked about the so-called fun films. In *Safar*, where Rajesh Khanna played a painter and sang '*Jeevan se bhari teri aankhein . . .*' his performance was unforgettable. The guru kurtas that he wore throughout the movie had become a rage. Nonu and I wanted similar kurtas. We bought khadi fabric from Khadi Bhandar, took Didi's kurta, accordingly cut our own two kurtas and stitched them on Mama's sewing machine in the veranda. We then put on our home-made creations and went off to see the movie—we were that crazy about Rajesh Khanna.

∞

The year 1969 was also the season of 'adult' films. It was the month of August when a much talked about English film called *Blow Hot, Blow Cold* released with its steamy posters all over town. It allowed entry to only those aged eighteen and above, and we were seventeen something. But with a title like that, we needed to go check out what all the hot and cold stuff was about. So, all we girls got dressed in saris, and made bouffants with stuffing in our hair in order to look older. We did turn a few heads as we walked through the lobby. But at the entrance, one look at us, and the usher recognized us right away. We were the bunch who was forever there at the theatre for all new releases. He saw through our little act and turned us right back from the door. Feeling like a bunch of buffoons with bouffants, we came back terribly disgruntled. But one year from now things would be different.

Chetna was a serious adult film. Everyone was talking about the two college girls who become call girls out of choice. It was a scandalous subject and we couldn't afford to discuss it at home. The poster had a girl in a miniskirt standing on a bed with her legs apart, and in between the legs was the figure of a man looking away. This time we entered the theatre, matter of fact, as if it was a routine thing for us to watch movies like this. We walked in confidently, as legitimate eighteen-year-olds, and saw our first adult film.

∞

Six years after *Sangam*, the most awaited Raj Kapoor film, *Mera Naam Joker* finally arrived. It released in the December of 1970 in the same Ashoka Cinema, but this time the hall was empty. But I loved *Mera Naam Joker*. It was nothing like any other film I'd seen so far—or like the films of our time—hero and heroine falling in love, singing songs, having misunderstandings, and then eventually getting married, and living happily ever after.

Mera Naam Joker was about a clown who uses his own pain as a means to make his audience laugh. In different phases of his life, he falls in love with different women, but always ends up losing his love. The three women that he loved all come back to see his final performance at the end; a visual representation of the acceptance of that loss. I was very moved by the sequence where Raj Kapoor camouflaged his pain, holding a joker puppet in his hand, his own tears hidden behind dark glasses, sings, '*Jeena yahaan marna yahaan . . .*' and recalls all the people in his life he'd loved and lost.

In all honesty, I feel it was a landmark film of my youth, a film ahead of its time. The song, '*Jaane kahan gaye vo din . . .*' was a song for all times, never to be forgotten. It was a four-hour-long film and just before the interval Joker implored his audience: '*Joker ka tamaasha khatam nahin hua, jaiyega nahin . . . jaiyega nahin . . .*' A most insightful film it was, and I wondered why the seats around me were so vacant. This film had so much to say about life. When I found myself crying in the theatre, I remember telling myself, 'Why am I crying? I *know* how shootings are done'. But this film was beyond all that. 'The show must go on', was the message I came back with. *Mera Naam Joker* conveyed a philosophical message and was a lesson in living.

∽

The year 1971 brought with it more films. *Kati Patang* was based on the famous Gulshan Nanda novel of the same title. At this time, we had just a few months to leave for the US and there was lots to do. But with Rajesh Khanna singing a song like '*Jis gali mein tera ghar na ho baalma . . .*' how could we miss out on the movie? On 30 January, first day, first show, we somehow managed to get to the theatre despite the jostling crowds. When Bindu came on the screen trying to intimidate Asha Parekh, gyrating to the song, '*Tumhara naam kya haaaaiiii? . . . Neena, Meena, Anju, Manju,*' the whole house went trilling: *YAAAA . . . . MADHUUUU!*

Anand released in March that year, when the date of our departure had been fixed and there was hardly any time left. There were lots of things to look into—the whole winding up process was in full swing.

Nevertheless, I went one last time to a movie hall in Amritsar to see a Rajesh Khanna film. It was a poignant film and had some beautiful songs: 'Kahin Door Jab Din Dhal Jaye' and 'Zindagi Kaisi Hai Paheli'. Rajesh Khanna was completely endearing in the film. Along with him was a new actor, a very tall, lanky young man whom Rajesh Khanna addressed as Babu Moshai. At once candid and intense, he was an extremely compelling performer. 'Who is this actor?' I asked Santosh sitting next to me. 'His name is Amitabh Bachchan,' she said.

∽

Many things would change for me shortly after moving to America. I would not be able to look at cinema in the same way ever again. All the popular Hindi films of the 60s would be clouded over and replaced by the *Taxi Drivers*, *Serpicos*, and *Deer Hunters* of the 70s that I would be seeing in the theatres of Manhattan, and watching actors like Al Pacino, Robert De Niro, and Meryl Streep. But *Mera Naam Joker* would remain embedded in my heart as the one film I would never forget as it had come at a turning point in my life.

30

America, the Land of Dreams

An incident happened in Amritsar that left a deep wound in the heart of the walled city. The streets were the darkest that day, darker than they'd ever been. My parents had not uttered a word all evening. Mama and Piti just sat together in the veranda in complete silence; they were in a state of shock. Then I heard my father say, 'How can the *students* do this? To a *teacher*! Their *own* teacher?'

I quietly sat upstairs, waiting to hear what had happened. It was later, as the evening turned into night, that I learnt of the unfortunate incident.

Professor Kumar, one of my father's colleagues had been garlanded with a jooton ka haar, string of shoes, by his students and paraded through the gullies. My father had always been very close to Professor Kumar and looked up to the man for his uncompromising values. He had always been an excellent teacher and a strict disciplinarian, something that never did go down well with some of his students. It so happened that the professor had refused to pass a student, one who was known to be a big goonda, because the boy didn't deserve the marks he demanded. The students ganged up against the professor and decided to teach him a lesson. The whole thing turned into a dark, ugly situation. The boys pulled up a donkey, dragged the poor professor to it, threw a garland of shoes around his neck, and flogged him through the narrow gullies, beating on drums.

That night, Guruaan di Nagri, the city of the Gurus, was shocked into silence. Only the last train could be heard chugging past the Railway Bridge. Never could one imagine a more ruthless act, never a sadder sight.

∽

To my impressionable mind, the incident acted like a catalyst. It was soon after this that my parents announced to us the life-changing decision of leaving Amritsar and emigrating to the US. But the fact remains that they had been contemplating moving to America for a long time.

In the year 1966, the American government opened its doors to professional Indians—doctors, teachers, engineers, etc., to become permanent residents of the United States of America. For days there had been discussions at the dining table. My parents had decided to emigrate back then itself. And so in 1970 when we were told of their final decision to leave for the US, it came as no surprise to Didi and me.

Pitaji left in the summer of 1970. At that time Badi Mummy came to live with us. On the day of his departure, a final family photo was taken at Prabhat Studio. We all got dressed up and went over to Dhruvji's Photo Studio to get ourselves photographed one last time together in India.

∞

As I have said earlier, my father, in order to provide us with better opportunities, decided to emigrate to the US at the age of forty-eight, at a time when his colleagues at Hindu College were planning to retire in the hills of Dalhousie and Mussoorie. He gave up a well-respected job as the head of the English Department to start his life from scratch in a foreign land. I have always admired my father for having the will and courage to leave home with no security whatsoever, or even the promise of a job. He set off for New York with just twelve dollars in his pocket and a dream of a better life. Here, as I have said earlier in the book, he would go back to pursue his studies and obtain a PhD in the field of linguistics at the age of sixty-four, a full forty-four years after completing his MA honours in Lahore.

As a first-generation immigrant, my father started with nothing. His first year was especially hard—he had to work as a librarian by day and as a watchman, an ordinary guard in a factory in the Bronx, by night, earning $1.75 an hour. His guard duty required him to do his rounds every hour, and then ring a bell periodically to show he was awake. None of this was easy and I have deep respect for his grit and determination to first save enough money to send air tickets for all of us to join him in the US, and more generally to make a go of it in the land of opportunity. That one year has always remained an inspiration for me.

∞

America, the land of dreams—the land of skyscrapers and escalators and lots of lights like on Diwali nights. In my mind I was no longer a small-town girl. I was soon going to belong to the cosmopolitan world, a world where people of all colours and races mingled and interacted, a land where millions of people had come together to form a nation called America! And I was going to be one of them.

I recall the first time when Piti had gone to America in 1961, the arrival of his blue aerogrammes would send a ripple through the house. But this time, the tone of my father's letters was different. I remember he wrote that we'd all have to work hard to sustain ourselves there—and was I prepared! In one of the letters he said, 'Deepi, if you could learn some basic skill, that would enable you to get a job here right away.' Though his letters to us were cheerful and full of exciting details, it was from a letter addressed to 'My dear Winnie' that I learnt of my father's real struggle in America.

'I'm working during the day at the Bronx Library. That, I don't mind so much, at least I'm surrounded by books. Then at night I've picked up another job as a watch guard, it helps me make extra dollars. But the winter here is severe. It's freezing cold and the nights are chilling. Each time I open the door, the draught hits me. At times my eyes well up, thinking how far away I am from home . . .'

I became silent. *My father*, having to work as a *watch guard*? Something shifted within me. I became more determined, more driven to make a go of things. When I reached New York, the first thing I would do is to take up a job so I could pay for my own college and not be a burden on my father. I would work nine to five, and attend night school. I wrote to Piti, asking him what kind of job would I be able to get once I landed in New York. The return aerogramme said only one sentence. 'Deepi, learn to type.'

I sprang to my feet. The closest typing class was at the end of the lane where Madhubala . . . suddenly Madhubala appeared as a stepping-stone in my life. My father's letter in hand, I sped down to the printing press at Regent Talkies Chowk and stood at the wooden threshold.

'I need to learn typing. When can I start?' I asked with urgency.

'Today.' Came the prompt reply.

That evening I joined the typing class.

I can't remember much of what was going on around me at the time. All that mattered was that I was going away to America and I was busy with my typing classes . . . which finger on which letter. The typewriter was an antique Remington with a keyboard that required some pressure on each key to strike it down. Q W E R T with the left hand moving towards the right, and P O I U Y from the right to the left. Not only did I learn how to type, but I was soon able to type at great speed. It somehow empowered me. I felt a great thrill at being able to roll out words using all ten fingers and without looking at the keyboard. The sound of Pitaji's old Remington typewriter on the veranda was now replaced by the clickety-clack of the keyboard in my head. It spelt a ticket to America, a job in midtown Manhattan, walking on the streets of New York City, cafes, college, art classes.

At the end of one month when I was handed the little square document certifying me as a qualified typist, I finally took a long deep breath. As I stepped down, I turned to look at Madhubala's slant smile. For once, I was smiling back.

∞

While Piti was slogging away in the US, Mama was left all alone to wind up things back in Amritsar. Within a year we all were to join my father and there was much left to be done. There were a lot of tasks still remaining on Mama's 'wind-up' list. There was the Hammer sitting at Chatiwind Gate that desperately needed to be sold. That machine was a monstrosity; it wasn't easy to get rid of the white elephant. But my mother being my mother, decided to take on the herculean task single handedly. She spoke to various people, mistris, kaarigars, factorywallahs. Any clue she got, she made sure to follow up on in order to wind up that task. One day when Mama had to go on a scooter with the old Sardar mistri to Chatiwind to finalize the deal for the Hammer, she made my little brother sit with her on the back seat and rode off into the sweltering heat of summer. When she returned home that evening, we could see on her face, the Hammer had been *SOLD*!

∞

It was time now to escort Badi Mummy back to Mukerian. Saying goodbye to Bade Daddy and Badi Mummy would be one of the most painful things we'd have to do. Mama wanted to spend time with her parents, perhaps for the last time before she went far away to another country. We visited the Mukerian house just a few days before we were to leave for America. After spending as much time as we could with our grandparents, it was finally time to say our farewells. Mama was upstairs with Badi Mummy, both of them clinging to each other and crying, while Gugu and I were downstairs with Bade Daddy. In the tiny vehra of the old Mukerian house, Bade Daddy sat on a wicker chair, his walking stick slanted against it. His old blue-grey eyes were gleaming with unshed tears as he looked at Gugu and me standing before him, waiting to take his blessings. He patted my head and then with a trembling hand, he touched Gugu's face.

'This is my last look, son . . .'

As I turned at the threshold to look back one last time, I saw Bade Daddy sitting alone in the vehra of the old house, looking at us with liquid eyes, his right hand trembling on his thigh. At that moment, standing by the door looking back, I remember feeling, 'Why can't I say something appropriate to my grandfather at this moment? Can't I, give him ... hope? That we'll meet again?'

Bade Daddy

But that was not to be. I was never to see Bade Daddy again.

∞

It was spring when we learnt that Pitaji had finally got a job in his field. I knew it! That difficult phase of my father's life wasn't going to last forever. His best job, actually, had been of an editor. He'd been the head of a newspaper in the Bronx, a local paper. From there his qualification was picked up, and now he'd acquired the post of Associate Lecturer at the Lehman College, teaching English as a Second Language at the City University of New York.

Didi finally returned from Chandigarh and we girls decided to celebrate the news. We went to see the new film in town: *Anand*.

A ticklish memory from around this time surfaces, when Piti had sent us our first gift from America. When the parcel arrived from New York, there was much excitement. As Didi and I opened the packaging, two milky-beige nylon slips slithered out of the crisp paper wrap and fell on the bed.

'*Hai* ... so *soft!*' I loved the buttery feel of the fabric.

'Deepi, try it on?'

'Yes, let's!'

The stringy nylon slip fell just above my knees. I'd never worn anything as slippery and satiny as this. It felt wonderful on my skin. So now? Time to head to the mirror in Mama's room. Let's go! We stepped out of our room, and stopped.

'What if someone's peeping from the windows above?'

'No one's there, I'll keep an eye out. Go!'

Didi runs across the courtyard, straight into Mama's room, while I keep an eye above to make sure no one's peeping down. Quickly she runs back, blushing. Now my turn. She prods me, glancing up.

'Go, go, go ... No one's looking!'

Barefoot, I dart across the vehra, up the veranda, and stand breathless in front of Mama's full-length mirror. I'm looking at myself for a long moment; turning this way, that way, admiring myself from all different angles. I *like* this ... and the fabric is so *yummy*!

Badi Mummy

One more time Didi runs across, then me again, a second look.

Badi Mummy is sitting in the veranda in a white voile sari, pallu over her head, and maala beads in her hand, reciting the Gayatri mantra. She sees us zip past her, one first, then the other.

'What are you girls doing, running up and down, wearing little-little chemises?'

Once my friends come, the running intensifies. Nonu, Pemu, Kiran, Munni— each one of them wants to try on the nylon slips. One by one, they dart across the vehra, check themselves before the mirror, then zip back to our room and fall on the bed, giggling. So tickled were we seeing the skimpy-flimsy version of ourselves.

∽

Those were days when life was a joy ride on a white bubble balloon. I was going away to America, and that's all that mattered. It was our last day in the Chandraavali house. I ran up the stairs one last time and stood breathless on the barsati looking at the mosque. The pigeons roosted under the dome, a blue line of stillness. A sudden wind surfed the terraces. One last time I picked up a stone, and stood gazing at the pigeons nestled under the white petals of the dome. One last time I threw a stone and watched the pigeons fly. And I wondered, just like pigeons always come back home, would I return, too?

I closed my eyes for a moment, and looked out for Mai Sardi, for Bebbe, for the Faqir who would come singing in the winter and stand in front of the empty house, waiting for me to open the door. I looked out for my golliwog; I can't remember where, over the years, I'd lost him . . . I looked down and saw the little, cropped-hair version of myself, sitting behind Didi on a little tricycle, the two of us going round and round in the vehra . . .

Downstairs, Mama clung to the pillars of the veranda and cried.

∽

We left for Delhi by the Flying Mail. At one o'clock in the afternoon we were at the Amritsar railway station boarding the train. The next day, Air India would fly us to London. We'd get three days with my favourite Uncle Brian, and then leave for America, our scheduled arrival in New York being the Fourth of July 1971.

All my friends were there to see us off. I felt such mixed feelings— the excitement of going away, intermingled with the sadness of going away. Santosh spoke to me in hushed desperate tones as the train slowly pulled up on the platform.

'Deepi, in America you will get all kinds of fancy face creams and lotions for your skin—Max Factor and Revlon—all that, but remember to use *only* besan and haldi scrub on your face. You'll see, your complexion will glow!'

Nonu grinned. Santosh turned to her.

'Yes, there'll be traffic jam in America when she comes out in a hipster sari and her besan-glowing skin!'

Just then I saw Pemu appear last minute, waving frantically.

'Oh boy! I'd nearly missed you!' she said and hurriedly pulled out a book from her handbag.

'Here, this is for you.'

'Parting gift?' I looked at her expectant face, then turned the book around: Poems, T. S. Eliot. I hugged Pemu tightly.

'Okay, okay, now don't make me *senti*, yaar!' she pulled back, embarrassed.

'Bye Deepi, write . . . Don't forget!'

'Yes, Pemu! I'll write, I won't forget . . . I promise!'

'Write every week, about New York City, the people, the art galleries . . .'

A whistle went off and the train started to pull out slowly amidst goodbyes and waving of hands and tears. I quickly hugged Nonu, Kiran, Santosh, and got on. I looked back for Pemu.

'Write, letters, Deepi . . . letters . . . then one day when you become famous . . . I'll publish them!'

We both were at once laughing and crying. I waved back to one and all with the same enthusiasm. But one figure was pacing along the train holding on to the bars of the door. I heard the tearful voice of Toshi.

'Remember Deepi . . . the words of a true friend! Do it to America! Show them what a *simple Indian beauty* is!'

Through my own tears I waved back as the train had left the platform and was now moving on the gravel. Nonu stood on one side, in tears, but grinning. Mama was crying, so was Didi. Lots of people were being left behind. Toshi was running faster now, tears rolling down her cheeks.

'Nobody would have seen anything like it, when you cross the streets of New York in your sari and your glowing complexion . . . not white . . . not black . . . but the colour of bajra . . . the colour of gehu . . . . . . the colour of . . . colour of . . . *W . . . H . . . E . . . E . . . E . . . A . . . T !*'

⁂

Let me take a pause here, and tell you of something else I left behind in Amritsar—a blue-eyed boy who came into my life for a brief season like a whiff of autumn breeze, and then was gone . . .

One day, I opened the door to the thhada to find this light-eyed boy standing outside the door, lean, and tall, and good-looking. His eyes were more glacial-green than blue, I thought. He stood there, seeming a bit unsure. He had come to deliver a packet from his sister. I don't remember the details, but we spoke briefly through the flyscreen, and then he went away. I like to believe that as we set eyes on each other, somewhere far out, a bell chimed. I'm not sure if this was *that* moment, the one you wait for, but it was a moment that stayed.

He wasn't like the typical Punjabi boys I'd been averse to. He was different. Meeting someone like him seemed like a breath of fresh air. I soon found out that we were family friends. Gradually, he started to drop by on his way to his college next door, and I'd wait for him. Whenever he would come, I'd make coffee, the kind you whip up in a cup to a thick white froth, and then we would sit down and talk. Not that he spoke very much, and neither did I. He was the shy, quiet, intense type, the kind I always imagined I'd meet some day. It wasn't like the filmy onscreen romance at all. It seemed like the sound of a river coming from deep beneath the frozen ice bed, something pure, untouched.

It was autumn time. We both loved getting out in the open. I'd sit on his bicycle and we'd ride off towards the old airport road. In my mind that was the most romantic thing I'd ever done—sitting on the front of his bicycle riding along the empty road with green fields on either side. I remember going to his country farm once where I sat under the shade of the kikar trees, gazing at the dappled sunlight.

Could the feeling have grown? I didn't stay long enough to find out. When our ways parted, I regretted that we didn't get to hold hands.

Now when I look back at the autumn of 1970, I recall it as a brief season of, what can I say ... he was eighteen and I was eighteen, and we were this close to falling in love.

౼

As the plane took off the tarmac of Indian soil leaving the country of my childhood behind, memories began to unspool in my head like a top angle shot, in which I could see details of all that my life had been until this point in time.

The large dimly lit house, the dust rising and falling as little children flapped barefoot in the gully, the flight of pigeons, the white of the mosque, the grey of the clouds ... up on a terrace, two sisters, against the sunlit dome, wringing chiffon dupattas, flicking them dry in the breeze ... The sound of water pouring into the tin tub, the enigma of the dark staircases, the latticed windows, through which light fell on the walls breaking into little rectangles—all these seemed part of another world; a world I was looking at from the other side of the globe. And suddenly, everything that was the 'now' of my life became a memory.

Here's a bird's eye view:

A young girl sitting on her terrace in a house next to a mosque, surrounded by waves of houses and gullies fanning outwards through the walled city . . . Hall Gate with its clock tower in the chowk; bicycle shops and vegetable stalls next to the rickshaw stand; the bus stop which formed

the heart of the city from where one road wound its way up Bhandari
Bridge where you had to get off from the bicycle and walk up to the
circle going down on the other side, past Company Bagh from behind
the V. J. Hospital, all the way out to turn into Majitha Road, which then
rambled along for miles to reach the familiar red brick colonial structure
of Sacred Heart Convent School, standing aloof amidst green fields; a
dust track leading to the forbidden idol of Kali, enigmatic amidst the
golden mustard fields thick with the winter fog; all of this and more was
my hometown of Ambarsar, surrounded by a network of deserted roads
along which the occasional bullock cart would amble lazily, headed for
other destinations in a country of thousands of towns and villages . . .

Epilogue

In Light of Punjab

My mind goes back to the landscape of Punjab ...
By the end of March, the leaves return to the trees but the fog remains in the fields. It gets thicker, denser, intending to stay. The kikars along the road turn from black to green, a white film persisting between the sky and the earth. It is the light that has changed.

A white glow in the sky bounces back from the golden wheat, now nice and ripe, and spills over the earth. The sun is a smudge of soft gold behind the poplars. In the month of March, you can look into the sun. Little leaves appear on the tip of slender branches. The light behind the electric poles now intensifies and spreads like water in the fields, filling up the earth with white on white, till the yellow wheat blanches and soaks. Kikars stand crooked on both sides of the road turning the landscape into an impressionistic painting. A soft haziness prevails, a dull dreaminess. The air is cool, clear, and full of effervescent light flooding the fields as if a dam has broken somewhere beyond Mukerian in the foothills of Kangra valley.

On the horizon it is the thickest and whitest, the texture of marble, the glow of a pietà. The trees along the pond on either side bend and touch each other. The foggy far end is dense, like the light is here to stay. This is the early April light, moist with the sense of a cold winter gone by. In the cool, crisp white-light-flooded mornings, there is always a lone, lean figure of an old Sardar in an onion coloured kameez and salwar, walking along the roadside, barefoot, his arms clasped behind him.

The flood of light now recedes and curdles at the horizon making way for shadows. Streaks of dark spill through the trees to cut the road intermittently, and stretch on to the cow-dung-caked walls, the background blurring into infinity. The fog begins to descend on the world once more, blotting out the sienna of the wheat that remains frosted in white, and the world becomes again what it once was ... luminous, opaque, unfathomable ...

Acknowledgements

First, I wish to thank my cousin Manisha Gangahar who has been hearing of my book for ever and ever and has stood by me for years, seeing me struggle to put things together. I thank Ginny for her precious contribution to my book and for being on the same page with me.

I cannot thank enough my publisher David Davidar for believing in my book, for meticulously working at it in order to give it some shape and form, and particularly for guiding me to structure the storm of childhood memories that form the substance of this book. I would also thank the entire team at Aleph Book Company for their hard work in bringing my manuscript to its finale.

I need to thank my dear friend and writer Vijay Singh for allowing me to disrupt his work every now and then and make him read passages I needed instant feedback on. I owe Vijay a big thank you for teaching me to be ruthless with myself.

I thank Bhagyashree Verma, for helping me with 'films from my childhood', going meticulously over dates and other important details. I am grateful to Sanjana and Anushree for their contribution in the final stages of my book. Let me not forget to thank Ambika for sitting with me for hours together, going back and forth, reading and re-reading chapters and for urging me to say it my way.

Among my family members, I so need to thank dear Uncle Brian, who helped me reconstruct scenes of the exodus from Burma when he was only a boy of fourteen on an ardous journey to India, trekking haplessly across the Assam hills. My thanks to Lily Aunty, Mahinder Uncle, and Georgie Gangahar for filling in the gaps while I was cross-checking little details of their life in Mandalay.

I'm indebted to Bindu Uncle for narrating to me in detail the life of my paternal grandparents, details only he knew, and fondly reminisced.

How can I not be grateful to Indu Bhaiya for helping me research family history and recalling my years as a young girl growing up in the city of Amritsar, and . . . and most of all, for inspiring me to *have a dream*!

I so thank with all my heart, Deepika Mehta Devichand and Rouma Devichand for giving me their gracious approval, knowing how hard it has been for them, to write about their beloved sister Neeta Devichand and to bring her endearing life to light.

I am grateful to my school friends Kiran and Nandini, for being there for me all through the time I was trying to reconstruct our days together at the Sacred Heart Convent of Amritsar, for going down memory lane with me and recollecting little instances; Jyoti, Madhu, Rita, and Daman—I thank you all for sharing with me the *joy of being girls*.

I thank Atul Puri for being a huge support over the years, for accompanying me to Jalalabad, my grandfather's birthplace, and for being by my side as I roamed the little gullies of the once small teela where Bauji as a young boy walked barefoot to school and back, and for helping research on Partition and the tragic incident at the Beas River.

I was greatly touched by the people of Jalalabad for welcoming me with such warmth and for going out of their way to confirm the exactitude of all the stories from my family history.

I'm grateful to Billu Mehra for driving me around the city of our birth now so different, for revisiting all the landmarks of our younger days, and finally walking inside the Amrit Talkies of Katra Kanhaiya and discovering the place once forbidden.

How can I forget Babulal of Mochistan—the neighborhood in which we both grew up at the same time, on either side of the big iron gate—for taking me inside Khairuddin's maseet where we sat around the dome, delightfully recalling people we both knew as children living across the gully from each other. I thank Babulal for the lovely gift of a handmade Rajasthani jutti, one I wouldn't wear, lest it should wear out.

People I lost during the writing of this book: Raj Aunty, Gogi, Binder, Bindu Uncle, Sneh Bhua, Kamal Bhaiya, and most of all my dearest childhood friend, Munni, whom I lost recently during the lockdown, who was there for me at any odd hour of the day or night, to exchange notes, to live and relive memories of our shared childhood—Munni, without whom I wouldn't have been able to complete this memoir. I thank her for standing by me, for holding me up whenever I ducked down remembering the good old days, or recalling painful incidents and raking up memories . . .

I thank my dearest friend Pemu for sharing with me my girlhood years, for understanding me like no one ever did, and for prodding me to write . . .

It was to pay homage to the two beautiful souls who are no more in this world today that I had set out to write this memoir—my dear dear Mama and Piti, my wonderful parents. How can I ever, in this life *and* beyond, thank you both enough for bringing me into this world, for being my guiding light, and for giving me the splendid gift of a *memorable* childhood!